Golden
PANTHERS

Golden PANTHERS

PITT'S TEN-YEAR AFFAIR WITH FOOTBALL PROMINENCE (1973–1982)

SAM SCIULLO JR.

AMERICA THROUGH TIME®
ADDING COLOR TO AMERICAN HISTORY

Front cover image courtesy of The Times-Picayune/New Orleans Advocate.
Back cover images courtesy of University of Pittsburgh Athletics.

America Through Time is an imprint of Fonthill Media LLC
www.through-time.com
office@through-time.com

Published by Arcadia Publishing by arrangement with Fonthill Media LLC
For all general information, please contact Arcadia Publishing:
Telephone: 843-853-2070
Fax: 843-853-0044
E-mail: sales@arcadiapublishing.com
For customer service and orders:
Toll-Free 1-888-313-2665

www.arcadiapublishing.com

First published 2020

Copyright © Sam Sciullo Jr. 2020

ISBN 978-1-63499-275-6

Typeset in Sabon
Printed and bound in England

ACKNOWLEDGMENTS

The author wishes to express his appreciation to the following individuals who were kind enough to be interviewed directly for this project.

Benjamin "Buck" Belue, Dean Billick, Jim Bolla, Charles "Chaz" Bonasorte, Lou "Bimbo" Cecconi, Frank Cignetti, Sr., Ralph Cindrich, Jim Corbett, Jimbo Covert, Billy Daniels, Jeff Delaney, Wayne DiBartola, Jerry DiPaola, Tony Dorsett, Chuck Fusina, Dave Garnett, Hugh Green, Dave Havern, Robert Haygood, Bill Hillgrove, Roger Huston, Ed Ifft, Dave Jancisin, Alex Kramer, Joe Macerelli, John Majors, Mark May, Greg Meisner, Chris Peak, J.C. Pelusi, John Pelusi, Al Romano, Bryant Salter, Stan Savran, Jim Sessler, Jackie Sherrill, Bob Smizik, Rick Trocano, Vicki Veltri, Lloyd Weston, Clair Wilson, and Tom Yewcic.

Other quotations attributed herein were derived from the many interviews I have conducted over the years, along with weekly Pitt press conferences and postgame interviews and transcripts.

I would also like to thank E. J. Borghetti and Celeste Welsh from Pitt's Department of Athletics for their assistance, along with Ryan Tomazin of Tomazin Scanning Services.

Special thanks are extended to Alan Sutton, Kena Longabaugh, and Joshua Greenland of Fonthill Media for their guidance and instruction throughout the process. Finally, I must thank my late parents, Sam and Ryta Sciullo. Dad, you created so many opportunities for me, and opened so many doors to Pitt sports. I cherish the times we spent together and the countless memories. Mom, you instilled in me a love of reading and a curiosity for words for which I am eternally grateful.

CONTENTS

INTRODUCTION

By the end of the 1972 season, the University of Pittsburgh's football program was on life support. The Panthers had just completed a 1-10 season, the only time Pitt has lost that many games in a campaign. Attendance for home games at aging Pitt Stadium, the team's home since 1925, was sparse, media coverage was largely disinterested and sarcastic, and membership in the newly created Golden Panthers booster club was small.

Faced with the prospect of either moving its football program to a lower level of competition or disbanding it altogether, university officials decided to make a major push to restore Pitt to heights it had not enjoyed over an extended period since the glory days of Coach Dr. John Bain "Jock" Sutherland during the 1920s and 1930s.

Enter Johnny Majors, a legendary player in his native Tennessee during the 1950s, fresh from a rebuilding effort at Iowa State University in the rugged Big Eight Conference. Majors brought virtually his entire staff of assistant coaches with him—young, aggressive men with close ties to the South, recruiting ground virtually unheard of and unattainable for all previous Pitt coaching regimes. Four years later, Majors had taken Pitt's football program from near extinction to a 12-0 season and the 1976 national championship. Jackie Sherrill, who had been a member of two national championships while playing for Paul "Bear" Bryant at Alabama in the early 1960s, and who would succeed Majors as Pitt's coach following perhaps the most spectacular four-year revival in college football history, kept the winning going in five subsequent seasons. To date, Sherrill has the highest winning percentage of any football coach in school history.

By the late 1970s, Pitt had established itself as one of the nation's most successful programs. All American players, major individual award winners, TV appearances, and bowl game victories abounded.

The remarkable period from 1973 through 1982 began with a freshman halfback named Tony Dorsett and ended with senior quarterback Dan Marino, who had grown up in the shadow of Pitt's campus in the Oakland section of the city. Marino capped his prolific career when the 1982 Panthers finished the season ranked No. 10 in the nation—a lofty status Pitt has not reached since.

In the nearly four decades afterward, Pitt football has produced some of the greatest players the game has known, including Bill Fralic, Chris Doleman, Craig "Ironhead" Heyward, Curtis Martin, Larry Fitzgerald, and Aaron Donald, but the ten-year stretch beginning with Dorsett and ending with Marino remains surrounded by an invisible cocoon. Pitt has had its share of thrilling victories since 1982, but has not enjoyed the overall success that its long-suffering fans believe is their birthright.

To understand and appreciate where Pitt football landed later in the 1970s, it is important to understand whence it came. The late 1960s and early 1970s are generally glossed over in any study of Pitt's football history. But the program struggled through survival just as this country was experiencing some of the greatest turmoil in its history, making it inevitable that the two forces would converge.

1

TROUBLED TIMES, TROUBLED PROGRAM (1966–1972)

We had a lot of guys who were more academic than athletic. I hate to say that, but it was true.

Lloyd Weston

I'm sure, I'm positive, there were real racial inequities back in those days. Anybody who denies it is a liar. Everything was crazy. Everything was unsettled.

Dave Havern

"Go to the loser's locker room," noted newspapermen Bill Heinz and Jimmy Breslin liked to say. "That's where you'll find the best stories."

Had the local Pittsburgh media heeded that advice, they would have spent plenty of time in the locker rooms of the Pitt football teams from 1966 through 1972. How bad was Pitt football then? Two coaches—Dave Hart and Carl DePasqua—tried their luck at reviving what had become a stale program, but neither man produced a winning season. Pitt never appeared on network television during those years, and interest and attendance at Pitt Stadium continued to founder.

When Pitt celebrated 100 years of football in 1990, it produced a commemorative video titled "Paths of Glory." The Hart-DePasqua years received a scant fifteen seconds' mention in passing.

Those unlucky seven years of football were preceded by the end of John Michelosen's eleven seasons as coach of the Panthers. Michelosen, who had played for Jock Sutherland from 1935 through 1937, was an ardent protégé of Sutherland, and he succeeded his mentor as coach of the Pittsburgh Steelers following Sutherland's sudden death in 1948. He was named Pitt's coach in 1955, and took the team to bowl games in his first two seasons, but none thereafter. Pitt surprised the college football world by going 9-1 in 1963, the only winning season any of the players on that team enjoyed at Pitt. But the Panthers slumped to 3-5-2 in 1964 and 3-7 the next year, losing several games by ridiculous margins: West Virginia outscored Pitt, 63-48; Syracuse cruised to an easy 51-13 victory; and Notre Dame rolled the Panthers, 69-13.

Pitt defeated Penn State, 30-27, in the season finale at Pitt Stadium when Frank Clark kicked a game-winning field goal in the final seconds, but Pitt athletics director Frank Carver had seen enough.

"I'm getting so many letters complaining about Mike [Michelosen] that I can hardly sleep nights," Carver told *The Pittsburgh Press*.[1]

Carver entered Pitt as a freshman in 1927 and climbed the company ladder from student worker in the publicity department to becoming athletics director in 1959. He resided in Beaver, Pa., a community approximately 30 miles northwest of Pittsburgh. He would take the train to and from his job at Pitt. Carver would be charged with hiring a new coach to replace Michelosen. A holdover from Michelosen's staff, Lou "Bimbo" Cecconi, had been a standout player at Pitt in the late 1940s. In a 19-0 win against Penn State in 1949, Cecconi threw for two touchdowns, ran for another and intercepted three passes. He was outspoken in his desire to become Pitt's head coach in late 1965. Cecconi said: "It's their [athletic committee's] decision. They know how much I want the job, and they know that I understand Pitt's problems better than others who have been mentioned."[2]

Other names brought up in the search were Penn State assistant Joe McMullen, John Chickerneo (a member of Pitt's famed Dream Backfield in 1938), and Dave Hart (a Connellsville, Pa. native who was then an assistant coach at the Naval Academy). Hart had been a highly successful high school coach in Pennsylvania.

Dave Hart was named Pitt's new coach on December 5, 1965. He was given a three-year contract. He was thirty-eight years old and eager, full of energy and optimism.

"Every time a guy gets a job—this is apt to sound trite—he feels he can whip the world," said Hart. "I'm no exception."[3]

"The reason we picked him is his obvious drive and energy," said Carver. "He's a dynamic man. He sticks his chin out and still is pleasant to deal with. He's a fine recruiter."[4]

Hart's introductory press conference was held at Frankie Gustine's restaurant and lounge on Forbes Avenue on the Oakland campus. He let it be known that the football talent rich region of Western Pennsylvania would be his immediate priority.

"We're going to cover that area like it's never been covered before," said Hart.[5]

Hart assembled an eager, aggressive staff of assistant coaches, including many who would later become head coaches themselves. Frank Cignetti, Sr. (West Virginia and Indiana University of Pennsylvania), Bill Lewis (East Carolina), Dick Bestwick (Virginia), and Leeman Bennett (Atlanta Falcons) look good on paper now, but upon reflection, they were the right coaches at the wrong time for Pitt. Hart and his staff were faced with a monumental rebuilding job in the face of considerable obstacles, both financial and more tangible to football.

After assembling his staff in Pittsburgh, Hart sought help from the university to secure temporary housing for his coaches until they and their families could get settled. Hart was told his assistants would have to live in the Spartan dormitory rooms that had been constructed inside Pitt Stadium. They would also have to pay a rental fee for the cots.

Dean Billick, a 1963 Penn State graduate, where he had been sports editor of *The Daily Collegian*, was named Pitt's sports information director in 1966 at the age of twenty-four, following nine months in a similar position at Bucknell University. He soon discovered what an impossible task Dave Hart faced. Dean Billick said:

> Pitt didn't have the money to be competitive in football. I guess I was kind of naïve about the financial situation at that time. The facilities, the locker room—what they were paying the coaches—they just didn't have the money. It was that simple. It was a time of uncertainty at the university. The previous chancellor [Edward Litchfield] had these grand academic designs, but he didn't have the money to back it up.

Billick also had to face a few challenges upon taking over at Pitt, where he replaced Carroll "Beano" Cook, who previously had been Pitt's SID. "I had a secretary, and that was it," said Billick. "I also had about a bushel basket of unopened mail left over that hadn't been opened since Beano left. Plus, I had to get a football media guide out, and I started at work on July 1."

Pitt held its preseason training camp at Allegheny College in Meadville, Pa., and it was there where Billick recognized the enormity of his new responsibilities. Dean Billick said:

> The big college football writer at that time was Gordon White of *The New York Times*. He would go around to the various colleges and training camps prior to the season. He came to Meadville to watch us and write a story about the team. He walked in a conference room where all the coaches were, and I couldn't introduce him to them because I didn't know all their names. It was very embarrassing. I tried the best I could. I didn't know one player, and I didn't know Dave Hart.

Pitt's upper campus was a cramped place in the 1960s. Billick's office, as well as those of the football coaches, were at Fitzgerald Field House. From 1964 through 1969, Pitt shared Pitt Stadium, which had a natural grass playing surface, with the NFL's Pittsburgh Steelers, guaranteeing worsening field conditions as their seasons progressed. The Steelers practiced at South Park Fairgrounds prior to Three Rivers Stadium being built, while Pitt held its weekly workouts at Trees Field on upper campus, or across the field in the area behind the end zone at Pitt Stadium.

Pitt and the Steelers were kindred spirits in losing; neither team had a winning season from 1964 through 1971. Dean Billick noted:

> I overheard a tremendous argument one day coming from the football offices for about forty five minutes to an hour, arguing about how they wanted the center to snap the ball. I don't know too much about the Xs and Os, but I figured we were a long way from having a competitive football team if they were going to spend that much time arguing about how to snap the ball from the center to the quarterback.

On paper, Dave Hart's resume appeared appropriate to the challenge he was about to encounter. He enlisted in the Air Force in 1943 during World War II and flew thirty bombing missions over Europe during that time. He was honored with the Distinguished Flying Cross and Air Medal with Oak Leaf Clusters. Hart understood what real pressure was, and recognized what he and his staff were up against when he saw his team during spring practice. He was brutally candid, telling writers he could not understand how some players had even been given scholarships.

"We lack everything you need to be a major college football team except for three ingredients—pride, enthusiasm and desire," said Hart. "On paper, it doesn't look like we'll win a game."

Hart made a few aesthetic touches, actually designing new uniforms for the team. For the first time in program history, a panther head decal would adorn the team helmet. Hart even designed new uniforms for Pitt's cheerleaders.

But none of the cosmetic touches made a dent in the enormous task Pitt football and Dave Hart faced. Hart's 1966 Panthers went 1-9, the only victory coming in the fourth game of the season, a 17-14 win against West Virginia at Pitt Stadium. UCLA defeated Pitt, 57-14, at Los Angeles Coliseum in Hart's debut, a stinging defeat punctuated by UCLA's attempt at an onside kick with the Bruins well ahead in the fourth quarter. UCLA coach Tommy Prothro apologized to Hart after the game, calling it a communications "mix up."

Pitt gained only 9 yards on the ground in a 33-7 loss at Syracuse. The Panthers had the gamblers on the edges of their seats when they visited Notre Dame. The Fighting Irish beat Pitt 40-0. The spread had been thirty-nine.

Despite the poor inaugural season, Hart and his assistants hit the recruiting trail hard, searching for talent to bring a winner to Pitt. Dean Billick stated:

> That was an amazing young staff that Dave had. I don't know how they recruited anybody with the facilities we had. I remember we held a press conference and thought it was big time when we put a Universal weight machine in the middle of the locker room. One! One Universal Gym! And I thought that was big time. Dave Hart had to hustle the boondocks to get the money to pay for that.

Billick was optimistic at the outset of Dave Hart's term:

> At the time it actually looked like a good hire for Pitt. He was energetic. He had a lot of good ideas. Dave really took over an abysmal situation at Pitt. And they didn't have any players. He was a bright guy, very outgoing. He was a PR guy, a front guy. He was very sensitive to that sort of thing.

Dean Billick is not the only person associated with Pitt who remembers Dave Hart in a positive light. More than fifty years later, several players who fell under Hart's recruiting spell recall the coach in glowing terms.

"Dave Hart was great," said Dave Havern, a smallish quarterback from Montour High School who played his first two seasons (1967 and 1968) at Pitt under Hart, and his final two campaigns (1970 and 1971) for Carl DePasqua. Havern noted:

> I thought he had a great vision for where he wanted the program to be. He was hit with a huge rebuilding job. He impressed me, and my parents. As soon as he threw that letter of intent on the table at Webster Hall Hotel, I was ready to sign. He took me to Mt. Washington and pointed to downtown and said, "This is where a lot of corporate offices are. This is your home. You can be a part of that. You can make a difference for Pitt." It was a very compelling message.

Another member of Pitt's 1967 recruiting class was Ralph Cindrich, a star football player and wrestler at Avella High School who played several seasons professionally before becoming an attorney and highly respected sports agent. He acknowledges the new coach was instrumental in his decision to attend Pitt. Cindrich had attended but two football games—Pitt's 24-12 loss at Navy in 1963, and a Pitt-Army game in Pittsburgh—prior to college.

"No question it was Dave Hart," said Cindrich. "He was the ultimate recruiter. He said everything that needed to be said to get you to go to the school."

Pitt had only one black played, running back Dewey Chester, on its 1966 roster, Hart's first season. That changed when Hart and his staff went through their first full season of recruiting during the 1966 season. Dave Garnett, J. D. Lewis, Larry Watkins, Lloyd Weston, and Bryant Salter joined Havern and Cindrich as members of a strong freshman class. Garnett and Salter came to Pitt on track scholarships to provide additional scholarships for football.

"He [Dave Hart] was the best," said Garnett. "When Dave Hart talked to you, you could hear people screaming in the Orange Bowl. He was the consummate recruiter."

Garnett came to Pitt from all black Buffalo East High School, where he was president of both his junior and senior classes, as well as Student Council president. He admits that his time in Pittsburgh was defined, to a large degree, by race relations.

"That was the central part of it,' said Garnett. "When I got to Pitt, it was a very different experience. I was defined by my experience with my freshman coach, who I wanted to choke."

Pitt's 1967 freshmen reported to camp a few days earlier than the veterans, and held a series of workouts. Garnett started as a wide receiver, and caught the ire of his coaches in the process.

"I caught a couple passes for touchdowns," Garnett recalled. "At a black high school, we celebrated and talked a lot of stuff. Next thing I know, this guy's fighting me."

That ended Garnett's experience at wide receiver. He was moved to running back, where he had a violent collision with a linebacker, resulting in another skirmish. Dave Garnett said:

> The coach said, "We're gonna run until Garnett apologizes." We started running wind sprints. I'm thinking to myself, "Doesn't this stupid son of a bitch know I'm here on a track scholarship." I could run all day. The coach said, "Dave, all you have to do is apologize." I said, "Not as long as I'm black."

Eventually, the other players were told they could sit, but Garnett had to keep running:

> I started to get a little sideways with the coaching staff there. I had an issue with facial hair. I had a mustache which I would not shave. The other issue was the afro. I had a huge afro. They just saw that as a sign of defiance. I should have switched to defense. The only reason they didn't want me on offense was because they didn't want a black person scoring touchdowns. That was sort of the unwritten rule at the time.

Bryant Salter was another outstanding track man who entered Pitt the same time as Garnett, Havern and Cindrich. A graduate of Pittsburgh's South Hills High School, Salter grew up in the Beltzhoover section of the city, and developed a social conscience at an early age.

"When they passed the Civil Rights Act [in 1964], I went to my parents and asked them why they waited so long to do it," said Salter. He remembered what is was like riding the street cars (trolleys) around Pittsburgh as a youngster. Bryant Salter noted:

> We'd get on the street car and it would be virtually empty. Four of us would sit in separate seats. By the time we got to our destination, the

street car would be full, but the seats beside us would be empty. It was a little different for people of my generation, because we weren't willing to accept any of that nonsense.

Salter remembers a story his Pitt roommate, J. D. Lewis, a football and tennis player from North Carolina, would tell him. "He (Lewis) said how the water fountains there in the department stores were separate for whites and blacks," said Salter. "They would never do that in Pittsburgh because they'd be fearful that the blacks would do something to the whites' fountains."

Ralph Cindrich experienced the racial tension from the other side during his years at Pitt. After being involved with a skirmish with a black player at practice, several black players approached him in a threatening manner.

"I said, 'C'mon,'" Cindrich remembers now. "They were my teammates. We were buddies. They looked at me, but I didn't cower from that. I didn't want to be lumped into that (racism), and I wasn't going to be intimidated."

Another time, Cindrich found himself surrounded by a small group of blacks in the lobby area of one of the Towers dorms. "I laid 'em out," Cindrich said. "I knocked the shit out of them. I was full of piss and vinegar in those days."

Today, Dave Havern is grateful for the timing of his playing career at Pitt:

One of the best things that ever happened to me was going to Pitt and playing with and getting to know the black guys. When you're a kid, you grow up with a lot of preconceived notions about people, but then you get to be with them and live with them and find the truth.

Those historic occurrences—Vietnam, Civil Rights, protests—probably outweighed the academic hardships while we were in college. Looking back now, what a great time to be in college. It was a pretty cool time to be nineteen, twenty years old, especially in Oakland, in an urban setting.

Dave Garnett said:

There were seven blacks on that team. You know who the seventh was? Dave Havern. He was the brother from a different mother. He's a guy we loved. He and [fullback] Phil Sgrignoli. Sgrig and I were on the kickoff team. They'd call a play and we'd say, "Screw that, we're gonna run what we want to run." On the kickoff team, that was our chance to play, so we would improvise.

Along with Ralph Cindrich, defensive lineman Lloyd Weston was one of Dave Hart's most celebrated early recruits, one of the nation's most coveted high school players. Weston entered Pitt following a stellar career at Westinghouse High School, a traditional powerhouse program in the Pittsburgh City League. Weston, who later worked in Pitt's academic support office for athletics, also remembers what it was like to be a college student during the late 1960s and early 1970s. Lloyd Weston said:

> It was a different time. You had the Viet Nam War, plus all the protests going on in the country. Then, a couple years later, you saw people getting naked and loving everybody at Woodstock. It was a crazy time on campus. You had people on the street in front of the Towers [dorms], passing out magazines and pamphlets about how we were gonna change the world.

Weston was an exception for admission to Pitt, which had stringent academic standards and entrance requirements at the time. "I had to have tutoring," he said. "The athletes weren't getting many breaks from the university, then, that they would later. They didn't have the Learning Skills Center. That was something we developed later."

"The academics were extremely difficult, as far as getting people into school," said Frank Cignetti, Sr. "The requirements for admission were tough. There were great players we couldn't touch because of academics."

Pitt undergraduates were required to take two years of a foreign language along with so many credits in the sciences.

"I had fourteen credits of French, but I don't speak French very well," said Havern.

Cignetti soon realized what an uphill climb he and his fellow coaches faced. "We had a great staff," he said, "but the schedule was just murderous." Pitt played UCLA, Notre Dame, Penn State, Syracuse and West Virginia in Hart's three seasons. Frank Cignetti, Sr., said:

> The facilities weren't there. You didn't have a great indoor facility. Actually, there was no indoor facility. You didn't have a great weight room. You didn't have things in place to put in a good offseason program

for the players. You compare that to what Pitt has now. It was a very, very difficult situation.

"Pitt didn't recruit certain kids then," said Weston. "I was one of the few people that they took a chance on."

Despite the handicaps, Hart maintained a brave front, dogged and determined throughout the 1966 season. He brought his players to every campus pep rally the day before home games. "The glory was there on Friday afternoon, but the power rarely came on Saturday," observed *The Owl*, Pitt's annual yearbook. Lloyd Weston noted: "Pitt was always talking about football players who became dentists and doctors, which is fine, but a lot of them weren't the athletes you needed to compete at that level. You need people who can play the game."

Hart also took his team to the annual Varsity Letter Club Dinner, which was held at the Webster Hall Hotel on a Friday night before a home game. The Pitt band would play "Hail To Pitt" while the players walked across and lined up on the stage. Hart would speak for several minutes, giving a rousing speech to the former students and athletes in audience. Thus inspired, the Panthers would lose, usually big, the next afternoon.

Every home game was played on Saturday afternoon during the Hart-DePasqua years. Each game started at 1:30 p.m. No Pitt game was broadcast on live television during Hart's tenure. Pitt games could be heard on WWSW AM, with WIIC TV sports director Charles "Red" Donley calling play by play, and local media personality Jack Henry providing color commentary. Twenty stations comprised Pitt's radio network.

Pitt had a new chancellor in 1967, Dr. Wesley W. Posvar, a Rhodes Scholar who had graduated first in his class at West Point in 1946. He let it be known that a successful athletics program could exist within a strong academic curriculum. Posvar said: "Pitt is one of the finest universities in the country. That's a fact, and we intend to keep it that way. But let me tell you something—we're going to have sports teams to match, and that goes for every sport, starting with football and working down the line. That's a pledge."

Pitt welcomed another newcomer to the scene in 1967. Bagheera I, a live, baby panther, was purchased by the Beaver County Pitt Club and donated to the football program to serve as a mascot throughout the 1967 season. It was held on a leash and maintained by Pitt's cheerleaders, and it lived at Highland Park Zoo during the week. Bagheera I was a fixture on the Pitt sideline during 1967 and part of the following year.

Entering the 1967 season, Hart was optimistic—in a cautionary way. "We will be one hundred percent improved. Of course, that may mean we'll only lose 20-0 and not 40-0."

Pitt had one of the nation's most attractive home schedules that year, including dates with UCLA (Gary Beban), Notre Dame (Terry Hanratty), Syracuse (Larry Csonka), and Miami (Ted Hendricks). The Panthers lost those four games by a combined score of 150-15. Pitt's only victory, and the only road win during Hart's term as coach, was a 13-11 decision at Wisconsin in the fourth game. Senior quarterback Bob Bazylak came off the bench to lead a second half rally in Madison.

A particularly bleak performance came in Morgantown where the Panthers managed only two first downs in being shut out, 15-0, by the West Virginia Mountaineers. Punter George Medich, who became more prominent as baseball pitcher and physician "Doc" Medich, punted twelve times for Pitt that afternoon.

The disappointing season finished at 1-9, but Hart was looking forward to 1968, when his strong freshman class from the year before would join the varsity. The newcomers would include Havern, Garnett, Weston, Cindrich, and Salter. "The Year The Panther Begins to Growl" was Pitt's battle cry for 1968. Hart could not contain his optimism. Hart said:

> What a difference! We have more football players both in numbers and ability. There's no question we're a much, much better football team than the past two years. We simply have more football players, more size, better speed and more depth. Barring injuries and getting the expected improvement from our young players, we could have a non-losing season.

Dean Billick shared Hart's enthusiasm entering the 1968 campaign. "The win a year pattern of the past two seasons should come to a halt," he wrote in the season outlook. "It should be the start of Pitt's return to football prestige."

Pitt's opening game of the season was set for September 21 at UCLA. Televangelist Billy Graham was in Pittsburgh in the time leading up to the game. Dave Hart invited Graham to come to Pitt Stadium to say a few words of inspiration to the Panthers before their trip to California. Graham was happy to do it. He made his speech, impressed Pitt's players and coaches with his message, but it failed to help the Panthers, who were defeated 63-7 by UCLA.

The following week, West Virginia beat Pitt, 38-15, at Pitt Stadium before the Panthers downed William & Mary, 14-3, in Pittsburgh in the next game. A small group of cynical Pitt students managed to bring down one of the goal posts after the game.

Playing at Syracuse, Pitt trailed 21-17 at halftime, but ended up losing 50-17. Navy edged the Panthers, 17-16, in Annapolis. Joe Spicko missed a short field goal attempt that could have given Pitt's its second win of the season. But time was drawing short for Dave Hart and his staff when Pitt traveled to play Notre Dame on November 9. Trailing 40-0 at halftime, both Hart and Notre Dame Coach Ara Parseghian, in conference with game officials, agreed to allow the clock to run uninterrupted in the second half. Pitt lost, 56-7.

A Pitt Stadium crowd of 31,224 assembled on a beautiful fall day, November 23, 1968, to watch what would be Dave Hart's final game as Pitt's football coach. Havern, Pitt's starting quarterback that season as a sophomore, broke out his white football shoes for the season finale. His shoes made it through the afternoon, but his jersey did not. A Penn State tackler tore Havern's No. 17 in the first half, and he had to wear No. 33 for the rest of the game. The wardrobe adjustment mattered little; the Nittany Lions drubbed Pitt, 65-9, capping a perfect regular season for themselves. Coach Joe Paterno called off the dogs as the game progressed, ordering his quarterbacks to keep the ball on the ground.

"In a complete mismatch, sympathy was the only thing Penn State gave Pitt yesterday," Russ Franke wrote for *The Pittsburgh Press*.[6]

Following the disastrous loss to end the season, Hart remained upbeat, looking ahead to the recruiting effort while telling reporters after the game he did not believe he would be fired because "they wouldn't kick me when I'm down."

Hart was wrong. He was kicked out as Pitt's coach a few days later. His dismissal saddened many of his players and supporters, who thought Hart deserved better.

"The crowds were small at Pitt Stadium," said Dean Billick, "The stadium was worn down. I don't blame anybody at Pitt. They just didn't have the money. It was hard to be competitive."

"I think things would have been quite different if he [Hart] had stayed," said Dave Garnett.

"I thought Dave was an excellent football coach," said Frank Cignetti, Sr. "He was a great recruiter. His timing on the Pitt job was not right."

"If Hart would have been given some resources, I think he might have made a go of it," said Havern. "Who knows?"

Hart never coached football after leaving Pitt. He did, however, enjoy a long and successful career as an administrator. He worked at Robert Morris College before becoming athletics director at Louisville, followed by a similar stint at the University of Missouri. Hart's final stop in athletics was as commissioner of the Southern Conference. Dave Hart died in 2009.

"Frank Kush Named Pitt Coach" read the headline in the January 5, 1969 edition of *The Pittsburgh Press*. Kush, the highly successful coach at Arizona State University who hailed from Windber, Pa., had agreed to come back to his home state to try his hand at reviving Pitt's dying football program. From all appearances, new Pitt athletics director Casimir Myslinski had scored a coup in his first big act as successor to Frank Carver, who announced his departure from Pitt shortly after Dave Hart had resigned. Kramer said: "Frank Carver was a very nice person. He was a gentleman, always well dressed, but I can't think of a single thing he did to improve Pitt's football program. He was passive. He was willing to accept losing records and poor attendance at Pitt Stadium."

Kramer became involved with Pitt football as a student manager in the late 1940s. His college roommate at one time was Pitt great Joe Schmidt, now a member of the Pro Football Hall of Fame. Kramer, and anyone else with an emotional stake in Pitt's fortunes in the late 1960s, watched in disbelief when, several days later, Kush reneged on his decision and decided to remain at Arizona State. Pitt also courted coaches Lloyd Eaton (Wyoming) and Dee Andros (Oregon State), but neither man wanted the job. Pitt, coming off three consecutive 1-9 seasons, had become the laughingstock of college football. "Doesn't Anyone Here Want This Football Job?" one national publication asked in its headline.

That was the burning question on the mind of Cas Myslinski, who was named to his new position at Pitt on Christmas Eve 1968. Myslinski had been an All-America lineman for Col. Earl "Red" Blaik at West Point in the early 1940s. He had grown up in Steubenville, Ohio. His mother never saw him play a game of football. His father had to be coaxed into attending the Army-Navy game when their son was a senior at the academy.

Following his Army experience, Myslinski later entered the Air Force, and retired from it as a lieutenant colonel in August 1967. He had been selling real estate in California when he was tabbed by Pitt officials.

"There's no doubt about it," Myslinski said at his introductory press conference. "We intend to be major league, and we intend to win."

"It was a time of great uncertainty at the university," said Dean Billick.

Pitt reached back in its football past to hire Carl DePasqua, aged forty-one, as its new football coach. DePasqua had been an excellent football and basketball player in Williamsport, Pa., and excelled as a Pitt football player in the late 1940s. He became the seventh former Pitt player to be named to coach the school's football program. He had been a member of John Michelosen's staff at Pitt, and had coached in Canada. He worked in the pizza business for two years, then had two very successful seasons as coach at NAIA Waynesburg (Pa.) College, where his 1966 team went undefeated and won the national championship. His two-year record at Waynesburg was 17-1. He left there to coach the defensive line for the Pittsburgh Steelers in 1968.

Bimbo Cecconi, who also had been an assistant to Michelosen, joined DePasqua's staff, along with two other Pitt men—Serafino "Foge" Fazio and Steve Petro. Petro was a holdover from Hart's staff. Cecconi was DePasqua's offensive coordinator, while Fazio and Petro worked with the defensive line. DePasqua said: "We're going to play fundamentally sound football—Western Pennsylvania style. I won't make any predictions, but I promise you this. We will know how to block and tackle. We'll do our talking on the field."

Dave Havern had been Pitt's starting quarterback as a sophomore in 1968, but when DePasqua saw his team for the first time at 1969 spring practice, Havern failed to make a good impression. Havern said:

> I wore those damn white shoes as a sophomore [in 1968], and when I walked into spring ball that first season wearing those shoes, I was about sixth on the depth chart. They gave me a pair of black high tops to wear. Then I took an elbow to the eye from [halfback] Denny Ferris at practice, which required about forty stitches. On top of that, I got sick that summer, so I ended up being redshirted. My introduction to Carl wasn't a good one. His impression of me was not a good one. We were alike. I think that was part of the problem. I don't think we had a particularly good relationship.

Pitt's quarterback during the 1969 season was Jim Friedl, a transfer from The Citadel who was a senior that year.

Lloyd Weston was entering his junior season when DePasqua was named Pitt's new coach. Decades later, he recognized the good and the bad in the hire:

> He [DePasqua] had come from the Steelers, and he had a more sophisticated approach to football than Dave Hart, but I don't know

that his communications skills were the greatest. When he lost, he penalized people. I got along with him, but he didn't get along with certain ballplayers. He could have won more. That year [1970] we were five and one, we could have been seven and three or something like that.

Dave Havern said:

Carl had done well at Waynesburg. He had a good reputation. He was a Pitt guy. He was a tough assed guy, Western Pennsylvania guy, but I don't think he had the vision that Dave Hart had. He probably knew more football than Coach Hart, but at the same time, he took an entirely different approach.

There was one glaring similarity, other than the losing records, between the Hart and DePasqua regimes. The heavyweight schedule remained. Pitt made its third trip in four years to Los Angeles to meet UCLA in the season opener, and came home a 42-8 loser. The Panthers traveled to Oklahoma—featuring Heisman Trophy-winner Steve Owens—and were beaten soundly, 37-8. "It was about 110 degrees out there," Lloyd Weston remembers. "I thought, 'Let's get the hell out of here.' They had a field day against us."

Playing its third road game in as many weeks, DePasqua registered his first victory at Pitt in a 14-12 defeat of Duke, holding the Blue Devils to negative rushing yardage.

Pitt opened its home schedule with an impressive 46-19 romp against Navy, with Denny Ferris scoring four touchdowns. It was the first time since 1963 that Pitt had won consecutive games. The winning streak was stopped when the Panthers blew a 22-0 lead at home against Tulane, losing 26-22.

West Virginia defeated the Panthers, 49-18, the next week in Morgantown, notable because it was the first football game Pitt played on artificial turf. Pitt defeated Syracuse for the first time since 1963 in a thrilling 21-20 victory against the Orange and later defeated Army, 15-6, at West Point, giving the Panthers their second road win of the season, another milestone the program had not enjoyed since 1963.

Pitt played undefeated Penn State in the 1969 season finale at Pitt Stadium. The Nittany Lions had won nineteen consecutive games entering the contest, but Pitt played one of its most inspired halves of football.

The game was tied 7-7 at halftime before Penn State took control after intermission, holding Pitt without a first down in the second half on its way to a 27-7 victory. Pitt ended DePasqua's first season 4-6, but the record inspired some hope for Pitt's future.

Another battle cry, "The Pitt Panther Is Back," heralded the 1970 football season and the beginning of a new decade. At a June press luncheon at Trees Hall, Cas Myslinski announced that Astro Turf, at a cost of $280,000, was being installed at Pitt Stadium to replace the natural grass playing surface. Pitt also moved across the radio dial to WTAE AM. Sports director Ed Conway would call the play by play with Bill Hillgrove serving as color analyst. Pitt also had a black assistant coach, Warren Sipp, for the first time in program history.

The 1970 Panthers lost to UCLA, 24-15, but showed a competitiveness that had been missing against the more prominent teams on its schedule. Pitt won its next five games and stood at 5-1 in late October, ranked No. 18 in the nation by Associated Press, the first time Pitt had appeared in the polls since 1963.

Sophomore John Hogan won the starting quarterback position, but it was Dave Havern who engineered the game winning drive in a 15-10 victory at Baylor in the second game of the season. Havern relieved Hogan two weeks later at Navy when Hogan injured a knee on a play deep in Midshipmen territory. Havern directed a fourth-quarter drive ending in Joe Spicko's field goal to give Pitt a narrow 10-8 victory.

Havern was under center from the start for Pitt's October 17 Homecoming game with West Virginia at Pitt Stadium, although a little unreported drama had infested the Pitt team in the days leading up to it. "The 36-35 game was the game where they punished a lot of the black players because we were gonna boycott," said Dave Garnett, noting that they were held out at the start of the game.

As reported in the 1971 *Owl*, several of the black football players, along with athletes from other sports at Pitt, had aired their grievances about mistreatment by coaches, the publicity office, local media, and *The Pitt News*. After the season, Pitt's Black Action Society called a press conference in December to raise public awareness.

"The struggle was in our face on an ongoing basis," Garnett recalled. "Some of our [white] classmates took over the computer room on campus during that time."

The black football players agreed to participate in the Homecoming game, and it was a contest none of them, or any of Pitt's players, will ever forget. The Mountaineers raced out to a 35-8 halftime lead, rushing for 351 yards in the first half.

WVU coach Bobby Bowden, in his first season with the Mountaineers, became conservative in the second half. Meanwhile, Carl DePasqua and offensive coordinator Bimbo Cecconi switched to a Power I formation in the second half, utilizing halfbacks Garnett and Denny Ferris in the same backfield with Tony Esposito. Havern ran the offense to perfection. Pitt scored on each of its four possessions in the second half, every drive in excess of 50 yards. Pitt ran sixty-one plays to WVU's fifteen. Ferris ran for 144 yards and two touchdowns on the day, Garnett scored on a 5-yard run and Esposito bulled over from 1 yard out. Havern threw a pair of two-point conversion passes to tight end Joel Klimek, a decorated Vietnam veteran who came to Pitt in 1965, but left school to join the Army, where he was awarded five medals, including a Bronze Star. The game winner came with fifty-five seconds remaining when, on a third and four from the WVU 5, Havern found end Bill Pilconis alone in the end zone to make the score 36-35. Inexplicably, DePasqua opted not to go for two points, but to kick the extra point, which failed. Luckily, Pitt's John Stevens recovered a Wayne Porter fumble in Pitt territory in the final seconds.

"This is the most fantastic comeback I've ever experienced in seventeen years of coaching," said DePasqua.

Havern, who led five fourth-quarter come-from-behind game-winning drives in his career at Pitt, still hears about it. He said: "That was my [Andy] Warhol moment. People die off. When people call me Davey, they're either from the [McKees] Rocks, or they're from Pitt. I'm reminded of that game maybe six times a year now. It was great. I remember everything about it."

Garnett used the racial turmoil leading up to the game as extra motivation. "It was the first time I ever played a football game where I was so pissed off," he said. "I looked across the line after I got going, and I could see the fear in the eyes of some West Virginia players."

Pitt defeated Miami, 28-17, the following week at Pitt Stadium to raise its record to 5-1. It would be the high point of Carl DePasqua's coaching tenure at Pitt. The Panthers would not win again in 1970. His teams were 9-7 in his first sixteen games, but won only four of his remaining twenty-six games as head coach.

The downfall began, fittingly perhaps, on Halloween afternoon 1970 on a cold, dreary day at Syracuse University's ancient Archbold Stadium where some men, rather than patronizing the cramped, rickety restrooms, chose to urinate against an outer wall of the stadium. The picture inside was not much better—not for Pitt nor for Syracuse. Veteran coach Ben Schwartzwalder had suspended nine black Syracuse football players for the season. They sat huddled together in end zone seats at Archbold. The players had aired their complaints about mistreatment and inequalities on campus.

Syracuse rolled to an easy 43-13 victory, and Pitt lost its final three games. What had begun as a promising season finished with a whimper at 5-5. It was a sad way for seniors Garnett and Bryant Salter to end their careers, and they have mixed emotions about their college experiences. Garnett said: "I love a lot of my teammates. I still have great relationships with them, but that coaching staff did not make it a positive mood for us. For thirty years after I left Pitt, I hated Pitt, until the institutional advancement person assigned somebody to us and started coming to us."

Salter, who later joined the United States Foreign Service as a consul and diplomat and is now CEO of his own international business consulting firm, played six seasons in the NFL, but is ambivalent about his four years at Pitt.

"I had a great [assistant] coach, Bill Lewis," Salter said. "He taught me to be a defensive back, and I've been grateful ever since. But it was a tough time going through those four years at Pitt. Very tough."

And how did the men who coached those Pitt teams see the strife and tension of the late 1960s and early 1970s? Did it affect their players and their approach to coaching? "Myself, it was not a factor. I did not sense it affecting the culture of the team. I could be wrong on that. People were aware of it, but I don't think it affected the staff, and I don't think it affected the culture of the team," said Frank Cignetti, Sr.

Bimbo Cecconi served as an assistant coach at Pitt after Cignetti had left, but his perspective is similar. "I never got involved in that aspect of it," said Cecconi. "I kept my feelings to myself. I listened to the problems that were going on, but I didn't try to solve them."

Dave Havern was a senior when he and his teammates traveled to California to open the 1971 season against UCLA, ranked No. 15 nationally in a preseason poll. The game was telecast locally in Pittsburgh by WTAE TV. Pitt led 14-0 early before the Bruins rallied to take the lead in the second half. Havern, again in relief of John Hogan, tossed a game winning touchdown pass to tight end Les Block in the final minutes of a thrilling 29-25 victory. But the win was a mirage, however, as UCLA finished the season 2-7-1. But it did nothing to diminish the Pitt legend of Davey Havern. Cecconi noted: "He [Havern] was a guy who got the most out of his ability as anybody I know. He had great confidence in himself. He wasn't the biggest, the fastest or the strongest kid. He wasn't the greatest passer, but I think it was his individual drive that made him a good quarterback. He had an air of confidence."

Havern said: "Bimbo, I'd give him my liver if he needed it. He was a good 'take a breath' kind of guy. He could tell when I was all fired up. He knew when to say, 'Hey, take it easy.' Cecconi was invaluable to me going through there."

Havern's competitive spirit got the best of him following a 33-8 loss to Tulane on a wet, muggy night in New Orleans on October 16, 1971. "Some scrawny guy was talking crap to me coming off the field," Havern remembers. "I hit him with a straight right hand. I got him where I wanted to. That was the end of it."

The 1971 Panthers won only two games the rest of the season, including a virtual repeat of Havern's heroics against WVU the year before. Pitt trailed Navy, 35-10, at halftime but Havern again choreographed four touchdown drives in the second half, capped by a six-yard scoring strike to Les Block to produce an identical 36-35 final. Once again, Pitt tried, and missed, the extra point kick rather than an attempt at a two-point conversion.

The season ended in Tallahassee, Fl., where Pitt played Florida State, the first season in which college football teams were permitted to schedule eleven games. Before a sparse crowd of 19,292, Havern donned his white shoes in honor of his final collegiate game. Bill Adams returned an interception for a touchdown to give Pitt a brief 7-0 lead, but the Seminoles roared back for a 31-13 win, ending Pitt's season at 3-8.

The trip to Florida also ended the Pitt career of Ralph Cindrich. Dealing with losing was a difficult experience for the highly competitive Cindrich:

If any of those guys on the grounds crew at Pitt were here today, they'd tell you that I used to cry around them because we were getting beat badly, and guys on our team were laughing and cheering for the other side. It was the most horrific experience I'd had in my life up until that time. For a young guy, it tore me apart. I have to watch how I say this because I hadn't had any catastrophic things happen to me at that point in my life. Those grounds crew guys, [Leo] Horse Czarnecki and the rest of them, I'd go into the tunnel there at Pitt Stadium and I'd eat hot sausage and kielbasa with them. We'd drink beer.

But as Cindrich and Dave Havern were leaving Pitt, another diminutive quarterback from Montour High School arrived on campus. Billy Daniels was a freshman in 1971, while Bob Medwid, who was one of the state's top quarterback prospects as a senior in 1969 at St-Rox High School, entered his junior season (1972) at Pitt with the inside track to run Pitt's newly installed Wishbone offense. DePasqua noted: "We are definitely committed to it [Wishbone] for the fall. We have the quarterbacks to operate it, and sufficient speed to make it go. Our players also like it and are sold on it. I'm confident we'll be improved over last year's record."

Billy Daniels was not so sure. "Did we run the Wishbone that year?" he said when reminded of it decades later. "I even forget that. Holy heck! I find that hard to believe. That surprises me. We didn't have the personnel for that."

"It [Wishbone] was the scheme of things at that time in college football," said offensive coordinator Cecconi. "I went to coaching clinics and heard other coaches give their views on it. I tried to transfer that to our boys. I don't think we did too bad, although we didn't have the best personnel then."

Pitt's Wishbone attack was scrapped after several games. The Panthers began the 1972 season with six straight losses before posting their only victory, a 35-20 decision against Boston College at Pitt Stadium in which Clair Wilson and Bruce Murphy scored on long runs.

The Panthers were 1-9 entering the season finale against Penn State at Beaver Stadium. Daniels, who had seen some action at quarterback in mop up roles and at returning punts and kickoffs, received a surprise announcement from DePasqua early in the week.

"I laugh about it now, but I remember DePasqua telling me before the Penn State game, that I was his quarterback going forward," said Daniels. "Then, a few days later, he was out of a job."

Daniels had a pass intercepted and returned for a touchdown in the first quarter, and Pitt later found itself trailing, 49-0.

"I was a young kid, and I was in over my head," he recalls. "They [Penn State] were loaded. They had [quarterback] John Hufnagel and [running back] John Cappelletti. They were really good."

John Hogan, in his final collegiate game, replaced Daniels and threw four touchdown passes, all in the fourth quarter, to make the score a seemingly respectable 49-27.

"John Hogan was a good quarterback on a bad team," noted teammate Dave Jancisin, a defensive tackle from West Mifflin, Pa. "He could really throw the ball."

But the die had been cast long before Pitt traveled to Happy Valley for what was Carl DePasqua's final game as a football coach. Pitt finished 1-10, the only time in school history Pitt has lost that many games in one season.

"There was a definite pall over that team toward the end of the season," said Daniels. "It was slowly building during the season."

Despite the losing, Daniels gives credit to the men he learned from during his first two years at Pitt:

Foge [Fazio] was the one who recruited me. Bimbo was the quarterbacks coach. Both of them I really liked and respected. They were fantastic. And Carl, too. He was a nice man, but he took a low key approach to everything. The practices were kind of low key. His whole coaching staff, they were great guys and they were quality football coaches, but they were older, more professional types. They were gentlemen who didn't get too excited about anything.

How do you get to be one and ten? I don't recall too many games being close. I thought we had some pretty good players.

Watching from a distance, but keeping close tabs on the Pitt situation, was Havern, who was coaching at Indiana University of Pennsylvania. "There was no excitement, no energy at all in the program by the end of Carl's tenure," Havern said.

"Some of the older guys were calling it in, but the younger guys, I was looking to get better, to improve," said Daniels. "Eventually, that paid off for me. Even at the end of that year."

Dean Billick said:

Things actually got worse under Carl, but I'm not blaming him or anybody else, but they didn't get better, so there had to be some changes made. It was an unrealistic view of big time college athletics by Pitt. Pitt played all those big name schools because that was the only way they could get anybody to come to the stadium to watch those games. To be perfectly honest, they were prostituting the players by putting them out there, and the coaches, by not committing themselves to a program against the likes of the schools they were competing against.

"You grow up thinking you're good, and that you can compete with anybody," said Daniels. "But the reality was we were a pretty bad football team at that point."

Cas Myslinski, his football program on the brink of failure, was charged with finding a replacement for Carl DePasqua, for hiring someone to orchestrate a major football revival on the Pitt campus.

"The next coach, whoever he is, will be the new messiah, the guy who finally will turn things around," Pat Livingston wrote in *The Pittsburgh Press*. "If he fails, heaven knows what Pitt will do."[7]

2

THE MAJOR CHANGE
(1973–1975)

*Over the years there have been funds set aside for a rainy day. It's
probably a substantial amount. I'd call this a rainy day. In fact, it's
pouring.*[1]

Bob Miller (1972)

*The Pitt football team, in one short and heated afternoon, transformed
itself from a question mark into an exclamation point yesterday and
that spells bad news for the opponents who have been knocking the
Panthers around for the last ten years.*[2]

Russ Franke (*The Pittsburgh Press*, September 16, 1973)

Feelings of dissatisfaction about the direction of Pitt's football program
were festering among the few hearty souls who followed the team's
fortunes during the early 1970s. The doom and gloom did not go
unnoticed by Cas Myslinski, who invited a small number of boosters to
travel with the team to Tallahassee for Pitt's final game of the 1971 season.

Among the invitees were C. R. "Bob" Miller and Sam Sciullo, Sr., two
of the founding members of the Pitt Golden Panthers booster club. Also
making the trip was Frank Knisley, a banker who had played football at
Pitt in the early 1940s, and whose son, Eric, was then Pitt's placekicker.
Charles "Corky" Cost, another former Pitt football letterman and CEO
of the construction company bearing his name, also attended, along
with Moe Lebow, a Pittsburgh jeweler. Roland Catarinella, a friend of

Myslinski who had been a member of West Point's powerhouse teams in the mid-1940s, also made the trip.

Although not a specific line item on the agenda, how much longer Carl DePasqua should remain coach of the Panthers did get mentioned. Two factions emerged as to whether DePasqua should be back in 1972, but Myslinski, as well as Chancellor Posvar, who also attended the meetings inside a Holiday Inn on the outskirts of the city, were willing to give the coach the 1972 season to right Pitt's sinking ship.

September 30, 1972 was an historic day in Pittsburgh, as Pirates' superstar outfielder Roberto Clemente collected his 3,000th career hit in a victory against the New York Mets at Three Rivers Stadium. Pittsburgh had already clinched the National League East.

Several miles away at Pitt Stadium, the 0-3 Panthers had a game of their own.

"We played Northwestern," Pitt radio color analyst Bill Hillgrove recalled. "There couldn't have been more than 6,000 people in the stadium. They just ran off tackle all day long and we didn't stop 'em. It was very discouraging."

Pitt lost, 27-22. Privately, Posvar and Myslinski had seen enough. DePasqua would serve as coach for the rest of the 1972 season, but the search for a replacement would begin immediately, unbeknownst to virtually everyone. Billick noted: "[Chancellor] Posvar wanted to win. I think he didn't know how. He didn't know what that meant. I'm not sure Cas [Myslinski] knew, either. They were tired of getting beat and embarrassed."

There were no high-priced headhunters or search firms to explore and vet candidates in the early 1970s. Pitt's quest to find a new football coach was strictly an undercover operation orchestrated by several key boosters. In early October, Myslinski invited Miller, Sciullo and automobile magnate Bill Baierl to his office. He told them that Pitt was going to look for a new football coach, and that they would be the men who would help him do it.

"Myslinski had become gun shy, particularly after the Kush affair a few years before," Miller said during an interview in 2004.

All three men were Pitt graduates. Miller, a Navy frogman in World War II, had a law degree, but never practiced, opting for a career in private business before serving for many years as an administrator at what was then Robert Morris College.

Baierl, who played basketball at Pitt in the late 1940s for legendary coach H. C. "Doc" Carlson, watched his family's automobile business grow from Baierl Chevrolet to a dealership empire in the North Hills suburbs of Pittsburgh.

Sciullo had both undergraduate and law degrees from Pitt, and spent close to thirty years representing countless Pitt students, athletes, coaches, and administrators. "If you were on the team and you got into trouble, you didn't call your coach," Ralph Cindrich remembered. "You didn't call your mom. You called Sam Sciullo."

The three men are deceased: Miller died in 2004, Baierl in 2007, and Sciullo in 2013.

Miller was Pitt's chief persuader, if not bidder. He went to former Pitt coach Dave Hart, asking for recommendations about coaches Pitt should pursue. Hart supplied three names: Frank Kush, the Arizona State coach who had backed out from his commitment to Pitt in early 1969; Homer Rice, a former collegiate head coach who was then athletics director at North Carolina; and Johnny Majors, a decorated player at Tennessee who was leading Iowa State's program to a level of success, including the school's first two bowl game appearances.

Rice showed little interest, and was soon scratched from the list. Kush sent an emissary to Pittsburgh to watch the Panthers in their final home game of the 1972 season against West Virginia, but nothing came of it. Kush later provided some insight into why he chose not to come to Pittsburgh in 1969, hinting that he had had a difficult time convincing some of his assistant coaches to leave the warmth of Arizona for the changing seasons of Pittsburgh.

But there was more, namely Pitt's restrictive academic standards. Frank Kush noted:

> There's an old philosophy that you don't check your transcripts on the goal line.
>
> It's important to have a program that a kid can master. Pitt talks about all its football players who are doctors and dentists, but so many people are just average. You have to provide an opportunity for them. These are the things that make a program.[3]

That left Majors. Myslinski did not seek approval from Iowa State officials to make contact with their football coach. The original call to Majors came from Dave Hart, who told Majors about Pitt's dire football situation. Hart explained that Pitt was willing to give it one more shot before perhaps considering some type of reduction of its program. Hart was aware of the

Bellefield Educational Trust Fund, formed in 1946, which later became known as The Panther Foundation. It had been established to provide loans to graduated Pitt athletes who wished to pursue graduate degrees. It would ultimately fund The Major Change In Pitt Football.

Dave Hart informed Majors that he should expect a phone call from one of the members of Pitt's secret search committee, and that was Bob Miller, who was running up expensive long-distance phone bills between his Pittsburgh home and Ames, Iowa.

Pitt was not the only school interested in Majors during the fall of 1972. Duffy Daugherty was retiring at Michigan State, and rumors were swirling that there might be openings at Kentucky and Purdue. But, unlike Kush and Rice, Pitt had piqued Majors' interest. He decided to send his brother, Joe—an attorney—to Pittsburgh for a preliminary exploration. Myslinski, Miller and Sciullo met John's younger brother at Greater Pittsburgh Airport and drove him to the Oakland campus, where they registered him under an assumed name at the Webster Hall Hotel, down the street from the Cathedral of Learning.

John Majors said:

> Joe was there under the ruse of being an adviser as far as what the Pitt people should do about getting a coach. [Chancellor] Posvar, according to what I know, did not know that he was John Majors' brother. My name never came out in the papers until right around the time I took the job.

The visit went well. Joe Majors reported back to his brother that he should take a serious look at the Pitt opportunity. Bob Miller, meanwhile, was relentless in his pursuit of Majors. Majors stated: "Bob Miller kept calling me. He's a great talker. He's such a charmer on the phone. We would usually talk later in the week—Wednesday or Thursday night. If it hadn't been for Bob Miller's charm, I never would have visited Pittsburgh." When Majors visited Pittsburgh, he went to Myslinski's house for a dinner meeting. Miller and Sciullo also were in attendance. Sam Sciullo, Sr., said:

> It was a little strange. At first, John seemed to be deflecting from himself. He mentioned a couple names of other coaches he thought would be good for the job. He didn't seem that anxious to want the Pitt job. Chancellor Posvar later joined the meeting, then left by himself. After

that, we started talking turkey. At one point I whispered to John, "John, he [Myslinski] wants you so bad he can taste you." I wanted John to be encouraged to make his own demands.

Majors returned to Iowa without making any commitment, saying only that he was interested. Myslinski and Miller later flew to Iowa and met with Majors at a hotel near the Des Moines airport, but could not get Majors to accept the job. Sciullo, Sr., said:

A while later, Bob, Cas and I met another evening at Cas's house. We were in his study, or library. We had to wait a while to call John because of the time difference in Iowa. Bob was sitting at the desk by the phone. Cas was sitting in an easy chair, reading something. Finally, Bob got Majors on the phone. Cas was making like he was reading, but you could tell he was more interested in Bob's conversation with John. At one point, Cas looked over at me and winked, as if to say, "It looks as if we got him." And he did. It was Bob Miller, nobody else, who got John Majors to come to Pitt.

In Memphis for his Iowa State team's Liberty Bowl date with Georgia Tech, Majors had a private meeting with legendary coach Bud Wilkinson, who was there to provide color commentary for the ABC telecast. Wilkinson advised Majors to take the job, noting Pitt's football tradition and the region's reputation as a fertile recruiting territory.

Myslinski flew to Memphis to meet with Majors, and secured a handshake agreement on Saturday, December 16, 1972.

Dean Billick was settling into a comfortable position on the floor of the living room at his Greentree apartment in anticipation of watching the December 18, 1972 Liberty Bowl game. A press conference had been scheduled for the following day at the Cathedral of Learning, and he knew the reason for it:

I remember the TV announcers [Wilkinson and Chris Schenkel] saying it's rumored Johnny Majors may be the next coach at Pitt. I thought to myself, "Okay, he's going to be our new coach. How can we talk about it? What can we call it?" The idea just popped into my head—"Major. Majors. Major Change!" I remember thinking, "This is gonna be a Major change in Pitt football." And it was all of that.

John Terrill Majors was born May 25, 1935 at his grandmother's house in Lynchburg, Tennessee. The oldest of six children (five boys and a girl), the Majors family later settled in Huntland, where John's father, Shirley Majors—a fine athlete in his youth—coached baseball, football, and basketball. John played all the sports, and showed a bent for leadership from an early age. He was the kid who organized most of the neighborhood activities, especially the games they played. Near the end of World War II, not only did John participate in a national military scrap iron drive, he collected more individual scrap iron than anyone in Huntland!

"My mother and father gave all of us what I would call a loving discipline," Majors recalled. "We were encouraged to think for ourselves and be individuals, but at the same time we knew that certain things were expected of us."

Two of John's brothers, Billy and Bobby, also starred for the Tennessee Volunteers, while brother Larry played collegiate football for his father.

Young John also developed a keen interest in college football as a boy. He favored the great Army teams of the 1940s, and made it a point to listen to the annual Army-Navy game while sitting on the floor. Throughout his coaching career, Majors would speak fondly of the service academies and their fierce determination on the football field. Upon his hiring at Pitt, he admitted to being intrigued by the fact that both Wesley Posvar and Cas Myslinski had graduated from West Point.

Whenever John and his younger brothers attended baseball games, they made it a point to arrive early. "We wanted to see everything," Majors said. "Batting practice, infield practice, the grounds crew getting the field ready for the game."

After playing for his father at Huntland, Majors took his skills to the University of Tennessee, where he overcame some initial doubt about his ability to play at that level to become one of college football's finest players in the mid-1950s. He finished second to Notre Dame's Paul Hornung for the Heisman Trophy in 1956 when he led the Volunteers to a 10-1 record and a No. 2 national ranking.

Following graduation, Majors spent the 1957 season as a graduate assistant at Tennessee before joining the staff on a full-time basis for two years. Following four seasons (1960–1963) as an assistant coach at Mississippi State, he joined Frank Broyles' staff at Arkansas, where he remained for four seasons before being named head coach at Iowa State in 1968. After breathing life into the ISU program and establishing it as a force in the Big Eight, Majors turned to Pittsburgh, where changes were in the offing.

Pitt had decided to break away from its "Big Four" arrangement with Penn State, West Virginia, and Syracuse, an agreement that, among other things, restricted the practice of redshirting. Myslinski often commented that he thought it was not the hindrance some thought it to be, but at his introductory press conference, Majors said he would not have taken the Pitt job if the university had remained part of it. He hinted at his conversation with Wilkinson as an influence in his decision to come to Pitt.

"I might not have anticipated coming here some time ago," Majors explained, "but I talked to some people who have knowledge of the game. They think I made a wise decision."[4]

"He [Majors] walked into a very poor program at Pitt," said Billick. "He may not have known how weak it was."

Majors did not make any bold proclamations. "I don't believe in making quick promises," he said. "My job is to make lemonade out of a lemon."[5]

Following the press conference, Foge Fazio, in coaching limbo following the dismissal of Carl DePasqua, took Majors to Hopewell High School to meet Tony Dorsett and his coach, Butch Ross. Dorsett, one of the nation's top running back prospects, was in his senior year, and Pitt was going to have to recruit hard and fast to secure his services. Dean Billick noted:

> That first night, I took John around to all the Pittsburgh television stations. After it was over, he told me, "You wore me out!" We went everywhere. But he liked that. If it had been somebody who wouldn't have liked that, it would have been a different story. But he was willing and he was eager to do it. He was terrific to work with, but it was a whirlwind and exhausting. He was probably that way with his entire staff, and that's probably what had to happen at Pitt in order to turn the program around. He was a lot of fun.

Upon his arrival at Pitt, Majors took a suite of rooms at Bruce Hall on campus. One evening, he convened a meeting involving several boosters, including Sciullo and Ed Ifft, a financial adviser who would become one of Majors' closest friends in Pittsburgh. During the meeting, a few of Majors' assistant coaches arrived, throwing their bags on the floor and positioning themselves in seats around a conference table.

"John asked what we thought was important to know about Pitt," said Sciullo. "He was looking for information he could use to tell recruits."

Ifft and another friend, Ron Puntil, met Majors for the first time at the Field Club in Fox Chapel, where Majors was meeting with WTAE TV executive John Conomikes to talk about a weekly show for Majors during football season. Pitt had never had one. Ifft said:

> One of the first things John said was a question. "Can we win here? Can we recruit good football players here?" Those persons who responded in a positive manner, Majors remembered. I said, "Coach, we've been waiting, looking for somebody like you to come to Pitt." Everybody I introduced him to, after he took the job, he asked the same question: "Can I win here? Can I recruit here?' He wanted to be around positive people.

Somebody like Majors was not what Pitt football had been accustomed to. He and the majority of the assistants he brought to Pittsburgh spoke in rich Southern accents. They had grown up and gone to school and coached at places far from the Northeast. They had made important contacts and connections in parts of the country Pitt had never recruited. Many of Pitt's past football coaches—and their assistants—had been men with strong ties to Pitt.

"I knew how to recruit football players, and I also knew how to recruit good coaches, and I knew how to recruit the right type of alumni to help us," Majors remarked many years later.

Majors' men were a hungry, aggressive bunch, led by assistant head coach Jackie Sherrill, then twenty-nine years old. Majors was first introduced to Sherrill in the early 1960s when Majors, then an assistant coach at Mississippi State, was on a recruiting mission during a basketball game at Biloxi (Miss.) High School, where Sherrill was a student.

Sherrill played fullback and linebacker for Paul "Bear" Bryant at Alabama before short coaching stints with the Crimson Tide and then under Frank Broyles at Arkansas. He was later hired by Majors to come to Iowa State.

Another member of the Iowa State staff was Jimmy Johnson, who had played at Arkansas. When Johnson left Iowa State for a job at Arkansas, Majors promoted Sherrill to assistant head coach.

"That was a fun loving group of coaches we had at Iowa State," Majors recalled. "But I can't ever remember seeing Jackie yawn during a staff meeting the next morning. He challenged the players. Nobody could ever question Jackie's work ethic."

Offensive coordinator George Haffner was a native Chicagoan who had originally gone to college at Notre Dame before transferring to McNeese State for his final year of eligibility. Line coach Joe Avezzano was a New Yorker who played collegiately at Florida State. He was instrumental in opening Pitt's recruiting pipeline to the Sunshine State, including five players—Arnie Weatherington, Cecil Johnson, Jim Buoy, and the Walkers, Elliott and Leverga, from Miami Jackson High School. They came to be known as Pitt's Jackson Five.

Defensive line coach Jim Dyar was from Alabama, and played college football at the University of Houston. Offensive backfield coach Harry Jones was an All-State scholastic quarterback in Oklahoma before starring as a safety on Arkansas' national championship team in 1964. Larry Holton was an Iowan who played for Majors at Iowa State. Secondary coach Joe Madden was from Washington, D.C., and played collegiately at Maryland prior to serving coaching stints at several schools, including Iowa State. Receivers coach Bobby Roper was another Texan who was a member of several outstanding teams at Arkansas in the 1970s.

Bob Leahy, who had a short term as a quarterback with the Pittsburgh Steelers, also was a member of Majors' first staff at Pitt. He had been an All-Conference player at Kansas State Teachers College.

The youngest members of the staff were Keith Schroeder and Bob Matey. Schroeder had been an All Big Eight defensive player for Majors, while Matey played high school ball at Chaney High in Youngstown, Ohio, where his brother, Ed, was head coach. That relationship would pay great dividends for Pitt. Youngstown Chaney sent standout players Matt Cavanaugh (quarterback) and the Brothers Pelusi—John (center), Jeff (linebacker), and J. C. (defensive lineman) to Pitt in the near future. Billick stated: "That whole coaching staff was a young, aggressive Southern football staff, something Pitt wasn't used to, and the players thrived in it. The program thrived in the public perception because John Majors made it thrive. He was everywhere. Television. In the newspapers."

Majors and his men caught the attention of WTAE radio talk show host, writer, and local legend Myron Cope. Hearing tales of one recruiting success after another, Cope delivered several dramatic commentaries set to the music of the William Tell Overture, more commonly recognized as the theme song for the old *Lone Ranger* TV series. One such commentary centered on Jackie Sherrill's recruitment of Dorsett, including the anecdote about Sherrill's mother, Dovie, preparing a homemade rhubarb pie for the young prospect. "Hiyo, Majors! Hiyo, Dovie!"

"Those commentaries were good for Pitt," said Bill Hillgrove. "It provided a spark. It caught the general public's attention. Majors brought in good, young coaches, and it opened up the South for us. We got faster. The speed and conditioning were things we had lacked."

Much of that had to do with Pitt's grossly inadequate facilities at the time of Majors' hiring. He was less than impressed by his first look at Pitt Stadium, both inside and outside:

Cas Myslinski picked me up at the airport one night and took me directly to Pitt Stadium. It was dark, so I couldn't get a true idea of what it was like inside the stadium, but the impression I had was that it was rather old. Then Cas took me into the locker room, and I recall that vividly. It looked as if nothing had been done to improve it since Jock Sutherland had left. It was in very bad condition. There was no weight room. They had one Universal weight machine in the middle of the locker room. I knew that there was an urgency to do something about the locker room facilities immediately. It looked very old, very decrepit, and very dark.

Majors admitted he had not been spoiled during his five seasons at Iowa State, but he had come from a rich football background, and had been exposed to quality football and coaches in both the Southeastern and Southwest Conferences.

In 1971, he led the Iowa State Cyclones to an 8-3 record and a spot in the Sun Bowl. He was named Big Eight Coach of the Year by both wire services, followed by the Liberty Bowl berth in 1972. Then it was on to Pittsburgh.

Majors was a master of organization, and brought consistency and thoroughness to Pitt's program. Dean Billick noted:

He really knew what the head coach's role was. As far as the Xs and Os, he coached the assistant coaches. He didn't coach the players so much. He was the face and voice of Pitt football, a Southern voice I might add. That was refreshingly different from anything Pitt had had. There was no effort to hide that fact that the South had taken over, and it needed to in order to get the program turned around.

Sam Sciullo, Sr. said:

John brought something to Pitt that was so lacking, and that was enthusiasm. He used to talk about "Pride and Enthusiasm" all the time, and while it sounded like a lot of baloney, it really was contagious, and he backed it up by going out and getting guys who could play football.

The holdover players from the DePasqua years soon realized things were going to be different with John Majors as coach. Defensive tackle Dave Jancsin was among the local players who went to Greater Pittsburgh Airport to serve as part of a welcoming committee for Majors.

"I couldn't even understand what he said in that Southern accent," Jancsin remembered.

"He [Majors] seemed even younger than his age [thirty-seven]," quarterback Billy Daniels said. "He was young, very positive and very personable."

"His dad once said that John's mind goes a mile a minute, and that he uses every bit of that mind," Mary Lynn Majors, John's wife commented in the 1973 Pitt-Baylor game program. "That's the best description I've ever heard of him."

In the final few hours of 1972, Majors, Myslinski, Miller, and Joe Majors and their wives celebrated New Year's Eve at the Castle Shannon home of Sam Sciullo, Sr. Earlier that day, Majors had attended the Steelers' AFC title game loss to the undefeated Miami Dolphins at Three Rivers Stadium on an unseasonably warm day. That evening, Pittsburgh Pirates superstar outfielder Roberto Clemente was killed in a plane crash off the coast of Puerto Rico. At Sciullo's residence, the men watched the first half of the Penn State-Oklahoma Sugar Bowl game before getting down to the business of Majors' first contract. Sam Sciullo, Sr., noted:

> I was taking notes throughout the meeting. I had to put the agreement into writing. At one point, when John stated a salary demand, Cas responded by offering a figure even higher! That's how bad he wanted John to be satisfied. We came to an agreement, and everything was settled. John always knew what he wanted, and I never had any problems with him.

With contractual details settled, including Pitt's decision to remove its foreign language requirement along with the beginning of an academic support services department for athletes, Pitt's new coaching staff engineered an historic recruiting campaign, due in large part to the availability of funds from The Panther Foundation. When the recruiting dust settled, Majors and his staff, in the final year before the NCAA mandated the maximum number of football scholarships a school could award in a given year, more than seventy players had been signed to grant-in aids to play football at Pitt. A university document discovered in the athletic department files at Pitt listed seventy-six such awardees. The 1973 Pitt football media guide listed sixty-nine recruits. John Majors recalled:

> I met with the chancellor [Posvar] and Cas Myslinski and told them that I wanted to be able to give fifty scholarships a year for four years. Pitt had been giving only as many as twenty-five. Sure enough, in January, right after I had taken the job, the NCAA came out with the rule limiting scholarships to thirty a year and 105 total. I knew I'd better sign as many as I could that first year because I knew that unlimited amount would soon be out the door.

The first high school player to sign up for The Major Change in Pitt Football was Canon-McMillan High School linebacker Joe Macerelli, who signed with Pitt alongside teammate George O'Korn; Macerelli noted:

> I got called to the office at school, and the rest is history. It was not a high gloss presentation. "Hi, I'm Jackie Sherrill" in that low, monotone voice. "We're gonna do something special here at Pitt. We want you to be a part of it."
> Next thing I know, Jackie came to my house. Then, Johnny [Majors] came with Jackie. Those two guys were different as day and night. Jackie was the earthy character. Johnny was the high energy, more outgoing person. "We're gonna do this at Pitt. We're gonna do that." It swept a young kid off his feet. It definitely worked for me.

During his official visit to Pitt's campus, Macerelli's host was rising senior lineman Dave Blandino. Macerelli noted: "That was a godsend. If one of the crazy guys had taken me around campus, I might have thought differently about going there. Dave being who he is, just a special guy, he and I are great friends to this day." Blandino eventually became a geriatric doctor; Macerelli an attorney.

The precise number of recruits in that first class is probably lost to history, but there can be no doubt as to which recruit was the most important—young Anthony Drew Dorsett. "We had a lot of players in that first recruiting class," said Jackie Sherrill, "but we didn't have any player with Tony's ability."

John Majors credits Sherrill with being chiefly responsible for recruiting the future Heisman Trophy winner to Pitt. Pitt was a late entrant in the Dorsett Derby, and Sherrill hustled to make up ground, making countless visits to Hopewell High School.

"He [Sherrill] almost practically lived at the school," was how Dorsett put it.

Somewhat overwhelmed by both the number and frequency of the visitors who came to see him during school hours, a Hopewell administrator named Barney Waters came to serve as a buffer between Dorsett and the college coaches. Waters did not take to Jackie Sherrill, not initially. "He [Waters] came into the room, so I introduced myself," said Sherrill. "He said, 'Are you from Pitt?' I said 'Yes,' and he told me to get out. He actually chased me out of the school."

Sherrill admits he had a hard time getting back in, but luckily for Pitt, he eventually won over Barney Waters as well as a number of faculty members at Hopewell. "I was there every day at the school," he said.

Not only at the school. Sherrill was a frequent visitor to the Dorsett home in Aliquippa, and even spent an entire overnight awake in his car outside the house because he wanted to be there to confront any Penn State representative who might come calling. Sherrill said: "Tony was a very shy person, very quiet but very polished. One thing I noticed when I went into his home that really got my attention was how clean and neat it was, even though he lived in the projects. Not too many white people went into the projects at that time."

Dorsett was not the only player from Hopewell who caught the attention of Pitt's coaches. Senior defensive lineman Ed Wilamowski also was on Pitt's recruiting radar. Jackie Sherrill said:

Ed and Tony were very close. Tony probably looked up to Ed. Tony was at their house a lot. They would go on visits together. Of course, everybody wanted Tony. Not everybody wanted Ed, even though Ed was a very good football player.

When they would visit places, they [schools] would separate them. I didn't separate them. They roomed together. They also went out together.

Although Dorsett later divulged that it was not a sure thing that he would follow Wilamowski to his college of choice, he did say that he and his teammate were "pretty tight" in high school. Sherrill played a hunch: "I just had a feeling that if I could get Ed to commit, Tony would follow Ed, and that's what happened. When Ed committed to Pitt, Tony felt very, very comfortable about doing the same thing."

A longstanding relationship between Sherrill and Dorsett evolved over the years. "I came to know and trust him [Sherrill] like an older brother," said Dorsett. "Jackie Sherrill meant an awful lot to me."

Dorsett and the rest of that first recruiting class comprised a football roster in and of itself. It included players from twelve different states as far reaching as the Deep South, New England, and the Pacific Northwest. But before the vast majority arrived on campus, Majors and his staff were able to assess the returning players from the 1972 team. The first part of that process, an offseason conditioning program labeled The Fourth Quarter, was an experience none of them—those who stayed and those who left Pitt's program—will ever forget. There had not been any conditioning program in place between the end of the season and the start of spring ball during Carl DePasqua's term as coach.

Majors' assistant coaches coordinated the workouts, which included weightlifting at Pitt Stadium, followed by a more intensive program uphill at Fitzgerald Field House. Daniels noted: "We had to run from the stadium up to the Field House—this was the middle of winter—and we saw the linemen, who had been going through agility drills, gasping for air. A lot of us were thinking, 'My God, these guys are out of shape!' But forty-five minutes later, that was us!"

Clair Wilson, a senior who enjoyed a stellar scholastic career at Kiski Area High School, might have been Pitt's starting tailback if not for Tony Dorsett in 1973. He remembers the conditioning routine:

It was intense. It was a very high level stressful situation. You went from having no winter workouts to organized workouts. Before Majors, you just worked out on your own. When Majors came in, that all changed.

When we would run sprints, you know how you would lean forward afterward with your head down and your hands on your knees? Well, we weren't allowed to do that. You had to stand straight up with your arms up and put your hands behind your head. It was brutal. A lot of people left the team after that.

Dave Jancisin was entering his junior season as a starting defensive tackle. Upon reflection, he realizes he did not have any better alternative to enduring the workouts. "It was either make it through there, or maybe go to Vietnam," he said. "It was very grueling, but Majors used to say, 'Those who stay will play, and those who play will rise to the top in life.'"

"We did everything imaginable," Daniels remembers. "Crab crawling across the gym floor, various stations, jog along the track then sprint the straightaways, jog the turns." But nothing compared to the drills conducted inside the wrestling room:

> That was brutal. That was Jackie Sherrill's station. You'd do all kind of agility drills on all fours, and then you'd do up-downs until you could hardly get up anymore. And then he'd have people wrestling. You'd pair up with someone.
>
> The last part of the whole thing, after down-ups, he would call one guy out, and that guy would have to lie in the middle of the circle on his back. He would call another name out, and that guy would dive on the guy and pin him. The first guy couldn't really defend himself. Then he [Sherrill] would blow his whistle, and the guy on the bottom would have to get up. The rest of the guys were around you, yelling and screaming. It was hysteria. Guys were hyperventilating, throwing up.

Jim Bolla was the starting center on Pitt's basketball team at the time. Almost fifty years later, he has vivid memories of football players in various states of exhaustion.

"We [basketball players] would be on the court getting ready for practice, and we saw the football players straggling along, completely drenched in sweat," said Bolla. "Some of them would be puking. Others had blood on their shirts and shorts."

Pitt's basketball coaches then were head coach Buzz Ridl and assistants Fran Webster and Tim Grgurich. Ridl and Webster were mild mannered, middle aged men; Grgurich was the younger, more emotional member of the staff, but even his brand of energy could not compare to what Bolla saw in some of Pitt's new football assistant coaches.

"Jackie Sherrill, Joe Avezzano, Jim Dyar—they'd be yelling and screaming at the players," said Bolla. "Billy Knight and I were watching some of this one day. We thought to ourselves, "These guys [coaches] are nuts.""

There was, apparently, a method to the madness, as Billy Daniels recalled:

> The coaches had elected a leadership council, or something like that, the first few days, and I was on it. So every day when I was in that

wrestling room, I was the one on my back. Guys much bigger than me—Rod Kirby, Mike Bulino—they'd be diving on me. There was a lot of pressure put on us during that program. You had to respond, and you got a lot tougher mentally and physically. As an athlete, you want to respond to a challenge. Those are the kinds of traits you like to think you're developing as a football player. That helped me improve from a toughness standpoint.

Daniels will never forget the experience—or Sherrill.

"Jackie scared the hell out of everybody," he said. "He really did. We were petrified of him. I came to the conclusion that he would push us to the point where we would pass out. That's as far as you can go, so what are you worried about?"

"Jackie was the hit man, the tough guy on Johnny's staff," Dave Jancisin added.

Sherrill, who always had a keen eye for spotting physical talent, also recognized players who possessed intangible qualities. Such was his feeling for the undersized quarterback who led the Panthers during the first two seasons of The Major Change.

"The one guy who probably played better than his ability, and had a lot to do with changing Pittsburgh into a winner was the little quarterback, Billy Daniels," said Sherrill.

"If I had a son, I'd want him to emulate Billy Daniels," said Joe Macerelli. "He had a strong inner drive to be the best at everything he's ever done."

Sherrill, a man not prone to excessive laughter, chuckled plenty many years later when reminded of Daniels' recollections of that conditioning regimen:

Today, as a coach, your ass would be fired for doing something like that. Back then, you're talking about a very physical game. But if you're not mentally tough, you're not gonna be physically tough. It was more about building their mental toughness and taking kids and showing them they can go further than they think they can go.

During his days as a player at Alabama in the 1960s, Sherrill went through the same type of conditioning routine under the direction of assistant coach Howard Schnellenberger.

"I'd get in there [at Pitt workouts] and challenge them, and do the same things they would do," said Sherrill. "In life, unless you pay the price, then you really don't understand the rewards. Those kids at Pittsburgh had never paid the price at all."

With the winter conditioning program behind them, Pitt's coaches and players moved downhill to Pitt Stadium for the opening of spring practice. It would be the first time for Majors to do some actual coaching on the stadium's artificial surface, which looked much better to him on the inside during daylight hours than it had during his earlier nighttime tour given by Cas Myslinski.

Pitt returned a number of starting players in 1973, including most starters from both the offensive and defensive lines. Carl DePasqua's first full recruiting season (1969) had been a good one. Those players would be the seniors in Majors' first season at Pitt. Bill Hillgrove noted:

> We played Tulane down there [New Orleans] in 1971. I saw one of our former coaches. I can't remember his name, but he was doing some scouting for an NFL team. I asked him, "How many kids are you looking at?" He said, "About a dozen. Three Tulane players and nine Pitt players." And we weren't very competitive in that game [33-8 loss]. In other words, we had some players, and a few of them made the pros.

"I think he [Majors] was shocked, at spring ball, by the caliber of talent on hand," added Dean Billick. "It was much better than what he expected."

As a major Eastern independent, Pitt had complete freedom in scheduling, but typically played the same seven or eight traditional opponents, with several new teams added each season.

"He [Majors] had come from Iowa State, where he had to deal with Oklahoma and Nebraska all the time, both on the field and in recruiting," said Billick. "Here, sure, you had Penn State, but he knew he could compete and to make a name for himself, and to win some football games."

Their approach to coaching was radically different from what Pitt's veteran players had seen from Carl DePasqua, Bimbo Cecconi, and the rest of the previous coaching staff.

"Carl [DePasqua] didn't have the resources," said Jancisin. "His assistants were very nice guys, very gentlemanly, but they were still living in the dark ages as far as recognizing the importance of speed in the game of football. Majors brought in depth, and he did get a halfback named Tony Dorsett."

"It was like going from a Division III football program to what big-time college football was all about," said Clair Wilson.

Dave Jancisin recalled:

We never ran to the football. We hadn't been in good shape. Under the
previous staff, it was coached like it was 1963. Things change, times
change, and the black athlete was becoming more popular in the South.
Majors and his staff recognized that, and used it to Pitt's advantage.

These guys [Majors' staff] fought each other. If you didn't run to the
football, you had to run the stadium steps along with your coach. Before
1973, we had thunder, but we had no lightning.

Before the 1973 Panthers left campus for training camp in August on the
campus of Pitt-Johnstown, the entire squad, including the newcomers,
assembled at Pitt Stadium for some light workouts. Billy Daniels noted:

We were in shorts and T shirts before we went to camp. There were all
these kids that no one had seen before. A lot of 'em. You're trying to
pick Dorsett out among all these new guys. It was unbelievable. What
a culture shock. Somehow, he [Majors] got us all together, and we did
pretty well that first year.

John Majors had his first look at Dorsett in live action at the annual Big
33 Game in Hershey, Pa., in August. The details of how and where he
responded to a brilliant run by his prized recruit remain cloudy. Majors
claims he waited until he was back in the privacy of his motel room, where
he shut the door behind him, and let out a whoop, "Hoo-ray! We have a
tailback!"

Dean Billick remembers it differently.

"I was sitting next to Majors," said Billick. "Dorsett made a great run.
Majors jumped up, screaming, 'We got a football player.' He screamed
so loud, and he was embarrassed because I know [Penn State coach Joe]
Paterno heard him. Paterno was a few seats down."

Billick remembers a similar incident at training camp in Johnstown. "Tony
ran for a long touchdown early in camp," said Billick "Majors ran, his funny
little legs the way he ran, all the way down along the field with Dorsett."

After another scrimmage in which Dorsett displayed some impressive
moves, Ed Ifft had a conversation with defensive coordinator Jackie
Sherrill. "He [Sherrill] asked me, 'What do you think about Dorsett?'
I said, 'Either your defense is pretty bad, or that kid [Dorsett] is pretty
good.' Jackie said, 'My defense isn't that bad.'"

Recognizing the greatness in the freshman back, Billick knew the young player was about to become the focus of increased media and public attention. Billick had his first meeting with Dorsett at training camp, telling him he wanted to use a play on initials, calling "TD Dorsett."

"He didn't say, 'No,'" Billick recalls. "He was very quiet. He was very cooperative, but I can't tell you that he wanted to do it. His personality was within himself. That was when we knew him as DOOR-sit. He later changed the pronunciation in a 1976 interview with a female reporter on the lawn of the Cathedral of Learning."

Bill Hillgrove saw the considerate side of the freshman Dorsett toward the end of the 1973 season. "We did an interview with him [Dorsett] in Arizona before the Fiesta Bowl," said Hillgrove. "He helped us carry the equipment back to the car. I said to myself, 'What a nice kid he is.'"

"I tried to help him so he didn't get overwhelmed by all the requests," said Dean Billick, "but after his freshman year it did become overwhelming."

Majors and his staff appreciated the hot weather during training camp in Johnstown. The Panthers were scheduled to meet Georgia's Bulldogs on September 15 at Sanford Stadium, noted for its hedges surrounding the playing field. "Between the Hedges" is how the locals describe a game played at Georgia.

When the Pitt team arrived at the stadium to begin a new era in the school's football history, it was met by a howling sea of red—boisterous Georgia fans out for blood. Nose tackle Gary Burley, playing his first game as a Panther, rallied his teammates:

> I pulled all the guys together and we said a prayer. I remember saying, "Hey, we're just about the only people here who are going to support us." In the locker room right before the game, we really weren't sure what to expect. We were like a bunch of nomads who had come together under Coach Majors and his crew.

Billy Daniels said:

> That [Georgia] game is the one I probably remember more than any. There was a little contingent of Pitt fans, and they were making a lot of noise. When we ran out on the field, fans were calling us "Dog Food, Dog Food." [Offensive lineman] Ray Olsen and [defensive tackle] Glenn Hyde were yelling back at them. It was a lot of fun. We had every opportunity to win that game.

After holding the Bulldogs on downs to start the game, Pitt drove 62 yards on eleven plays, capped by a 17-yard touchdown run by Daniels. Georgia tied the game with a touchdown in the second quarter. Neither team scored in the second half. Pitt missed a chance to win the game when Carson Long, in his first game as a Panther, missed a 33-yard field goal with 3:10 remaining in the fourth quarter. Both Long and freshman punter Larry Swider handled every punt and kick from placement from 1973 through 1976.

Despite the 7-7 tie, Pitt players and fans had reason to celebrate.

"After the game, we were all sitting on tables getting IVs," said Jancisin. "Jackie [Sherrill] said before the game that if we won, he was gonna go over and do what that bulldog mascot usually does to the hedges. Well, we didn't win."

A bit of trickery caught the Bulldogs by surprise. According to Jancisin, Georgia's coaches had been watching Iowa State's films from 1972 to get a better idea of what Majors and his coaches would do. They also saw Pitt's spring game, well before the newcomers arrived on campus. Georgia coach Vince Dooley gave his version of the story many years later. Dooley said: "We knew going in what type of player Dorsett was in high school, but the guy who made an even greater impact was the nose guard [Gary Burley] they had recruited from a junior college in Texas. He gave us all kinds of trouble. He caused all kinds of havoc."

"The thing I'll always remember about that game was how silent their crowd was later in the game," said Burley.

Hillgrove noted: "We listed Gary Burley at linebacker on the depth chart, and he lined up at nose guard.... We played Georgia tooth and nail, and had a couple chances to get out of there with a win, but a tie, under the circumstances, was a major accomplishment."

"Gary was big and fast," said fellow lineman Jancisin. "And he's one of the nicest guys you'll ever meet. He wasn't mean. He was real quick. And we also had two freshman linemen—Al Romano and Don Parrish—who worked their way in later that season."

In his collegiate debut, Tony Dorsett ran for 101 yards on twenty-six carries. The performance capped a memorable weekend for the freshman. His son, Anthony, Jr., was born the day before Pitt played Georgia. Anthony Dorsett, Jr., played for Pitt as a defensive back in the 1990s.

Billy Daniels noted:

Every bit we should have won that game. We were in unbelievable physical condition. We had new uniforms and mesh jerseys, tear away jerseys. Majors got us visors to wear because it was so hot down there. Every time we came off the field, we put on those visors on the sideline. We thought we were the coolest things.

Clair Wilson, whose role at tailback was reduced almost entirely because of Dorsett, played on the punt coverage team. He has fond memories of the opening game of The Major Change: "That first game at Georgia was one of the greatest days of my life. We had the new color scheme in our uniforms, and white shoes. I think some of us are still walking on air because of that game. That set the tone for a very memorable season."

Perhaps Dean Billick had the greatest appreciation and understanding of the new beginning for Pitt's football program. Having been an eyewitness to all that had happened from 1966 through 1972, he could not contain his excitement at what he was witnessing that day in Georgia:

I was in the press box sitting next to John Conomikes, and I remember him looking down at the field at one point and saying to me, "Is that us? Is that Pitt? We're as quick as they are. We're just as fast? That has to be a mistake. That's Pitt?" It was an amazing transformation. After the game I thought to myself, "Wow, did this really happen?"

Ed Ifft was at Sanford Stadium on that steamy September afternoon in 1973, and he shared the exhilaration Billick and other Pitt fans and administrators were experiencing following the near victory.

"I remember feeling so elated when we came away from there," said Ifft. "It was a tie, but we looked at each other and said, 'We have a semblance of a football team.'"

In 2020, it is almost inconceivable to believe that none of Pitt's eleven regular season games were on live television in 1973, but that was the case. Action from that memorable season exists on grainy game films, which was the video shown during the Johnny Majors Show on WTAE TV each Sunday evening throughout the football season.

The television show was not the only addition to Pitt's football scene that year. A major refurbishment to the locker room was made, including a traditional weight room to replace the single machine. Majors and his staff brought excitement and innovation to the program. They introduced fun at practice. During the week leading up to the October game at West Virginia, the players were served Mountain Dew. John Denver's hit song, "Country Roads," blared from the public address system. Prior to a home game with Syracuse in November, Jackie Sherrill had oranges dropped in the urinals of the locker room bathroom. Before playing at West Point in November, Sherrill rode into practice one afternoon at Pitt Stadium atop a mule. Majors also rode the animal.

Carson Long and Larry Swider, a couple of pranksters, later rigged a bucket of water atop a door in the locker room—it splashed all over Sherrill.

Every Tuesday night was designated "Soul Food Night" at the team's training table, designed for the pleasure of the blacks Pitt had recruited from the South. Line coach Joe Avezzano had his players, known as FOOLS—Fraternal Order of Offensive Linemen—up to the Mt. Washington apartment he and Sherrill shared for a brief time. There, he would prepare an Italian dinner for them.

The fun and hard work paid immediate dividends for Pitt in 1973. The Panthers went 6-4-1 in the regular season, defeating four opponents—Northwestern, West Virginia, Navy, and Syracuse—it had lost to the season before.

Following the surprise tie at Georgia, the Panthers lost their home opener to Baylor, 20-14. Dorsett scored his first collegiate touchdown on a 32-yard run in the third quarter. Pitt's defense, playing without an injured Gary Burley (ankle), yielded 323 yards rushing. But, as a harbinger of what was to come for Pitt's football fortunes, the Baylor loss was the only time, from 1973 through 1983, that Pitt lost a game to any team that finished the season with a losing record.

Tony Dorsett burst on to the national scene the following week at Northwestern, running through the rain and wind for 265 yards and a pair of touchdowns (6 and 79 yards) in a 21-14 win, the first of the Majors era. In setting a Pitt single game record for rushing yardage, Dorsett earned Back of the Week honors by *Sports Illustrated*, AP, and UPI.

The first win also meant the beginning of a new tradition in the life of John Majors. Friend Ed Ifft presented the coach with a bottle of champagne after the victory, and would repeat that particular bit of generosity following each Pitt win through the end of the 1976 season.

Pitt turned the ball over seven times, and Dorsett injured his back after rushing for 59 yards on his first three carries—in a 24-6 home loss to Tulane, but the Panthers hit their stride the following week with a surprising 35-7 win against West Virginia at old Mountaineer Field in Morgantown. Pitt's players carried Majors off the field, and doused each other with Ginger Ale and Mountain Dew in the locker room afterward.

It was Pitt's first win in Morgantown since 1963. Daniels ran for two touchdowns in the first half, while Dorsett added three of his own in the second half, rushing for 153 yards on twenty-four carries.

Consecutive wins against Boston College, Navy, and Syracuse followed. The Midshipmen rallied from a 16-0 halftime deficit to take a 17-16 lead in the fourth quarter, but Daniels scored on a 3-yard keeper with thirty-three seconds left in the game to give Pitt a hard fought win.

Dorsett ran for 211 yards as the Panthers defeated Syracuse, 28-14. Pitt amassed 576 total yards of offense. It was the seventh time he ran for more than 100 yards, giving him 1,139 yards through eight games as a freshman. At 6-3, Pitt reached No. 20 in the Associated Press rankings after that victory.

Pitt welcomed undefeated Notre Dame to Pitt Stadium before a sellout crowd at Pitt Stadium on November 10, 1973. The Irish boasted the nation's top rushing defense entering the game, but Tony Dorsett ran through and around it for 209 yards, the most individual yardage an Irish team had ever allowed in a single game. But turnovers on a cold, snowy day proved too much to overcome, and the Irish—the eventual national champion in 1973—left Pittsburgh with a 31-10 victory. Pitt came away with the knowledge that it could be competitive with one of the best teams in the country. The legend of Tony Dorsett had been born.

"Tony Dorsett is not merely a man among men," Bob Smizik wrote in *The Pittsburgh Press*. "He is THE man."[6]

"He's the most outstanding back I've ever witnessed," Majors remarked after the Notre Dame game.

"We couldn't have had a winning season that first year without Dorsett," said Dave Jancisin. "We would have struggled to win four or five games. We went out to Northwestern on a windy, rainy day and he ran wild. He was the difference."

Clair Wilson, who spent seven years as a schoolteacher before a thirty-year career in pharmaceutical sales, roomed with Dorsett on the road that season.

"He [Dorsett] was a very down to earth person," said Wilson. "We talked a lot during the road trips, but I wouldn't say we were close. I was a senior and he was a freshman—a very special freshman."

Billy Daniels said:

As good as Tony was, he was still a puppy. He was not the biggest kid, either. Running that option offense, we were out there getting pounded. I greatly respected his toughness. Here's a 155-158 pound freshman who's carrying the ball twenty-five times a game. I witnessed the hits he was taking. From a seniority point, I felt I kind of had to look after him to protect him to the extent that I could.

But it was a blast being on the field with somebody like that. That's a once-in-a-lifetime opportunity for all of us, especially when you look at what he did throughout the rest of his career. We participated in that. We were there with him near the beginning.

"You could see that he had greatness written all over his performance," Wilson added. "He could do things that normal people couldn't do. You could see that he was exceptional."

"He was special," said Daniels. "When you watched him on film the next day, you were amazed at his quickness and elusiveness and the things he could do. His toughness was amazing to me."

Dorsett did take a beating as a freshman. He later admitted that he never weighed more than 155 pounds as a freshman. "I was getting tattooed," he once remarked when asked about his freshman season.

But he stuck it out, and ran for 161 yards and a pair of touchdowns in an easy 34-0 win against winless Army at West Point in the next to last game of the regular season. Defensive back David Spates, a junior college transfer from Seattle, Wash., returned an interception 86 yards for a touchdown. Following the game, Pitt accepted a bid to play Arizona State, coached by Frank Kush, in the Fiesta Bowl. It was Pitt's first bowl invitation since 1956.

Spates was one of four transfers Majors brought in to start on defense in 1973. In addition to nose tackle Gary Burley, junior college defensive back Jeff Hartin earned a starting position, as did linebacker Kelcy Daviston, who had been a highly touted linebacker from Duquesne, Pa., who took went to Arizona State originally before coming back to Pittsburgh, where he enrolled in night school and walked on at Pitt in time for spring practice.

Tony Dorsett was the only newcomer to start on the offensive side of the ball in 1973.

Pitt ended the regular season by visiting Penn State on November 24. It would be the opening salvo for a natural rivalry that would grow much fiercer over the next twenty-five years. Joe Paterno had had his way with Pitt since becoming head coach of the Nittany Lions in 1966. He had two perfect seasons (1968 and 1969) on his Penn State record, and was about to register his third. He was 7-0 against Pitt; in fact, Pitt had never held a lead against Penn State in any of those games.

The Lions featured that year's Heisman Trophy winner, halfback John Cappelletti. After Chris Bahr gave the Lions a 3-0 lead with a field goal, Dorsett countered with a 14-yard touchdown to give Pitt a 7-3 lead. Carson Long added two field goals in the second quarter, including one from 50 yards on the final play of the half. The Panthers took a 13-3 lead into halftime, and actually led, 13-11, entering the final quarter before Penn State's strength and depth prevailed. Penn State won, 35-13. It was Pitt's only road loss in 1973; the Panthers were 4-1-1 away from Pitt Stadium.

Pitt's defense made a valiant stand late in the third quarter. Leading 13-3, Penn State had a first and goal at the Pitt two, but needed seven plays to score a touchdown, aided by a questionable pass interference call in the end zone on third down when Pitt defensive end Jim Buckmon was about to sack quarterback Tom Shuman. Shuman unloaded the ball to nobody in particular. Pitt defenders thought, mistakenly, that intentional grounding would be called.

With the satisfying regular season over, Pitt prepared for its first bowl game in seventeen years. The experience was something new for Cas Myslinski, if not John Majors and his coaching staff.

Jackie Sherrill noted:

> I went in to see Cas one day while he was trying to prepare the budget and what the per diem should be for the players, and so forth. Cas was getting frustrated. He was looking in the NCAA rule book. He took it and threw it at me across his desk and said, "Here, you do it and bring it back to me when you're finished."

Dorsett ran for a touchdown to open the scoring, but they were Pitt's only points. Arizona State won, 28-7. Pitt finished the season with a record of 6-5-1, an impressive mark following the 1-10 campaign in 1972, but a little backstory, one which could have been a crippling blow to the program, had been brewing throughout the season. Tony Dorsett, for all his toughness, was thinking about quitting.

"Several times that season, Tony would get banged up and hurt and come over, and I'd say, 'You know, Tony, you have to play,'" Jackie Sherrill recalled. "He thought about leaving after that season. I told him, 'Tony, we're recruiting you help. We will get you help.'"

Dorsett remembered one particular time when he left the practice field, discouraged, and headed for his room on campus. Soon, there was a knock on the door. "I knew who it was," Dorsett said, laughing. "It was Jackie Sherrill."

The brilliant freshman said he changed his mind about quitting largely through the efforts of his mother and Sherrill, whose "belief and confidence" in him were important.

Dorsett rushed for 1,586 yards and twelve touchdowns as a freshman, the greatest rushing performance (yardage) by a freshman in college football history at the time. He also was a first team Associated Press All American.

Looking ahead to the 1974 season, Majors was quick to sound an advance warning to his players. "We have to continue to grow and not be self-satisfied," he said on the eve of his second campaign at Pitt. "We can't rest on our laurels."

To be sure of that, the winter conditioning program returned to campus.

"I remember after we came back from the Fiesta Bowl, even though we'd had our butts kicked by Arizona State, we were feeling pretty good about ourselves," said Joe Macerelli.

Macerelli, whose career at Pitt was cut short by back surgery prior to the 1975 season, could not escape the winter workouts at Fitzgerald Field House.

"That experience uniquely prepared [fellow Canon McMillan product] George O'Korn and me for what to expect at training camp at Johnstown later on. It was something else for a young man to go through that."

Pitt's winning season did pay significant dividends in its recruiting efforts. Majors and his staff signed four players—quarterback Matt Cavanaugh, defensive lineman Randy Holloway, offensive lineman Tom Brzoza, and defensive back Bob Jury—who would be honored as All Americans during their collegiate careers.

Cavanaugh was already familiar with Pitt center John Pelusi, who had grown up a few blocks away from the Cavanaugh home in Youngstown, Ohio. Pelusi remembered when Majors paid a recruiting visit to his home in early 1973.

"My dad was insistent that I wasn't going to Pitt," Pelusi said. 'That team was one and ten last year! He's not going there.' We were in our basement. My dad was making martinis. He and Coach Majors were drinking wine. My dad challenged Coach Majors to a game of pool. If he won, I would go to Pitt. My dad won, but I went to Pitt anyway."

Jackie Sherrill said:

The talent level kept building. A winning season gives you the credibility to recruit more talented players. When we went through the first recruiting year, the only player we beat Penn State on was Tony Dorsett. When I came back to Pitt later, they were scrambling to beat me on some players. It was very hard for Penn State to beat me on a player.

The first big class we signed going into 1973, Tony [Dorsett], Al Romano and all those guys, they set the stage for what was to come.

A sad development struck Pitt's football followers between the 1973 and 1974 seasons. Ed Conway, Pitt's play-by-play radio announcer for the previous three seasons, passed away on May 28, 1974. He was only forty-eight. Bill Hillgrove spoke of Conway:

He [Conway] had been sick before that. He said to me, "I think I have The Big C," meaning cancer. We were rooming together, and he said that to me. I didn't say anything back. He was so nice to me. He knew he was on his way out at WTAE. Jack Fleming had kind of pushed him out of the TV side of things. He was great to me. He drummed into me, "Watch the official. He will tell you the story."

Hillgrove was the obvious choice to step into Conway's role as Pitt's play-by-play man, and he has been doing it ever since. Pitt's new radio color analyst was Johnny Sauer, a West Point graduate and longtime football coach who had been doing broadcast work of NFL games on CBS, but was looking for something different.

"Johnny Sauer taught me more about football than I thought I could ever know," said Hillgrove. "He could tell you a team's game plan after two series. That's how much football knowledge he had."

The 1974 Panthers added one more victory to the win total, finishing the season at 7-4 but without a bowl bid. Dorsett barely topped the 1,000-yard mark, gaining 1,004, but became the leading rusher in Pitt history, passing Marshall Goldberg, in Pitt's third game of the season.

Pitt opened the campaign with a pair of road wins at Florida State and Georgia Tech, continuing a pattern of road games to begin the season. From 1973 through 1976, Pitt never played its first game at Pitt Stadium. And, it was not until 1976 that Pitt played more games at home than on the road.

Pitt defeated Florida State, 9-6, in a game telecast back to Pittsburgh. The game had an interesting twist; FSU coach Darrell Mudra, nicknamed "Dr. Victory," always coached his team from the press box, not because of any incapacity, but by choice. Dr. Victory did not win enough games, and 1974 was his last season in Tallahassee. He was replaced by Bobby Bowden, who left West Virginia for the job with the Seminoles.

The Panthers went to 2-0 with a 28-14 win on a steamy Saturday afternoon in Atlanta. It was the program's first 2-0 start since 1963, setting up an intersectional clash with the University of Southern California at Pitt Stadium. The game was billed as a showdown between TD East (Dorsett) and TD West (USC's Anthony Davis). Some of Pitt's players, who were accustomed to playing national powers Notre Dame and Penn State, saw a noticeable difference in coach John McKay's traditional powerhouse team. Billy Daniels and Dave Jancisin were Pitt's co-captains for the game. Daniels noted:

> Notre Dame had big, heavy, fat guys. They were just bigger and stronger than we were. USC had big guys who were agile. That was the biggest difference. They were scary athletic. When we went out for the coin toss, [linebacker] Richard Wood was one of their co-captains, along with Anthony Davis. Richard Wood looked every bit a grown man. He scared the hell out of you just looking at you. He chased me out of the pocket a few times that day. We had a very difficult time moving the ball against them.

"That USC team was loaded," said Jancisin. "At the coin toss, Anthony Davis only came up to the middle of my chest, but he was some player. Ricky Bell was the blocking back."

In its final regular season game that year, USC spotted Notre Dame a 24-0 lead before running off fifty-five unanswered points to defeat the Irish, 55-24. Pitt lost by a more respectable 16-7, but was never really in the game. The Panthers were overmatched along the line of scrimmage, but the Trojans hurt themselves with numerous turnovers. USC quarterback Pat Haden was injured in the first half, but his replacement, run oriented Vince Evans, proved to be more difficult for Pitt to defend. Davis finished the game with 149 yards rushing; Dorsett had 59.

USC was crowned national champion at the end of the season, and had fourteen players selected in the 1975 NFL Draft.

The Panthers dropped to 2-2 with a 45-29 road loss at North Carolina the following week, but then defeated West Virginia, Boston College,

Navy, Syracuse, and Temple in succession to raise their record to 7-2—and a No. 15 national ranking. The Temple game was significant because it was the only game Dorsett missed during his four years at Pitt. Freshman Elliott Walker stepped in and ran for 167 yards and four touchdowns in a thrilling 35-24 victory against the Owls, back on Pitt's schedule for the first time since 1946.

Pitt then traveled to South Bend to meet defending national champion Notre Dame. It would be a bittersweet day for Billy Daniels, then a senior, playing against McKees Rocks native Tom Clements, in his final season as quarterback of the Irish.

Clements threw a touchdown pass on Notre Dame's first possession to give his team a 7-0 lead, but the Pitt defense kept Notre Dame from scoring until very late in the fourth quarter. Pitt was driving for an apparent tying touchdown, but Dorsett lost a fumble at the Irish 1-yard line in the second quarter. Daniels had his moment of misfortune a short time later, one which ended his college career; in the second quarter, the Panthers called a trick play:

> We were seven and two and had a lot of confidence going into that game. Bad things happen. It was a play where Dorsett was throwing the ball to me. That's how I got hurt. We'd been practicing it all year. It was called "Quarterback Throwback" where I pitch the ball to Dorsett like he was gonna run a sweep, and I quietly go out to the other side. While he's running right, I'm running left. It was especially successful against teams which ran man-to-man defense, which Notre Dame did. I'm strolling out there. At one point I was about fifteen yards away from anybody. Unfortunately, Tony threw a wounded duck. I had to reverse field and come back toward the line of scrimmage. I was thinking, "I'm gonna go up and show these wide receivers how to go up and get a ball." Unfortunately, several people collided, and I injured my knee.

Daniels' day and career were finished, but redshirt senior Bob Medwid, another McKees Rocks quarterback, entered the game and scored on a short fourth down run late in the second quarter to tie the game 7-7.

It stayed that way until the final play of the third quarter, when Carson Long's 52-yard field goal in the misty rain gave Pitt a 10-7 lead.

Tom Clements ran for the go-ahead touchdown, giving the Irish a 14-10 lead with 2:49 remaining in the game, but Medwid brought the Panthers downfield quickly with three completions to senior wingback Bruce Murphy.

Pitt drove as far as the Irish seventeen, but Medwid's final two passes to the end zone were incomplete. The third down pass, intended for speedster Karl Farmer, was broken up at the last instant by Notre Dame's Reggie Barnett.

"I have never been prouder of any team than I am today," Majors told reporters after the game. "Even though we didn't win, this game gave us the boost we need to go ahead in the years to come."

Pitt football returned to the national spotlight on Thanksgiving Night 1974 when ABC selected the Pitt-Penn State game for a prime time telecast. The game was shifted from Pitt Stadium to Three Rivers Stadium because Pitt's home facility did not have permanent lights until 1985.

A bowl game the previous year, and now a national TV game. Prominent television appearances have become commonplace today, but it was heady stuff for Pitt in 1974. Everybody wanted to get into the act. Pitt cheerleading captain Vicki Veltri went to Cas Myslinski asking for approval to order blue and gold shakers and other game favors so Pitt could put on its best face for the TV audience. Myslinski approved.

Penn State spoiled Pitt's party with a decisive 31-10 victory. Bob Medwid, in his final collegiate game, was making his first start since the 1972 season. Pitt led, 10-7, at halftime, but the Nittany Lions dominated in the second half. ABC would select Pitt-Penn State for national TV from Three Rivers Stadium in both 1975 and 1976, and the results would be much more dramatic.

Majors had his second winning season in as many years, a feat Pitt had not enjoyed since 1959 and 1960. The departing seniors, those who had endured two awful years before experiencing success, at Pitt, appreciated the experience.

"I thank Johnny [Majors] for what he did for my life in the future," said Dave Jancisin. "Jackie [Sherrill] taught his players that there's no such thing as entitlement in football. If there's someone better than you, they'll put you right on the bench."

Meanwhile, Elliott Walker's rushing performance against Temple in the absence of Tony Dorsett convinced Pitt's coaches to modify their offense in 1975. Quarterback Billy Daniels and blocking fullback Dave Janasek had graduated. Replacing Daniels would be junior speedster Robert Haygood from East Point, Ga., the first black quarterback in Pitt history. Haygood came to Pitt on a football scholarship, but also found time to be a point guard for the Panthers' basketball team. He would get the first crack at the quarterback position, with sophomore Matt Cavanaugh trailing him, but not by much.

Pitt went to the Veer attack in 1975, utilizing the abilities of both Dorsett and Walker in the same backfield, along with Haygood, who had the speed of a running back. A key freshman recruit, wide receiver Gordon Jones, arrived from East Allegheny High School, and provided Pitt with another dangerous weapon as a receiver and punt returner. He finished his first season at Pitt ranked sixth in the country in punt returns, averaging 13 yards per return.

The new offensive system produced as advertised. The Panthers ran for a school record 4,483 yards, averaging 275 rushing yards per game. Haygood and Cavanaugh split duties at quarterback; Haygood started the first seven games before an injury forced him to the sideline. Cavanaugh started the final four games of the regular season before John Majors pulled a surprise switch and had Haygood start against Kansas in the Sun Bowl.

Many of Majors' first recruiting class had earned spots in the starting lineup. Up front, John Hanhauser, John Pelusi, Joe Stone, and Jim Corbett were entrenched in the offensive line. On the defensive side, Don Parrish, Al Romano, and Ed Wilamowski were entering their third seasons at Pitt, along with linebacker Arnie Weatherington.

But Pitt's 1975 season will best be remembered for the continued brilliance of Tony Dorsett, as well as some of the most exciting wins and heartbreaking losses in the program's history.

Robert Haygood returned to his home state, and the Panthers to the venue of the first game in The Major Change in Pitt Football, to meet Georgia in the season opener. Georgia did not come to Pittsburgh for a game; in fact, in the seventy-five-year history of Pitt Stadium, the Panthers never hosted any opponent from the Southeastern Conference.

Pitt's Veer attack was grounded in the first half, which ended with Georgia leading, 7-0 on a wet, rainy day in Athens. Carson Long's two field goals and touchdown runs by Haygood and Walker after intermission were the difference in the Panthers' 19-9 win. Dorsett ran for 104 yards on fifteen carries.

The Panthers traveled to Norman to face Oklahoma following an off week. The Sooners were serving the third year of NCAA probation in 1975, but that mattered little when Pitt absorbed its worst loss (46-10) of the Majors era. The Sooners, ranked first in the nation entering the game, limited Dorsett to 16 yards on twelve carries, the lowest rushing total of his career.

Pitt opened its home schedule with consecutive shutout wins—the first time since 1945—against William & Mary (47-0) and Duke (14-0).

Dorsett ran for 142 yards against the Indians and Walker added 105. In blanking the Blue Devils, Pitt allowed only 33 rushing yards.

Junior cornerback J. C. Wilson had a memorable performance in a 55-6 rout of Temple at Veterans Stadium the following week. The junior cornerback intercepted two passes (returning one for a touchdown), made two fumble recoveries and returned a blocked field goal 52 yards for another score. Gordon Jones scored his first touchdown on a 75 yard pass from Haygood, while Dorsett ran for 114 yards.

On a rainy afternoon at West Point, Dorsett rewrote Pitt's record book by rushing for 268 yards—218 in the first half—to lead the Panthers to a 52-20 win against the Cadets. He scored on touchdown runs of 14, 66, 21, and 35 yards. Walker contributed 107 yards on sixteen carries as Pitt set school records for total offense (610) and rushing yards (530).

The remainder of the season had a distinct pattern. Pitt alternated losses and wins over its final six games, starting with a disappointing 17-0 home loss to Navy one week after routing Army. Haygood was injured late in the game, and Matt Cavanaugh received his first collegiate starting assignment the next week at Syracuse. He handled it well, and Pitt registered its third shutout (38-0). Cavanaugh threw three touchdown passes, including one for 73 yards to Gordon Jones. Dorsett rushed for 158 yards.

Pitt suffered its only loss to West Virginia from 1973 through 1982 the following week in Morgantown. After a scoreless first half, WVU took leads of 7-0 and 14-7 but Pitt rallied to tie the game twice on touchdown passes from Cavanaugh to Jones and Dorsett. The Mountaineers handed the Panthers a bitter defeat when Bill McKenzie booted a 38-yard field goal as time expired. The game was not without intrigue; it was later discovered that, under the direction of an assistant coach, West Virginia had been filming Pitt's sideline at earlier games in Pittsburgh to get a read on the team's offensive signals.

Pitt's players and coaches had to put the heartbreaking loss aside when Notre Dame visited Pitt Stadium on November 15, 1975. Pitt had not defeated the Irish since 1963, coming up short in a gallant effort at South Bend in 1974. This time there would be no doubt—Tony Dorsett saw to that. Dorsett ran for 303 yards, including a 71-yard touchdown run, and caught a pass from Cavanaugh and raced 49 yards for another score. Majors, so fired up about the win, could not get to sleep that night: "I wish I had something bright to say. Of course, I was always hoping for something like this. But never in my wildest dreams did I envision that much yardage. No other win in my entire life compared to this."[7]

Bill Hillgrove said:

To amass that kind of yardage against Notre Dame, I had been to games against Notre Dame during Dave Hart's time as coach, and certainly as a broadcaster when Carl [DePasqua] was the coach. Notre Dame could have just called the scores. Finally, we were competitive, just as good as Notre Dame, and maybe even better, and that was a great realization.

Hillgrove overheard an interesting comment from a member of the Notre Dame contingent following Pitt's 34-20 defeat of the Irish.

"[Notre Dame athletics director] Moose Krause was coming down from his perch in our press box," Hillgrove recalled, "and I heard him say to somebody, a Notre Damer that 'we didn't make any adjustments.'"

Irish coach Dan Devine, in his first year on the job following the retirement of Ara Parseghian, begged to differ with his boss when he met with the media after the game. "We tried to make normal adjustments," said Devine. "But one guy [Dorsett] kind of made them inadequate."

Many years later, Majors, looking back, recalled the victory against Notre Dame: "In my first stay at Pitt, the 1975 game against Notre Dame was great. We never won a bigger football game than that one. That did a lot for our program. It gave us confidence—that game, and the Sun Bowl win against Kansas—going into the championship season."

After defeating Notre Dame, Pitt accepted a bid to play Kansas in the Sun Bowl. But before that, the Panthers would attempt to end another long series losing streak, this time against Penn State on November 22 at Three Rivers Stadium.

Pitt dominated the statistics, and led 6-0 (its extra-point kick was blocked following a touchdown run by Elliott Walker) until Penn State's Steve Geise put the Lions ahead with a 29-yard run with eight minutes remaining. The Panthers drove to the Penn State six, but Carson Long's 23-yard field goal attempt was wide, as was a kick from 45 yards with eight seconds left. It was Pitt's tenth straight loss to Penn State, but probably the first time Pitt's players and coaches truly believed they were the superior team.

"When I get home, I'm going to church real quick-like," was how Penn State coach Joe Paterno summed up his team's good fortune to reporters after the game.

In El Paso preparing for the Sun Bowl game with Kansas, Majors called quarterbacks Haygood and Cavanaugh together to inform them that the starting nod in the Sun Bowl would go to the player who looked better in practice.

Kansas expected Cavanaugh, but got Haygood instead. Pitt's Veer offense ran close to perfection with Haygood (101), Dorsett (142), and Walker (123) leading Pitt to an impressive 33-19 win against a Kansas team, which had defeated Oklahoma earlier in the season. Haygood earned the game's Most Valuable Offensive Player award and nose guard Al Romano was named Most Valuable Defensive Player.

After the game, Jackie Sherrill announced to the team that he was leaving Pitt to accept the head coaching position at Washington State. A few days before the game, Majors permitted Sherrill to address the team in the locker room as a head coach would. Majors was in the back of the room observing from where the players could not see him.

Tony Dorsett was not very happy that Sherrill was leaving. He later explained that when he signed with Pitt, "Jackie told me he would be there all four years while I was there." Dorsett paid a visit to Sherrill's hotel room later that evening.

"Tony came to my room, privately, and said, 'Coach, I understand,'" Sherrill recalled. "Several players gave me their helmets after the game."

Dorsett finished his junior season with 1,544 yards and fourteen touchdowns. He placed fourth in the Heisman Trophy balloting. Ohio State's Archie Griffin won his second Heisman award that year.

Pitt finished the 1975 season ranked No. 13 by UPI, and with seventeen projected starters returning in 1976, expectations would be significant.

"We'll be rated high for 1976, and there's not much I can do about it," Majors stated following the Sun Bowl victory.

3

PITT IS IT! (1976)

I don't think I've ever seen a team that won a national championship that had more complete balance. We had the complete arsenal in 1976.

John Majors

Junkyard Dogs, my eye. Give me the Blast Furnace Cats!

Furman Bisher (Atlanta Journal-Constitution, January 2, 1977)

Wire service polling to determine a college football national champion began in 1936 when the Associated Press (AP) put out weekly rankings throughout the season. Pitt, with a record of 8-1-1, highlighted by a 21-0 victory against Washington in the Rose Bowl, claimed the No. 3 spot at the end of the season.

The following year, the Panthers rolled to a 9-0-1 mark and were ranked No. 1 by season's end. The only stain on the team's record was its third consecutive scoreless tie with Fordham. All three of those games were played at the Polo Grounds in New York City. Pitt's players, still smarting because of a perceived lack of consideration from upper levels of the school's administration regarding expense money at the Rose Bowl the year before, voted not to accept any invitation after the 1937 season.

The growing discord concerning the direction Pitt was headed, and the football program's role within the university's philosophy, were enough to force coach Jock Sutherland's hand in 1938. He resigned his position as head coach. Pitt finished 8-2 that year, and ranked No. 8 in the final AP

Poll. Not until Pitt's 9-1 team in 1963 finished third in the nation had a Pitt team attained such a lofty position.

As preparations for Pitt's 1976 season—the nation's bicentennial year—began, there was no shortage of optimism about the team's prospects. Its players, and Majors, knew what was at stake, and realized they were on the verge of completing perhaps the most stunning turnaround of a program in college football history.

"We believed going into that season that we could go undefeated and win the national championship," said John Pelusi, the senior starting center. "It was a senior-oriented veteran team with a lot of confidence in itself and in each other."

Indeed, Pitt's entire offensive line was back from the year before, along with quarterbacks Robert Haygood and Matt Cavanaugh, plus receivers Gordon Jones and Willie Taylor. Karl Farmer was the only starter lost, but junior Willie Taylor had gained experience in 1975.

"We had all played together, and we had a lot of confidence in ourselves and in each other," said junior free safety Bob Jury. "Having someone like Tony Dorsett on your team also helps."

Interestingly, following a 46-10 loss at Oklahoma in 1975, Jury and a few of his teammates received what amounted to an endorsement from a few of the Sooners.

"Coming off the field, some of the Oklahoma players were telling us we were going to win a national championship real soon if we continued to stick together and play hard," Jury recalled.

"We felt we had the depth and the talent to win at all," Robert Haygood said in an AT&T Sports documentary about the 1976 Panthers. Pelusi said: "After the [1975] Sun Bowl game, Coach Majors called all of us [seniors] in and said, 'We have a chance to be something special next year. We all need to work hard in the offseason and come back ready to go.'"

Pitt returned most of its defensive starters from 1975, but needed to replace ends Tom Perko and Randy Cozens along with safety Dennis Moorhead. An unexpected loss occurred during the spring, however, when senior linebacker Arnie Weatherington—Pitt's all-time leading tackler—was dismissed from the team by Majors following his arrest on theft charges stemming from an incident at his place of employment. Weatherington did not appear in Pitt's 1976 media guide previewing the team and season. Sam Sciullo, Sr., said:

John Majors found out about it and called me one day in the summer. I told him I thought it would be taken care of, but they held him [Weatherington] for court anyway. That meant I had to face the court system. When the hearing came, I had worked out with the assistant district attorney that we could give the kid ARD—Accelerated Rehabilitative Disposition— where you keep your nose clean, behave yourself, and your record would later be expunged. It usually comes up in cases in which there was no violence or moral turpitude. After the hearing, the judge asked Arnie, "Are you going to beat Penn State this year?"

The judge agreed to the recommendation of the attorneys. That weight was lifted from Weatherington. Still, there was the matter of his expulsion from the team. Sciullo, Sr., noted:

I told Arnie, "You have ARD. You don't have to go to jail. You won't have a criminal record. You go up to Majors' office, but I have a hunch that when he looks at his depth chart and doesn't see anybody behind you who is as good as you are, and he needs you, give him an opening so he can very gracefully take you back on the team. When you hit the door, you hit the floor and you crawl and you ask for forgiveness, and see what happens."

Close to the beginning of training camp at Pitt's Johnstown campus, John Majors reinstated Arnie Weatherington. Majors had his team in place.

"Many coaches are conservative in their public estimation about their teams, but I did say publicly, probably more so than any other year in my life, that I thought we had the makings of an outstanding team," said Majors.

Prior to the start of camp in August, Majors called a meeting of squad committee members, John Pelusi and senior tight end Jim Corbett among them. Majors recalled:

I said to the seniors, "Fellas, before I go and talk to the squad tomorrow, I'd like to find out if there's anything you have that you'd like to volunteer that you think would be helpful to the staff about what your thinking is." I don't know who it was who spoke up, but he said, "Coach Majors, you just tell us what you want done, and we're gonna get it done. We don't have any suggestions right now. You just tell us what you want to get done now."

Although the biggest question to be answered in camp centered on whether Haygood or Matt Cavanaugh would be the quarterback, preseason workouts took on an additional sense of excitement because Pitt was set to open its 1976 season against Notre Dame in South Bend on September 11. Originally, the Panthers were to have met Louisville at Pitt Stadium on that date, but ABC TV stepped in and, seeing a classic opening matchup, persuaded the schools to reschedule. There was no hesitation on Pitt's part.

"We went out to Notre Dame for that opening game with all the confidence in the world," said senior nose guard Al Romano. "We knew we could beat Notre Dame."

Dean Billick said:

ABC called the shot on that, and at the time there was a significant amount of money at stake in taking that game for television. It was a no brainer. There was no fear on our part on playing at Notre Dame. We were better than Notre Dame, and we knew we were better. There was a lot of excitement before the season because we knew we had a shot at it. We had good enough players and good enough coaches.

John Pelusi noted:

We knew that was a great opportunity being able to go out there and play Notre Dame on national TV. It was a lot of fun. I've never liked Notre Dame, so that game was always extra special for me. Going out to South Bend, we knew that if we played the way we were capable, that they couldn't beat us.

"We're gonna beat 'em [Notre Dame] anyway, whether we play them early or late," senior tight end Jim Corbett remembered telling Majors. "So just move it up and let's get on with it."

The Panthers were ranked ninth in both wire service polls when they left Pittsburgh for South Bend on September 10. They spent that overnight at the Holiday Inn in Elkhart, Indiana and bussed to South Bend for the game. Bill Hillgrove remembered:

I was sitting next to Johnny Sauer on the bus, and we were analyzing the game, trying to see how it might turn out. It got real quiet toward the end of the ride when we pulled up to the stadium, but as everybody's getting off the bus, who's the first person we see? [Legendary Pittsburgh radio personality George Jacob] Porky Chedwick! He's there greeting everyone, yelling, "Go get 'em, Pitt! Let's Go Pitt!" That seemed to relax some of us.

Inside storied Notre Dame Stadium, a bed sheet sign recalling Tony Dorsett's 303 yards against the Irish ten months earlier, proclaimed, "Hail Mary, Full of Grace, Tony Dorsett's Going No Place!"

The Irish, bent on revenge, were a slight favorite in the game, but one veteran Pittsburgh journalist proved prophetic. Pat Livingston of *The Pittsburgh Press* made his weekly predictions of key college and pro games in every Thursday edition of his paper during football season. He liked Pitt in the opener.

"The Panthers, mature and experienced, have too many guns in the skills positions to lose to the Irish," he wrote.[1]

There was concern that one of those weapons, junior back Elliott Walker, might not be able to play. Walker sustained a badly sprained left ankle after falling on a dormitory stairwell. The injury was not as serious as feared, x-rays were negative, and Walker was cleared to participate.

Pitt also had to contend with the tall grass—designed to slow Dorsett—at Notre Dame. "That was no story," Dorsett contended many years later. "It was true. That grass was high. It looked like it hadn't been cut in about a month."

Dorsett and fellow Hopewell High School graduate Ed Wilamowski, two of the cornerstone signings in the massive recruiting class upon Majors' arrival, represented Pitt at midfield for the coin toss on a brilliant, sunny late Saturday afternoon.

Not all Pitt supporters were as calm as the setting. Alan Sheps, a 1967 Pitt graduate and longtime loyalist, was so nervous about the game that he could not watch; he took in a double-feature movie presentation at a Squirrel Hill theater.

Sheps would have been beside himself when the Irish took the opening kickoff and drove downfield for a touchdown when quarterback Rick Slager hit tight end Ken MacAfee from 25 yards out. Slager, who might not have been the starter but for a shoulder injury to Joe Montana during training camp, connected on all three of his passes during the touchdown drive. He went three of nineteen the rest of the afternoon.

Notre Dame's 7-0 lead did not last long. Following a procedure penalty on its first play, Dorsett took a pitch from Haygood, who had earned the starting job at quarterback, and raced 61 yards to the Notre Dame 23. Five plays later, Dorsett took another pitch from Haygood and scored from 6 yards out to tie the game.

In a documentary about Pitt's 1976 season, Haygood remembered the dramatic Dorsett run to jumpstart the Pitt offense: "The defensive end took me, and I gave Dorsett the ball, on the dive. Ross Browner was the defensive end and he was kind of talking in my ear about how he had me, and what he did to me. I just told him, 'Look downfield.' And Tony was running about sixty yards."

Bob Jury and cornerback Leroy Felder intercepted Slager passes in the first half and Haygood scored a pair of touchdown on keepers from one yard out. Pitt's defensive front pressured Slager throughout the afternoon, and the Panthers won surprisingly easy, 31-10. Dorsett rushed for 181 yards, giving him a career total of 754 yards on the ground against the Irish. The win vaulted Pitt from ninth in the polls to No. 4 in the UPI ranking and No. 3 by AP. Credit was spread around during the postgame interviews.

"The defense won the game for us today," said Dorsett, as evidenced by Pitt's four interceptions. "We sputtered offensively, and it was encouraging to see the defense pull us out."

"It was a real manhandling of Notre Dame, which had never happened before for most of us involved with the program," said Bill Hillgrove. "It keyed a real great season."

The victory against the Irish was especially meaningful to Dorsett, whose performance served as a springboard for his Heisman Trophy aspirations. Dorsett stated: "I have my own special incentive when I play Notre Dame. I never said this before, but I heard that one of the Notre Dame coaches told Ara Parseghian that I was just a skinny little kid who couldn't make it in the big time."

"It [win against Notre Dame] set the tone for the season," added Matt Cavanaugh, who entered the game during the second half. Cavanaugh was needed sooner the following Saturday when Pitt traveled to Atlanta for a night game with Georgia Tech.

Haygood directed the Panthers to an early 14-0 lead highlighted by a pair of touchdown runs by Dorsett. But midway through the second quarter, Haygood, playing in front of friends and family members from nearby East Point, Ga., had his football career come to a sudden, painful end:

> I didn't pack the shoes I'd normally wear for AstroTurf, so we had to go out and get another pair of shoes. Those shoes had rubber cleats on the bottom, which you know are really not good on AstroTurf. I was just trying to scramble and get away, and I had to run. I saw the defenders

coming, and I pretty much rolled with the lick, but my left leg got stuck in the turf. And, at that moment, I kind of knew that that was it.

It was torn knee ligaments, which meant Cavanaugh was now Pitt's undisputed starting quarterback.

"Matt [Cavanaugh] had the experience and the talent to step right in and do the job," said John Pelusi, who knew better than anyone. He and Cavanaugh had been playing football together since both were in grade school. Pelusi was a year older than Cavanaugh.

Jim Corbett said of Cavanaugh:

Matt had a different style. He was a little bit taller than Robert. He was more of a pocket guy, but he could still move around and play the option. He would drop back and stand in the pocket and take command. He'd look around and see things. Robert was an amazing athlete, and he had a very nice arm. He ended up being an accomplished college basketball point guard [in 1977–78] for Pitt.

Cavanaugh stepped in and threw touchdown passes of 6 and 51 yards to Gordon Jones. Dorsett, who rushed for 113 yards, ran for a third score as the Panthers wrecked Georgia Tech, 42-14. It was a solid victory, but it came at a price. "It was a hot night at Grant Field in Atlanta, and there was a lot of sadness after the game because Haygood was out for the year," remembered Bill Hillgrove, then in his third season of calling Pitt football on the radio. "The team had to somehow go forward, and it did, in grand style."

The victory moved Pitt from fourth to third in the UPI Poll, trailing only Michigan (#1) and Ohio State (#2).

Pitt's home opener was Saturday, September 25 *versus* Temple at Pitt Stadium. Attendance had been growing steadily since the arrival of John Majors and Tony Dorsett in 1973. Home attendance averages increased from 33,609 in 1973 to 41,279 (1974) and 42,022 in 1975. More people were interested in Pitt football, but Majors wanted some pizazz. He met with Dean Billick.

"Majors said to me, 'Can we do anything to get the crowd more amped up? We need to have more excitement in the stadium,'" Billick recalled.

Enter Roger Huston, thirty-four years old, a relative newcomer to Pittsburgh as the Voice of The Meadows, a harness racing track in suburban Pittsburgh. Speaking of Huston, Dean Billick said:

I had heard him [Huston] on an interview with Myron Cope on Myron's show. He had played a tape of a race that he had called previously. It was a pretty exciting call, I thought. I made a trip out to The Meadows. I met Roger. He took me up to the booth from where he called the races. I got to know him and listen to him. I thought he'd be the right man, so we hired him.

Huston had grown up in Xenia, Ohio, where, as a boy, he kept statistics of Cleveland Browns games from an easy chair while either listening to or watching their games. He enrolled at nearby Wilmington College intent on becoming a teacher. He had an uncle who called races, and young Roger soon found himself announcing at county fairs throughout Ohio. He received a job offer—which was accepted—from the Red Mile track in Lexington, Kentucky the same day he received his diploma from Wilmington. Education's loss was horse racing's and football's gain. Huston said:

I met with Dean Billick on a Thursday morning. The first words out of his mouth were, "We're gonna win the national championship this year, and we want to bring more excitement and enthusiasm to the games at Pitt Stadium." He wanted to know if I'd ever done PA or broadcasting for football games. I told him I'd been doing both for a long time.

Huston replaced longtime Pitt football and basketball public address announcer Harold Neff, whose voice also was recognizable for his work at high school playoff basketball games at the Civic Arena.

"Roger obviously brought a different style of PA system than Harold Neff," said Billick. "It was a new era of Pitt football. I'm not saying anything against Harold. He did a very professional job for us, but we were looking for excitement, and Roger was certainly exciting."

With all of Pitt's home games kicking off at 1:30 p.m., the arrangement worked well for Huston, as his new duties at Pitt didn't conflict with his obligations at The Meadows. But while Roger Huston was bringing excitement during his first game behind the microphone, the Pitt football team was slogging its way to 7-6 halftime deficit against Temple. It would be the only time Pitt trailed at halftime of a game in 1976. The Owls' touchdown came on a blocked punt. "We didn't play well at all in the first half that day," said Corbett. "But Matt [Cavanaugh] really came alive in the second half."

Dorsett missed part of the game due to a bruised calf, but still managed to run for 112 yards and a touchdown. Elliott Walker gave Pitt the lead on a 1-yard run in the third quarter. Carson Long added two field goals and Pitt defeated the Owls, 21-7.

Cavanaugh and Pitt's receivers enjoyed a field day the following week during a rainy afternoon against Duke in Durham, North Carolina. Pitt's coaches added a wrinkle to the option game by having Cavanaugh come down the line as though to pitch the ball back. Instead, he paused, dropped back, and hit his open playmakers time and again for big gains and touchdowns. He completed fourteen of seventeen passes for 339 yards and five touchdowns, earning national back-of-the-week honors for his work. Gordon Jones and Willie Taylor each caught two touchdown passes, while Corbett had the other. Pitt won 44-31, much easier than the final score indicated. Pitt led 30-7 at halftime. Dorsett ran for 134 yards and a score.

Pitt moved up to No. 2 in both wire service polls as it returned home to face Louisville on another wet, dreary afternoon. The day before, walk-on quarterback Tom Yewcic threw a pair of touchdown passes to JoJo Heath to lead the Pitt junior varsity to a win against Potomac State—where Yewcic's father (Mike) had once played—at Pitt Stadium. His uncle, also named Tom Yewcic, starred at Michigan State and played professionally for the Boston Patriots in the old American Football League. His uncle, Russ Franke, happened to be the Pitt football beat writer for *The Pittsburgh Press*.

The Pitt varsity had little trouble with the Louisville Cardinals, building a 27-0 halftime lead. Cavanaugh ran for two touchdowns while Dorsett added a third on his way to a 130-yard performance. But while Louisville offered little in the way of resistance, another serious injury sidelined Pitt's starting quarterback. Cavanaugh noted: "It was a play where I was scrambling out of the pocket and kept the ball. Somebody fell on me from the side, and I could feel the pain. I remember being helped off the field, and finding out relatively quickly that it was a hairline fracture of the fibula."

Dave Migliore, a senior from Dover, Ohio, was inserted at quarterback. He threw an incompletion, and was replaced by Yewcic for most of the second half. Pitt failed to score following intermission, but won, 27-6.

Tom Yewcic, who had played quarterback at Conemaugh Valley High School near Johnstown, Pa., had grown up wanting to play football at Pitt. When he was a senior, father and son made an appointment to see John Majors at his office inside Fitzgerald Field House. Yewcic noted:

> My dad asked what it would take for Tom to play at Pitt. Coach Majors looked both of us in the eye and said, "A catastrophe would have to happen for Tom Yewcic ever to play football for the University of Pittsburgh." We thanked him for his time, got up and left and never said a word to each other until we got outside. We didn't know what to say. It was a little bit of a shock. One of us said, "At least he's honest." I decided to go to Pitt anyway.

Without their two primary quarterbacks, there was genuine concern about the team's chances for the remainder of the season. John Pelusi said:

> When Matt went down in the Louisville game, it was Tommy Yewcic's turn to play. We knew that Tommy wasn't able to throw the ball like Matt [Cavanaugh], and that he couldn't run like [Robert] Haygood, so we knew the offense would have to make some adjustments. We knew we'd be running the ball a lot and we knew we could get the job done.

"When Matt got hurt, there was a little bit of, 'Okay, where do we go from here?' said Jim Corbett. "I think everybody intuitively knew, 'We really have to step it up and execute here.'"

"When Matt was injured against Louisville, wow! I'll have to admit that we were concerned," said Al Romano. "Tommy Yewcic deserves all the credit in the world for what he did."

Majors and his staff had three candidates as Pitt prepared to host Miami on October 16, 1976. Dave Migliore, who had been the first man to replace Cavanaugh in the Louisville game; Woody Jackson, a scholarship freshman from Spotsylvania, Va., or Yewcic. It came down to Jackson and Yewcic. John Majors recalled:

> My thinking was that Yewcic and Jackson could do some kicking. We put in the shotgun. Yewcic was short, so that helped him, plus he could do some quick kicks if he needed to. He was heady, smart. Jackson could quick-kick, too. Woody Jackson had more quickness, but I made the decision to start Tom. Tom's father was a coach. His uncle had been a good player at Michigan State, so I thought to myself, "Here's a guy who has some osmosis working in his favor." He had some savvy to him. Tom was very confident.

And, of course, there was the comforting presence of Tony Dorsett behind whomever Majors had playing quarterback. The coaching staff switched offensive formations from the Veer to the I.

"From the I', we could at least turn and pitch the ball to Tony and let the fullback lead block," Majors explained. "We could also run the sweep, the sprint draw and some play action passes."

Unbeknownst, for a while, to Majors and his assistants, Yewcic was bearing the scars of an injury sustained in the Louisville game.

"I remember we ran a sweep left with Dorsett and Walker," said Yewcic. "They were twenty yards downfield looking for me! I was just rounding the corner. I got hit and slightly dislocated a joint in my right shoulder. I couldn't move my arm too well, but I didn't tell anybody until after the game." The injury complicated the situation. Yewcic was not able to practice until the following Wednesday, three days before the Miami game. "I couldn't throw the ball more than fifteen yards," he remembered. "But on Thursday, Majors told me I was starting."

The magnitude of the moment did not faze Yewcic, who had been the scout team quarterback his entire career until that week. He had never practiced with the regular offense. Majors had brought in Bill Cox to coach the quarterbacks. Cox replaced George Haffner, who left Pitt after the 1975 season. Yewcic noted:

> I stuck it out all those years. Coach Cox looked at me and he was honest about it. If there were six guys or sixteen guys, I was always last team quarterback because I was a walk-on. But he [Cox] gave me a shot, and the rest is history. It [playing for Pitt] was just something I wanted to do so badly. It was fun. If you're prepared, there really isn't any pressure.

With Tom Yewcic calling the signals, and Tony Dorsett rushing for 227 yards and three touchdowns, Pitt beat Miami, 36-19. Jeff Delaney and Leroy Felder picked off Miami passes and Pitt passed another crucial test in adversity.

"Tony Dorsett took the pressure off the entire offense while being keyed," Majors told reporters after the game. "Under the circumstances, I'd say this was his greatest game ever at Pitt."

"Pitt Will See Miami Again In The Orange Bowl; Need Five Tickets," read a sign at the game. Representatives from both the Orange and Cotton Bowls watched the Pitt-Miami game from the press box.

Heading into its game at Navy the following week, Tony Dorsett needed 152 yards to surpass Archie Griffin, then in his rookie season with the Cincinnati Bengals and winner of the Heisman Trophy in 1974 and 1975, as college football's all-time leading rusher.

The Panthers also had revenge on their minds; Navy had won 17-0 at Pitt Stadium the year before, and the Pitt coaches were leery of the Midshipmen.

"The coaches were so uptight all week going into that game," said Al Romano. "We had lost to them at home the year before, plus Matt [Cavanaugh] was still out."

Unannounced, the afternoon before the game, Romano and a few of his teammates left the team's hotel, the Sheraton Inn in New Carrollton, Md., to visit a friend or relative of one of Pitt's players. Romano said:

> We all got back late for the team meal the night before the game, and let's just say the coaches weren't too happy with us. They were on pins and needles as it was. I don't want to condone what we did. We were late, and we deserved whatever punishment we received, but my point is that we had so much confidence in ourselves, and knew how good we were, that we just went out and beat Navy without any trouble.

The coaches need not have worried. Yewcic tossed a 30-yard scoring strike to Corbett in the first half, then Dorsett scored from 6 yards out and Pitt led 14-0 at halftime. A field goal from Carson Long and Elliott Walker's 69-yard scoring burst made it 24-0 after three quarters.

The fourth quarter was all about Dorsett's quest to break Griffin's record. His 21-yard run made the score 31-0. Then, with the ball at the Navy 32, he dodged his way past Navy defenders all the way to the end zone to become the leading rusher in NCAA history. The entire Pitt bench raced to swarm and congratulate him. Dorsett accepted the game ball in the presence of his parents, Wes and Myrtle Dorsett. The Panthers won easily, 45-0. Bill Hillgrove stated:

> They [Navy] fired the cannon, which they never do for an opponent, and they [Midshipmen] doffed their caps, which they also never do for an opponent. They were very classy gestures on their part. I remember getting on the plane in Baltimore after the drive from Annapolis, and there were tears in my eyes. I'd been seeing the greatest back [Dorsett] in the history of the game, and I realized that this guy's place in history is secure.

"When Tony Dorsett does something, he does it in style," Russ Franke reported in *The Pittsburgh Press*.[2] Franke's nephew, Tom Yewcic, will be remembered as the man who pitched the ball to Dorsett for his historic run. Yewcic said:

> The play was Haw Option Nine from a slot formation. We ran it to the left side. It was designed to look like an option, but it was actually a sweep. He [Dorsett] rounded the corner, and he was just gone. Everyone in the country knew he was gonna get the ball. He must have run through their entire defense because everyone was shifted in that direction.

With the NCAA rushing record in hand, Dorsett's candidacy for the Heisman Trophy flourished. It became a race between Dorsett and University of Southern California running back Ricky Bell. Dean Billick, who managed the publicity efforts for Dorsett and Pitt's football team, thought Bell was the favorite at the outset of the season because the Trojans already had produced two Heisman winners in O. J. Simpson and Mike Garrett. The 1976 Trojans had lost to Missouri in their opener, but would not lose again. Dorsett's performance in the opener at Notre Dame, combined with the NCAA record, nudged him ahead of Bell, who was injured later in the season.

"We were playing for a national championship and we were running a Heisman Trophy campaign at the same time," said Billick. "There was national media attention coming from everywhere. A lot of national broadcasters were coming to our games, as well as *The New York Times*."

Dorsett, quiet as a freshman, came to know and understand how to play the media game. He was no longer a shy eighteen-year-old. "I was a communications major, so I was becoming more and more comfortable speaking and dealing with the media," Dorsett said. "The Heisman was pretty much between Ricky Bell and me, but then Ricky got hurt. I wasn't surprised that I won it, but it's still kind of a dream."

Billick staged a photo of Dorsett with Archie Griffin, holding a Tony Dorsett bumper sticker, on the field prior to a Steelers-Bengals game at Three Rivers Stadium. Dorsett, John Majors and his family also posed for a picture with President Gerald Ford at Greater Pittsburgh Airport when Ford visited the city. (At the time, Pitt was No. 2 in the nation behind Ford's alma mater, Michigan, where he had played football.)

"We knew it wasn't the local media that was gonna win the Heisman for him [Dorsett]," Billick said. "Number one, it was what Tony did on the field. Number two, it was making sure that the national media knew exactly what Tony was doing. That required a lot of effort on the part of not only me, but the coaching staff, the whole sports information office, and Tony."

As such, Billick had to balance Dorsett's time not only as a Heisman Trophy candidate, but as a football player and college student. He said:

> I had to make sure that we made allowances for Tony to be a student and a football player first, not a mega media star. But that was almost impossible. It became almost overwhelming. At the time, it was the first Heisman campaign we had run. It was more work than it was fun.

Billick arranged for Dorsett to come to the sports information office at an arranged time once or twice a week to return phone calls to media members. He sent out reams of notes listing Dorsett's accomplishments on the field, along with quotes from opposing coaches praising Dorsett. When Billick would go on the road to advance a game, he would arm himself with video clips of Dorsett which would go to every television station there. He would take action pictures to newspaper sports departments. "Newspapers were pretty big at that time, which they no longer are," said Billick. "And I'm not so sure if that's a good thing."

The Dorsett Heisman campaign required more in the way of effort and cooperation than dollars and cents.

"I don't think we spent a great deal of money on it," Billick said. "Tony and Johnny Majors took care of business on the field. That was the most important thing. We were secondary players, but we had a job to do, too." And that included winning the four remaining games—and a bowl game—on the schedule.

"Tony got national attention as a freshman with the season [1973] he had, and the way Pitt turned the program around," said Billick. "It was nice to win the Heisman, but the national championship drive was the most important venue."

The team's success on the field had much to do with how well the players related to each other off the field. It was an interesting collection of young men from divergent backgrounds and ways of life. Matt Cavanaugh said:

> It was an unbelievably close knit group of players. Sometimes it's hard to get that type of closeness at the college level, where you have a bunch of guys coming together from so many diverse backgrounds. But we were

all able to come together for a few hours a day and get the job done. The coaching staff deserved a lot of credit for that. They respected us like adults as we grew up together during those years.

Bill Hillgrove said:

> That team had great leadership. [Linebacker] Jimbo Cramer was just a real tough, tough guy who proved he could play with pain, and he did, and he brought that team the mental element. Dorsett did, too, but in his own way. Jim Corbett was a guy who liked to have fun. He was always willing to smile. [Tom] Yewcic, he was there just in case he was needed. John Pelusi was a leader on that team.

Al Romano was from a small town in upstate New York, but came to appreciate, and embrace, the relationships he developed in Pittsburgh.

"Coming to Pitt and meeting and making friends with the guys on the team was a great experience," Romano said. "It was just like coming into one very large extended family, where we all got along well."

Romano grew fond of his fellow nose guard David Logan, who was two years younger: "I can still see coming back to my place and opening the door, only to find Dave and however many friends and family members having what amounted to a cookout right in our room, some of them lounging on my bed, eating and drinking!" The camaraderie and positive vibes formed early during the tenure of John Majors at Pitt.

"We established an attitude and a feeing right away that we were winners," said Romano. "We were only going to get better and stronger." Don Parrish noted: "When I finished high school in Tallahassee, it would have been very easy for me just to stay there at home (Florida State). But I knew if I did, I'd never get a chance to grow up. I'm glad I came here. Pittsburgh is where I found myself, and it will always be special to me."[3]

The 1976 Panthers—some of them, at least—even adapted an unofficial theme song, "Do It, 'Till You're Satisfied" by B. T. Express. "Yeah, the brothers really liked to crank that up in the locker room and show their moves," remembered Romano.

Meanwhile, from Pullman, Washington, where Jackie Sherrill was in his first season as head coach at Washington State, *The Pittsburgh Post-Gazette* contacted the former chief aide to John Majors at Pitt to see how he was doing. Within the subsequent article, Sherrill made a prediction: Pitt would play Georgia in the Sugar Bowl for the national championship.

Sports Illustrated jumped on the Pitt bandwagon for its home game with Syracuse at Pitt Stadium, sending Myron Cope to write a feature about Dorsett relative to the game. Cope's story might have had an unhappy ending except for a controversial stand by the Pitt defense in the fourth quarter with the Panthers clinging to a 20-13 lead. A pesky sophomore quarterback named Bill Hurley, playing for the first time against Pitt, nearly sidetracked the Panthers' dream season.

Al Romano, from Solvay, New York, a stone's throw from Syracuse, was familiar with the Orange signal caller, and cautioned his Pitt teammates leading up to the game. "I told people that he [Hurley] could hurt us, that he could run all over the place," said Romano.

Hurley did, running and passing for a school record 303 yards of total offense. David Jacobs established a Pitt Stadium record with a 55-yard field goal in the third quarter to give Syracuse a 13-10 lead, the only time Pitt had trailed that late in a game during the season.

Dorsett, playing through a bruised leg and a sore elbow, carried the Panthers on his back, rushing for 241 yards and two touchdowns, including a 33-yard burst to give Pitt a 17-13 lead. Carson Long's 47-yard field goal extended the advantage to 20-13, but Hurley drove Syracuse deep into Pitt territory in the fourth quarter. The Orange found themselves at the Pitt 11-yard line on third down with a yard to go.

Romano, ironically, had grown up wanting to go to Syracuse. He intended to go there following one year at Staunton Military Academy ("I hated it there," said Romano), but Syracuse, still under the direction of coach Ben Schwartzwalder, would not plan a visit for him during his year away. In the meantime, Pitt began recruiting Romano, and scheduled a visit to the Oakland campus. He was recruited primarily by assistant coach Bobby Roper, got along great with Pitt's players, and decided that was where he was going to go play football in 1973. When Syracuse sent letter-of-intent papers to the Romano residence, Al instructed his mother not to sign anything. He was going to Pitt.

Jim Sessler was another Syracuse area player who grew up following the Orange. The Syracuse campus was about an hour's drive from his home in Waterloo, New York. His father had season tickets, and young Jim and his dad attended many games at old Archbold Stadium. Jim was happy when Schwartzwalder finally retired as coach after serving in that position from 1949 through 1973. "Schwartzwalder stayed at Syracuse about five years too long," Sessler said during a 2019 interview. "I was happy to go there [in 1974]. I figured if I played for a new coach [Frank Maloney], I'd be graded the same way as the current sophomores, junior and seniors."

Thus Sessler and Romano found themselves on opposite sides of the line of scrimmage with nothing less than Pitt's undefeated season and hopes for a national championship in dire jeopardy. Tom Coughlin was Syracuse's offensive coordinator.

On third down, Hurley turned and handed the ball to Sessler, who crashed into the Pitt defensive front. No gain—at least in the eyes of the officials. Sessler said:

> We were in a Power T, and it was a dive off the right hand side. We called that formation "Thunder." There's no question I made it on third down. I definitely made it on the third down play. The ball just had to be inside the ten-yard line, and it was a first down. My knees were over the line we needed. I was laying on the ground. The ref came and picked it up and took it back and set the ball right on the line, so there's no question it wasn't going to be a first down.

Romano was not as sure of the stop as Sessler was certain he had made it:

> If he did make the first down, it was on the third down play. Syracuse ran what we call a two hole. When Hurley ran that, I took out the guard, but the center shot out for [linebacker] Arnie Weatherington. The center tried to get a piece of me, but I slowed him up. I remember being at the bottom of the pile and grabbing for ankles. I figured, "This guy [Sessler] ain't going another foot." But it was Arnie who made the great play.

To bolster its front for the sequence, senior offensive tackle Joe Stone was inserted into the game. Hurley decided to try to fool Pitt at the line of scrimmage. Sessler noted:

> When we went back to the huddle before fourth down, Hurley said, "Look, I'm not calling twenty-four, but we're running twenty-four this time. We're gonna call it so that damn guy [Stone] thinks it's going someplace else." And that's what we did. He called a different audible, but we ran the same play. As an offensive lineman, he possibly understood what the audible was.

Film footage of the fourth down play, shot from behind the Pitt defense, shows Romano lifting his left arm and pointing in that direction, and that is exactly where the play went.

"The fourth down play I didn't get as far over, but I'm positive I did," Sessler insists. "The ref came in, grabbed the ball and put it back on the ten-yard line. That's history."

Livid after the call, Orange coach Frank Maloney drew an unsportsmanlike penalty, and later trailed one of the officials the entire distance off the field after the game.

The crisis diverted, Dorsett ran Pitt from danger and into Syracuse territory where Long kicked a 29-yard field goal for the final 23-13 score. A relieved John Majors explained to reporters how Syracuse had surprised his team throughout the afternoon: "They (Syracuse) mixed up their formations on us, so we started mixing things up, too. We began to adjust in the second quarter. It got down to a matter of outguessing each other. If you made the right choice, you were in good shape."

"Dorsett did some of the best running of his career to bring them out from deep in their territory," said Bill Hillgrove. "They weren't long runs, but they helped save the season. That's when I also realized that Dorsett was a lot more than just the ability and speed. There was a lot inside."

"That was the most critical part of the season, I would say," Majors acknowledged, many years later. "That was our most difficult game."

"We damn near lost to Syracuse," said Jim Corbett. "That was as close as it came for us. They were tough that day. They played us tough, and it was at our house, too."

Jim Sessler maintains a grudging respect for that Pitt team, but the disappointment is evident in his voice many years later. "It was a disheartening loss," he said. "Pitt had a great team. Urban legend has it that when Johnny Majors came in, he gave out seventy-some scholarships, and that's when the NCAA said, 'Hey, wait a second. We're not gonna do that anymore.'"

Sessler and Romano still stay in touch. Their sons played football together. Sessler kids Romano about a picture that appeared in a Syracuse paper, showing Romano holding his fingers a couple inches apart during the crucial part of the game.

"I tell him [Romano] I wanted to take that picture and shove it up his ass," Sessler jokes.

The Syracuse game also was the end of Tom Yewcic term as Pitt's starting quarterback. He retired undefeated after three games, maintaining his sense of humor. When asked who helped him the most in his career, he responded, "the two guys who hit Haygood and Cavanaugh."

Recovered from his injury, Matt Cavanaugh was in uniform for the Syracuse game, and indicated that he could have played in an emergency. It almost came to that. "Tom Yewcic came in and did a great job," said Cavanaugh. "The team rallied around him, and with Tony [Dorsett] in the backfield, you have a pretty good guy to hand the ball off to however many times a game."

"I don't know of any national championship team that's overcome the loss of its first two quarterbacks," said Majors. Tony Dorset noted: "Tommy did a great job. He'd been with us all along those four years, so we were comfortable with him. All of us on the offense—the backs and the linemen—knew we were probably going to have to rely on the running game most of the time."

Jim Corbett said:

Tommy did his part. He didn't fumble, he executed well and he threw the ball very well. Every pass he threw to me was right on the money. We didn't know him as well, but he stepped in and did everything the coaching staff asked him to do. He'll be remembered all through time as the guy who got us over the hump during a challenging period that season.

"Yewcic, as they say, rose to the occasion," said Alex Kramer. "He got the job done. And I must add that I was glad when Bill Hurley used up his eligibility at Syracuse. He gave us all kinds of headaches, but we never lost to them." In fact, from 1973 through 1983, Pitt was 11-0 against Syracuse.

Michigan and Pitt ranked No. 1 and No. 2 in both polls heading into each team's ninth game of the season. Pitt was set to host Army while, approximately 425 miles west of Pittsburgh, the Wolverines were visiting 3-5 Purdue. Notre Dame had fallen victim to a number of upset losses at Ross-Ade Stadium through the years; Pitt fans were hoping Michigan would meet the same fate.

The Wolverines had breezed through the first eight games on their schedule, outscoring their opponents 352-58, and were prohibitive favorites to make it nine straight wins against Purdue.

Matt Cavanaugh returned to the lineup for Pitt, grateful and relieved to have survived Syracuse's upset bid one week earlier. He showed few effects from the injury that kept him sidelined for the previous three games. Cavanaugh completed eight of twelve passes, including a 24-yard scoring toss to Willie Taylor. He also rushed for 76-yards, including a career high 49-yard dash. Pitt won, 37-7.

Continuing his stretch of brilliant performances, Dorsett ran for 212 yards and three touchdowns on runs of 4, 5, and 32 yards.

With the victory secured, most in the crowd of 45,753 turned their thoughts to West Lafayette, Indiana, where Purdue was giving Michigan trouble. In 1976, there were no cell phones, tablets, pagers, or other such devices where people could find current sports scores at their fingertips. There was no score ticker scrolling across the bottom of the ESPN screen because there was no ESPN. Some fans would bring little transistor radios to the game, holding them up to their ears to follow the live action and hear scores from others during the broadcast. Public address announcers would give a list of scores during breaks in the action, a practice virtually unheard of anymore.

At Pitt Stadium on November 6, 1976, public address announcer Roger Huston was the primary score provider for folks in attendance. Huston knew a secret he was about to tell everybody. The press box inhabitants, including Huston, knew something that the folks in the stands did not. Michigan had a chance to win the game in the final seconds, but Bob Wood missed a 37-yard field goal attempt.

"Knowing what had happened already, I decided to do a little recreation of the end of the game," Huston recalled. "'Michigan lines up for a field goal attempt. Here's the snap, the kick—it is wide left!'" Huston then gave the proper final score, and Pitt Stadium went wild, comfortable and delirious in the knowledge that, for the first time since the start of the 1938 season—Jock Sutherland's final season as coach—the Panthers were about to be rated the No. 1 team in the nation. With the ranking came additional attention, scrutiny, and responsibility. Matt Cavanaugh noted:

> We knew that with the number one ranking would come a lot of pressure, and the coaching staff at that point did a tremendous job of taking the pressure off the players, and that was very important. We had a veteran team for the most part, but still there were a lot of young players who hadn't been through that type of situation, so it was crucial that they have the right approach to the last few weeks of that season.

John Majors appreciated the excellence of his quarterback heading into the crucial, final weeks of the 1976 season:

Cavanaugh was a wonderful quarterback. He was one of the most ideal quarterbacks I've ever had on a college football team. He could see the field as well as anyone I've ever seen. He could see the overall field and know where to put the ball. He ran the option well enough to make it effective.

At 9-0, the nations' No. 1 team prepared to host West Virginia on November 13. It was the final home game for Dorsett and the rest of the special senior class responsible for resurrecting Pitt's football program. The Panthers had not forgotten the 17-14 loss to the Mountaineers in Morgantown the year before. That game had been televised regionally by ABC; likewise for the 1976 Backyard Brawl. It is hard to imagine, more than forty years later, that it was Pitt's first appearance on live television since the opener at Notre Dame, but that was the college football and television reality in 1976.

The Mountaineers came to Pitt Stadium with a new coach, but a familiar one. Frank Cignetti, the former assistant to Dave Hart at Pitt, had been WVU's offensive coordinator under Bobby Bowden. When Bowden left WVU for Florida State following the 1975 season, Cignetti was named head coach. He inherited a rebuilding job. WVU had lost thirty-two seniors from the 9-3 Peach Bowl team from the previous season.

A big part of the future for West Virginia's program was a high school senior prospect from South Charleston, West Virginia, named Robert Alexander, who was being recruited by virtually every school in the country. Alexander was on the sideline prior to the game at Pitt Stadium—on a Pitt recruiting visit—resplendent in a sharp suit, tie, and overcoat. He later signed with West Virginia.

A week earlier, in the magazine displaying Tony Dorsett on the cover, Alexander had appeared in the same *Sports Illustrated* "Faces In The Crowd" feature along with another scholastic running back, Pascagoula, Mississippi's Ray "Rooster" Jones and an aspiring young teenage tennis star named John McEnroe.

Alexander and the rest of the sellout crowd of 56,500—Pitt's only home sellout in 1976—settled in for a game much closer than Pitt fans had expected.

"That West Virginia game was a tough one," Majors later admitted. "Tony [Dorsett] was ejected from that game, but thank God he played most of the fourth quarter that day."

Pitt's 24-16 win was the only game the 1976 Panthers won by single digits. Pitt helped WVU's chances by fumbling five times. Although the final score was closer than the Syracuse game, the Panthers were never in serious danger of losing. They had an answer for each WVU threat. Tony Dorsett, Matt Cavanaugh, and Carson Long saw to that.

Cavanaugh rushed for a career high 124 yards and Long added a field goal in the third quarter to become the NCAA's all-time leading kick scorer. But it was Dorsett who stole the show.

Prior to the game, Dorsett had flashed the No. 1 sign while running in front of the West Virginia bench. At halftime, he had his jersey #33 retired—the first Pitt player to receive that honor—in a ceremony including Majors and Cas Myslinski. And with Pitt running out the clock at game's end, and Dorsett carrying the ball six straight times, he was ejected, along with West Virginia's Robin Meeley, for throwing the ball at Meeley in response to an apparent late hit near the sideline. Dorsett had 199 yards rushing on thirty-eight carries, and scored all three Pitt touchdowns.

"Tony came around the right side and somebody [Meeley] hit him late out of bounds, and he took the football and threw it at some kid's face," John Pelusi explained to reporters in the Pitt locker room after the game.

With a 10-0 record, the top national ranking and an off week prior to playing Penn State at Three Rivers Stadium on November 26, Pitt had a decision to make—which bowl game to choose. It had its pick of three—Orange, Sugar, and Cotton Bowl. This was at a time when there was no Bowl Championship Series or college football playoff of any kind. Bids would be extended on Saturday, November 20, before the end of the regular season. The Orange and Cotton Bowls each paid $1 million to their participating teams; the Sugar Bowl $750,000. Colorado (8-3) was the Big Eight champion, and would represent that conference in the Orange Bowl. Houston (9-2) won the Southwest Conference in its first season in that league. Georgia (10-1) claimed the Southeastern Conference title and automatic berth in the Sugar Bowl.

John Majors knew where he wanted to go, and realized he had to measure between his head and heart before making a recommendation to his team. "I wanted to go to the Orange Bowl in the worst way because it was a great game and a festive occasion, a first class deal," he said. "And, of course, we had a lot of Florida kids on the team, and they wanted to go to the Orange Bowl."

Majors was convinced he was coaching the best team in the country, and could beat anybody, and realized that a win against a one-loss team (Georgia) would resonate more positively with voters and the college football community than a defeat of a team with two or three losses.

He stated: "I had looked at Georgia on film and I knew that we were two touchdowns better than they were. If we played it equally—take out turnovers—we were at least a two touchdown better team." Realizing that some of the players would be disappointed, Majors informed the team of his wishes—to play the team (Georgia) with the best record. "I called the team together and told them we'd better ought to play Georgia," he said. "Some of the guys were a little disappointed, but they voted and said, 'Yeah, we'll go to the Sugar Bowl.' It turned out to be a great trip."

But first there was one final order of business in the regular season—beating Penn State, something Pitt had not done since 1965. "To reach a certain level or plateau of confidence, where you haven't been before sometimes involves beating a team, Notre Dame, you hadn't beaten before," said Majors. "Maybe it's Alabama—or Penn State."

Majors, Dorsett, and Pitt had lost their first three games to the Nittany Lions, none as bitter or painful as the 7-6 defeat the year before.

"That [7-6 loss] was really the first time that we outplayed them, and I don't believe in saying 'should have' and 'could have,' but we outplayed them that day," Majors recalled. "That was a game that we played better, outplayed them and let 'em off the hook."

Pitt's players were not buying into any jinx theories. They approached the game with supreme confidence. "Going into the game, we probably were the more talented team," said John Pelusi.

"We knew, deep down, that we were better than Penn State," said Al Romano. "When you look at where Pitt football had been before we got there, we realized just how far we had come."

One Pitt official was not as confident or optimistic as the players. Dean Billick noted:

> I wasn't sure we could beat Penn State, because it had been ten years. I knew we could beat Georgia. I knew we were better than anybody in the country, but until we beat Penn State I was not sure, because I couldn't help remember what had happened the year before when we were the better team but didn't win.

Even Penn State coach Joe Paterno, who hinted that a bit of good fortune or intervention had played a part in his team's win against Pitt in 1975, recognized things could be different in 1976. On his weekly public television show, *TV Quarterbacks*, Paterno stated that, since he had been coach at Penn State, this (1976) probably was the first time that Pitt entered the game with superior talent.

The days leading up to, and following, the 1976 Pitt-Penn State game turned out to be some of the most significant and dramatic times the program has ever experienced.

On November 22, 1976, four days prior to the Penn State game, Dean Billick approached Majors with a bit of news: Bill Battle had resigned as football coach at the University of Tennessee. Battle, then in his seventh season on the job, presided over a 6-5 record that season, including a 7-0 loss to Kentucky at Neyland Stadium two days before. The folks in Knoxville were not happy with the overall prospects of the UT program. Who better than Johnny Majors—a Tennessean by birth and one of the Vols' all-time great players—to come home and revive the school's football fortunes?

A couple years into Majors' term at Pitt, Billick had the coach provide a recorded message each weekday, relative to that day's practice session. The number was distributed to media only. The information provided gave writers and broadcasters tidbits of news for their stories and reports when they were unable to receive it for themselves, usually at practice. On this day, Majors addressed the rumors about the Tennessee situation: "I have not been contacted by the University of Tennessee, and my entire effort this week will be devoted to the Penn State game. I simply am not interested in discussing with anyone the Tennessee situation, or any other situation, until the conclusion of the regular season."

Two nights before playing Penn State, Pitt held a light workout at Three Rivers Stadium. *The Pittsburgh Press* published a photo of Majors with Tony Dorsett, with a smiling Dorsett waving, as if to say good-bye to the Pittsburgh fans. Majors, hands in front of him, unsmiling, seemed less sure; at least that is what *The Press* speculated.

In any event, Majors offered his take on the importance of Dorsett in the Pitt turnaround across four seasons. "Could we have done it without Dorsett?" he asked himself. "I doubt it. This year, maybe. Over four years? Never. He made Pitt a winner [in 1973 and 1974] when, really, we didn't have the personnel to win."[4]

A Three Rivers Stadium capacity crowd of 50,360 turned out on a damp, cool Friday night, November 26 to see if Pitt could finally beat Penn State—and head to the Sugar Bowl with a perfect record. Lost in the huge crowd was Frank Clark, whose field goal in the final seconds of the 1965 game at Pitt Stadium, had given the Panthers their most recent victory against the Lions.

It was Penn State's home game, with the Nittany Lions wearing blue jerseys while the Panthers wore their customary road whites. Penn State published the game program that, curiously, did not include a photo of Dorsett in the Pitt section.

Originally, the game was to have been played at Beaver Stadium in Happy Valley, but ABC again stepped in, wanting to feature the game in prime time the night after Thanksgiving. Neither Pitt's nor Penn State's home facilities had lights at the time. With the 1977 game already scheduled for Pitt Stadium, Penn State (Joe Paterno) agreed to the switch to Pittsburgh on the condition that Pitt would agree to play at Penn State in 1978, 1979, and 1980, which it did.

For Bill Hillgrove, about to provide play-by-play coverage of his third Pitt-Penn State football game, it was a long, trying day. "I had lost a dear friend earlier that day who had died at the age of forty," he recalled. "So here I am at thirty-six years old, and all of a sudden your mortality sets in. That whole game I was pretty emotional." Hillgrove could not have felt any better seeing Pitt's offense struggle throughout the first quarter.

Penn State scored the only points of the first quarter on a 21-yard pass from Chuck Fusina, another McKees Rocks quarterback, to Bob Torrey, but the Pitt defense kept the Lions off the scoreboard for the remainder of the game. Free safety Bob Jury intercepted two Fusina passes, giving him nine for the season, a Pitt record. J. C. Wilson picked off another. Jury said: "I had a lot of freedom to do things from my position, plus the fact that the rest of the defense always did a great job pressuring the quarterback. I always considered myself an aggressive football player, and a lot of times I just happened to be in the right place at the right time."

The Panthers tied the game 7-7 in the second quarter when Dorsett took an option pitch from Cavanaugh and reached the end zone from 6 yards out. It stayed that way until halftime. "Penn State did some things in the first half which had us a little surprised," John Pelusi admitted. "At halftime, Majors and [offensive coordinator and line coach] Joe Avezzano decided to switch Tony and Elliott in the backfield, and to run an unbalanced line. We ran all over them in the second half."

"I told the staff I was gonna put in the unbalanced line," said Majors. "That would change the blocking schemes, but we put in a couple simple plays with Dorsett at fullback."

Pitt made the switch in the third quarter, and with the game still tied 7-7 and the ball at the Penn State forty, Dorsett broke loose, aided by a finishing block by Gordon Jones on Penn State's Bill Crummy.

"They [Penn State] misadjusted in the middle of the line," Majors explained. "We hit the middle just right, and there was nobody in the middle. He [Dorsett] ran right past the goal post."

Dorsett ran straight through the end zone and flipped the ball to a surprised Pittsburgh police officer standing guard in his rain gear. Bill Hillgrove said:

> Once he [Dorsett] got loose in the secondary and was in control, then you had problems because he could turn people around in the secondary better than any player I ever saw. Once he broke the line of scrimmage from the fullback slot, it shocked the whole Penn State defense. They weren't ready to react to that.

Elliott Walker added a 12-yard touchdown run and Carson Long finished the scoring with a 47-yard field goal to secure the convincing 24-7 victory. Dorsett finished with 224 yards and two touchdowns, giving him 1,948 yards for the season, an NCAA single season record at the time. The Three Rivers Stadium scoreboard acknowledged Dorsett's 6,082 career rushing yards at game's end.

For Dean Billick, a Penn State graduate, the monkey had been lifted from the Panthers' back:

> By the end of the game I should have been running down to the locker room to do my job. I had to take on all the media who would be admitted to the locker room ten minutes after the game. But I got so engrossed when we won, I put my head down and cried like a baby. It was so emotional.

The honors and celebrations came rolling in. Majors was named Coach of the Year by UPI and *The Sporting News*. And, on November 30, 1976, Tony Dorsett received the word that he had won the Heisman Trophy. Unlike the extravagant ESPN production to announce the winner nowadays, Pitt officials and Dorsett received word a day in advance that they were needed to appear at a press conference at the Downtown Athletic Club in New York City. Dean Billick accompanied Dorsett to New York for the press conference. Dorsett's family members would travel to New York for the official acceptance ceremony dinner later in the month at the New York Hilton. Joe Paterno was the main speaker at that event.

Tight end Jim Corbett, who had been Dorsett's teammate for four seasons, marvels at the experience. "Tony Dorsett was probably one of the five greatest football players ever," he said. "He was probably the greatest college football running back ever. Every time he touched the football, you could score a touchdown. He was so quick and so fast and so strong."

Dorsett's demeanor and personality also left a memorable impression, as Jim Corbett recalled:

> As the years go by, I come to appreciate Tony's talent and demeanor even more. He hardly ever missed practice. He was always there. He wasn't one of those guys who thought, "Treat me right. I'm special. Do this. Do that." He was out there practicing. I would always marvel at how it never looked like he was trying real hard. Not because he was lazy. He could just do everything so effortlessly.

Two nights after Dorsett was named recipient of the Heisman Trophy, the Pitt football team banquet was held December 2, 1976 at the Pittsburgh Hilton. The following day, it was announced that Johnny Majors would, indeed, be marching home. He accepted the job as head football coach at Tennessee. It had been an agonizing period and decision for Majors, who said:

> It was a frustrating time because I did not want to leave Pittsburgh at all. If Southern Cal[ifornia] or Notre Dame had offered me the job, I don't think I would have looked at it. But being that it [Tennessee] was my *alma mater* was the only reason I did it. I wanted to go, but I wanted to stay.

There was no need for a secret search committee to seek a replacement for Majors at Pitt. Cas Myslinski set a December 21 deadline to name a new coach. Although George Welsh, then the head coach at Navy, interviewed for the job several days later, it soon became apparent that Jackie Sherrill would be leaving Washington State after one season and moving back to Pittsburgh. That, at least, was what some of Pitt's players were hoping.

"I'd like to see Coach Sherrill, if possible," said Matt Cavanaugh, who would be a senior in 1977. "I'd rather have somebody come that I know and who knows us. The team is close to him."[5]

"I really like Coach Sherrill a lot," said Jeff Delaney. "He recruited me, and I'd kind of like to see him come back."[6]

Sherrill flew to Pittsburgh for an interview almost immediately. He and Cas Myslinski were seated together at the Pitt-Virginia basketball game at Fitzgerald Field House on December 4. He was with Chancellor Wesley Posvar in a private box the following afternoon to watch the Pittsburgh Steelers play the Tampa Bay Buccaneers. His hiring seemed a foregone conclusion. At halftime, Posvar, Sherrill and Pitt administrator Bernie Kobosky huddled to discuss terms of a contract for the new coach. Without asking any amount, Sherrill demanded to be paid at least what Majors had been making.

Several football players had petitioned Myslinski to hire Sherrill, and some had gone so far as to plan a small rally in support of Sherrill's candidacy at the Pitt-Virginia basketball game. Sherrill got wind of it and urged the players not to do it.

"Jackie told me that if he weren't offered the job while he was here, to forget it," attorney Sam Sciullo, Sr., said in 2009. "He told me he wouldn't be coming back. I told that to Cas."

On December 6, 1976, one day after the Steelers hosted Tampa Bay at Three Rivers Stadium, Jackie Sherrill was named Pitt's twenty-eighth football coach. He was aged thirty-three at the time. The announcement came at a press conference at the Greentree Holiday Inn.

While Sherrill was standing by to assume his new duties at Pitt, John Majors spent parts of December shuttling between Pittsburgh and Knoxville, but when it was time for the Pitt team to depart for Biloxi, Mississippi, where it would train for a period before going to New Orleans, Pitt had Majors' full and undivided attention. Majors said: "When I got on the plane here to go to Biloxi, I remember saying, 'I am not doing anything for the University of Tennessee until this [Sugar Bowl] game is over. I will spend this last week enjoying this great team, and fully prepare it for this Sugar Bowl game.'"

Training in Biloxi turned out to be a wise move. Cavanaugh noted: "One of the most important decisions made was when Majors decided to take us to Biloxi for the first week of practice. In a college environment, it's tough to keep tabs on players twenty-four hours a day, and it was good for us to go away together like that."

The 10-1 Georgia Bulldogs had broken Alabama's string of five consecutive Southeastern Conference championships. They defeated the Crimson Tide, 21-0, in the fourth week of the season. Georgia claimed wins against three other ranked teams: California, Cincinnati, and Florida. It was a veteran team, and had registered four shutouts. Of its twenty-two offensive and defensive starters, twelve were seniors and ten were juniors. Conversely, Pitt had three sophomores (Gordon Jones, Matt Carroll, and Jeff Delaney) in its lineup.

Georgia's only loss was a 21-17 defeat at Mississippi (Ole Miss) one week after it had beaten Alabama. Georgia relied heavily on its running game, led by Uniontown, Pa., product Kevin McLee, who ran for 1,058 yards and six touchdowns. Coach Vince Dooley alternated quarterbacks. Ray Goff, who would start the Sugar Bowl game, was the more effective operator of the run option attack, while Matt Robinson was the better passer. Robinson completed a modest thirty-eight of sixty-one passes for 609 yards, seven touchdowns, and six interceptions for the season.

By the time the Pitt team party arrived in New Orleans, the city already was teeming with Georgia red. The Panthers were headquartered at the Marriott Hotel on Canal Street, several blocks from the famed French Quarter and Bourbon Street. Dean Billick said:

> New Orleans is a great place, along with San Antonio, to hold national events like that. It's easy to get around. You can walk to most places. It was just jammed on the streets. There was Georgia red all over the place. But it was the first time I had seen a lot of Pitt fans walking around in their Pitt jerseys, in their blue and gold colors. The arguments and shouting in the streets were amazing to see and hear. It was a lot of fun.

The Pitt players took advantage of the hotel's proximity to the bustling nightlife scene. For the first few nights, Majors established what could best be termed a "relaxed" curfew.

"Majors was quite liberal as far as letting our players go out at night," Dean Billick recalled. "The Georgia media couldn't believe it, even some of the national media. But the players didn't abuse the privilege."

Pitt's players were not the only ones enjoying the bowl experience. "When we were in Biloxi the week before, the coaches were out with us just about every night," said John Pelusi. "We saw them in different bars. There was no curfew. In New Orleans, we didn't have any curfew until it was Wednesday or Thursday."

The Sugar Bowl game was played on Saturday, January 1, 1977. Romano recalled: "A lot was said and written about our relaxed curfew. One night, or morning, a few of us [players] actually came back to the hotel when the rest of the team was congregating in the lobby waiting to board the bus for morning practice!"

"People wondered how we could have such a carefree attitude about town," said Matt Cavanaugh. "I think Georgia had a ten o'clock curfew every night, but we saw the Georgia players here and there. I think they broke curfew by position groups. I think the regimentation handcuffed them to a degree."

"That Pitt team wasn't regimented; it was free spirited," said Bill Hillgrove. "But when it came time to proving how good it was, it was able to do it. John [Majors] knew how to pull them in when it was necessary and time to pull them in."

Pelusi, one of the team leaders, recognized the team's ability to manage itself. "One of our practices for the Sugar Bowl, we were just supposed to go out in sweats," he said. "But we realized we hadn't had one of our better practice weeks the week before, so we decided to go out in full pads."

Pitt's players also were able to put aside the significance of the game they were about to play, and what was at stake. Pelusi said: "We didn't view that game any differently than any other game. It was just another game with the same routine. Obviously, we were in a different place other than Oakland. Relative to the things we were allowed to do, and what we did, it was no different."

But it was different for Pitt fans. The majority of them had not been going to Rose Bowl games when Jock Sutherland was the coach. Although outnumbered by the Georgia throng, Pitt sold its entire allotment of 12,500 tickets, without any public sale. The Golden Panthers booster club took care of that, and sent five charter airplanes to New Orleans for the game. Even "Tiger Paul" Auslander, more familiar for his outrageous cheering routines at Pitt basketball games, made the trip to New Orleans, and was spotted—arms flailing and perspiring heavily—leading a group of fans in a "Let's Go Pitt!" cheer in the middle of Bourbon Street.

Soon after the Pitt team arrived in New Orleans, WTAE TV filmed a short segment with Bill Hillgrove interviewing Jim Corbett and Cecil Johnson while the three were taking a horse driven carriage ride down Bourbon Street. Corbett announced his desire to get on with the game.

"I want to play," said Corbett. "I'm tired of practicing. We went out there today and seen all those Georgia boys with bald heads, but at the end of the game there's gonna be a lot more red on their head!"

Forty-three years after that carriage ride, Corbett was asked about that experience; he said:

Paul Martha looks for yardage during Pitt's 22-21 win against Penn State at Pitt Stadium in 1963. The 9-1 season was a rare bright spot during the 1960s. (*University of Pittsburgh Athletics*)

Helmets worn by Pitt in 1969 (left) to celebrate college football's centennial season, and in 1966 and 1967, with panther head decal. (Charles LeClaire)

1966 Pitt Coaching staff: Kneeling left to right: Walt Cummings, centers; Dave Hart, head coach; Bill Neal, defensive line; Leeman Bennett, offensive backfield. Standing: Frank Cignetti, ends; Dick Bestwick, linebackers; Bill Lewis, defensive backfield; Steve Petro, freshmen, and Jim Royer, offensive line.

Above: Dave Hart (front row, second from left) and his 1966 coaching staff. Leeman Bennett, Frank Cignetti, Dick Bestwick, and Bill Lewis later became head coaches. (*University of Pittsburgh Athletics*)

Below left: Running back Dave Garnett was an effective running back and kick returner at Pitt, but clashed with some of his coaches. (*University of Pittsburgh Athletics*)

Below right: Cynical Pitt students brought down the goal posts following Pitt's 14-3 win against William & Mary in 1968, the Panthers' only victory that season. (*Herbert K. Barnett*)

Above: Coach Carl DePasqua (far right) with running backs Denny Ferris (left) and Tony Esposito (middle) in early 1970s. (*University of Pittsburgh Athletics*)

Below left: Linebacker Ralph Cindrich receives instruction from assistant coach Foge Fazio during 1971 season. (*University of Pittsburgh Archives*)

Below right: Quarterback Dave Havern led Pitt to five victories during the fourth quarters of games Pitt had trailed in 1970 and 1971. (*University of Pittsburgh Archives*)

Above: Pitt *alumni* and Golden Panthers Bob Miller (hands in front) and Sam Sciullo worked behind the scenes to bring Johnny Majors to Pitt in late 1972. (*University of Pittsburgh Athletics and William J. Kovach*)

Below: Johnny Majors (middle) was introduced as Pitt's new football coach on December 19, 1972 by chancellor Wesley Posvar (left) and director of athletics Cas Myslinski (right). (*University of Pittsburgh Athletics*)

Johnny Majors was "kidnapped" by Pitt students as part of a campus charity event in 1973. (*University of Pittsburgh Athletics*)

Elliott Walker (far left), Robert Haygood (center) and Tony Dorsett each rushed for more than 100 yards in Pitt's 1975 Sun Bowl victory against Kansas. (*University of Pittsburgh Athletics*)

Above left: Johnny Majors (right) and assistant coach Jackie Sherrill hold 1975 Sun Bowl trophy. Sherrill announced after the game that he was leaving Pitt to become head coach at Washington State. (*University of Pittsburgh Athletics*)

Above right: Injured quarterbacks Matt Cavanaugh (left) and Robert Haygood on sideline prior to Pitt's 1976 game with Miami. (*University of Pittsburgh Archives*)

Offensive tackle Joe Stone (73) entered the game to help Pitt's defense stop Syracuse on a crucial series during the fourth quarter in 1976 season. (*University of Pittsburgh Archives*)

Above: Johnny Majors (kneeling) with coaching staff from 1976 national championship season. *From left to right*: Joe Madden, Bob Matey, Larry Holton, Bill Cox, Joe Avezzano, Jim Dyar, Harry Jones, and Bobby Roper. (*University of Pittsburgh Athletics*)

Below left: Quarterback Matt Cavanaugh (left) and running back Tony Dorsett in game action from 1976. (*University of Pittsburgh Athletics*)

Below right: Tony Dorsett with his parents, Wes and Myrtle Dorsett, at Annapolis on October 23, 1976 when Dorsett broke Archie Griffin's NCAA rushing yardage record. (*University of Pittsburgh Athletics*)

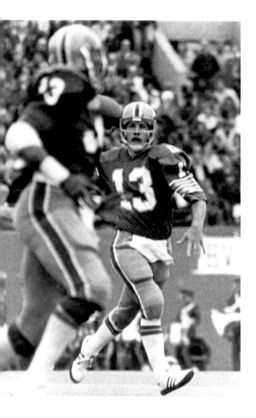

Above left: Quarterback Tom Yewcic (13) prepares to throw a short pass to Tony Dorsett. Yewcic led Pitt to wins against Miami, Navy, and Syracuse in the absence of the injured Matt Cavanaugh and Robert Haygood in 1976. (*University of Pittsburgh Athletics*)

Above right: Defensive lineman Al Romano was all set to attend Syracuse, but changed his mind and became an All-American at Pitt. (*University of Pittsburgh Athletics*)

Left: Robert Haygood entered Pitt on a football scholarship in 1973, but used his final year (1977–78) of eligibility to play point guard for the basketball team. (*University of Pittsburgh Athletics*)

Right: Jackie Sherrill and Jimmy Johnson (background) were a formidable coaching duo at Pitt in 1977 and 1978, but their time together in Pittsburgh did not end well. (*University of Pittsburgh Athletics*)

Below: Two of the greatest players in Pitt history, Hugh Green (left) and Dan Marino relax on the sideline as another victory is secure. The Panthers were undefeated at home during the 1978, 1979, and 1980 seasons. (*University of Pittsburgh Athletics*)

Above: The Pitt-Penn State rivalry became especially fierce during the Majors-Sherrill years. The game was played in late November, usually in rough weather conditions. Penn State won this 1977 game, 15-13, at Pitt Stadium. (*University of Pittsburgh Athletics*)

Below left: Pitt's sports information office produced this poster to boost the Heisman Trophy candidacy for Hugh Green in 1980. He finished second to South Carolina's George Rogers. (*University of Pittsburgh Athletics*)

Below right: Jackie Sherrill's Pitt teams went 50-9-1, including four Top Ten finishes and four victories in bowl games. (*University of Pittsburgh Athletics*)

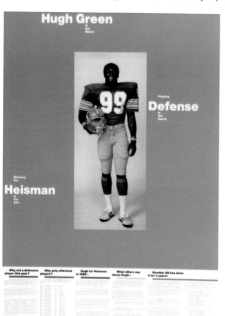

Above left: Bill Hillgrove (left) and Johnny Sauer provided radio coverage of Pitt football at a time when most games were not on live television. (*University of Pittsburgh Athletics*)

Above right: Alex Kramer was Pitt's administrative assistant to the head football coach from 1978 until 1995, but his involvement with the program began in the 1940s and continued well into the 2000s. (*University of Pittsburgh Athletics*)

Dean Billick had a front row seat to the awful, the great, and everything in between during his long career as an administrator in Pitt's athletics department. (*University of Pittsburgh Athletics*)

The Pittsburgh Press

Sunday, October 19, 1980

Sports

- Press Box 2
- X's & O's 2
- Scholastic 10
- Football Contest 11
- Outdoors 12
- Race Results 14

D

Panthers Climb Over West Virginia

Harassed all day, Oliver Luck is rushed by Greg Meisner, left, while Dwight Collins takes off on 53-yard touchdown pass play.

Press Photos by Donald J. Stetzer and Albert M. Herrmann Jr.

Marino Hurt, Trocano Stars In 42-14 Win

(Mountaineers run out of Luck — but not respect, Page D-4)

By BOB SMIZIK

For most college football teams the situation would have reeked of disaster. Their quarterback, the wonder sophomore who is what the team's offense is all about, has limped to the sidelines, finished for the day.

It could be just the emotional lift their arch-rival, already ahead by seven points, needs to stage a monumental upset.

But this is not an ordinary college football team when it comes to quarterbacks. This is a college football team which does not have the best No. 2 quarterback in the country, but one that does have the best quarterbacking free safety in the country.

After a brief fling with the No. 2 quarterback, over from the defense comes this free safety. Forget the upset. Forget the close game. Forget, maybe, about playing free safety.

At Pitt Stadium yesterday, Rick Trocano made them remember. He made them remember how he became Pitt's third all-time passer, and how for two seasons he led the Panthers to a 17-5 record.

Rick Trocano, pushed to defense by the brilliance of Danny Marino, came on to play quarterback in the second quarter and in slightly less than five minutes led Pitt to a four-touchdown eruption and the Panthers went on from there to a 42-14 rout of West Virginia.

Trocano had an incredible second quarter, completing eight of nine passes for 138 yards and two touchdowns.

"Ricky does things that no one else in the country could do," said Marino, whose injury was diagnosed as a mild sprain and who is questionable for next Saturday's game at Tennessee. "He just amazes me. No one in the country knows more about offense and defense than Rick Trocano. No one in the country could do the type of things he does."

A near sell-out crowd of 55,130 mostly moaned as West Virginia took a 7-0 lead when — ironically enough — split end Cedric Thomas got behind free safety Trocano in the end zone for a touchdown midway through the first quarter.

The crowd gasped later in the period as Marino suddenly was surrounded by trainers and doctors on the Pitt bench. Marino's tender left knee had given out on him as he walked to the sidelines following what he thought was a touchdown pass that was ruled incomplete.

Danny Daniels came on to direct the Panthers, who were on the 14-yard

(Continued on Page D-4)

Above: The 1980 Panthers rebounded from a difficult loss at Florida State to rout West Virginia in the 1980 Backyard Brawl at Pitt Stadium. (*Copyright Pittsburgh-Post Gazette, 2020, all rights reserved. Reprinted with permission*)

Below: Tailback Joe McCall (34) leads the way for quarterback Rick Trocano in Pitt's 1980 win against West Virginia. When Dan Marino was injured in the second quarter, Trocano switched to quarterback from his safety position and led Pitt's offense to four touchdowns in five minutes. (*Kennedy*)

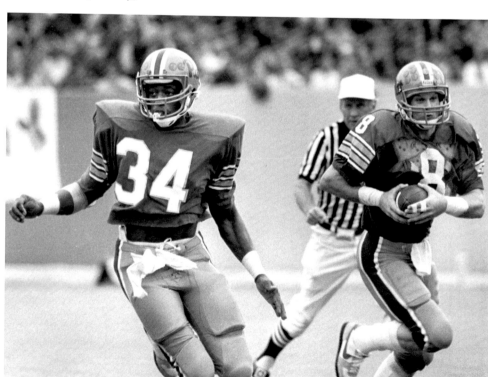

Above: Jackie Sherrill (kneeling) with his 1977 coaching staff. *From left to right:* Bob Matey, Don Boyce, Foge Fazio, Joe Moore, Otto Stowe, Bob Leahy, Larry Holton and Jimmy Johnson. Not pictured: Dave Wannstedt. (*University of Pittsburgh Athletics*)

Below: Pitt's 1980 defense led the nation in both rushing and total defense. One of the best units in college football history, eight of its starters made NFL rosters as rookies in 1981. (*University of Pittsburgh Athletics*)

Above: Hugh Green's jersey No. 99 was retired at halftime of his final home game in 1980, a 41-23 win against Louisville. Cas Myslinski (holding jersey) and Jackie Sherrill presided over the ceremony. (*Sam Sciullo, Sr.*)

Below left: Jackie Sherrill with senior defensive ends Hugh Green (left) and Rickey Jackson on the cover of *Game Plan*'s 1980 College Football magazine.

Below right: Offensive tackle Mark May came to Pitt from a small town in upstate New York, and left as the winner of the 1980 Outland Trophy. (*University of Pittsburgh Athletics*)

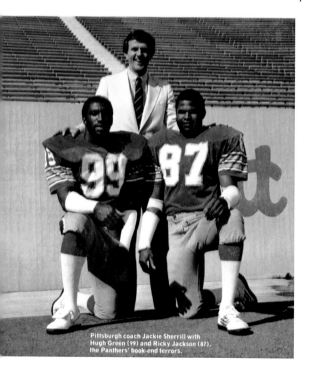

Pittsburgh coach Jackie Sherrill with Hugh Green (99) and Ricky Jackson (87), the Panthers' book-end terrors.

Above: Fullback Wayne DiBartola fights for yardage in Pitt's 26-6 win against Illinois in the opening game of the 1981 season. (*University of Pittsburgh Athletics*)

Below: John Brown (left) and Dan Marino celebrate their game-winning 1982 Sugar Bowl connection that beat Georgia, 24-20. (*University of Pittsburgh Athletics*)

Dr. Ed Bozik (pointing) pointing the way for Foge Fazio on cover of 1982 Pitt-North Carolina game program. Bozik and Fazio were in their first years as director of athletics and head football coach. (*University of Pittsburgh Athletics*)

Pitt players (left to right) Dave Puzzuoli, John Brown, Julius Dawkins, and Dan Marino were somber before leaving for Texas and the 1983 Cotton Bowl. Sophomore teammate Todd Becker had been killed in a fall from a dormitory window on campus a few days earlier. (*UCIR/Peter Nash*)

I look back and wish I hadn't said some of the things I said at the time. We were very spontaneous and we were full of life. I've never seen it as cockiness. I wasn't being flippant when I said what I did about Georgia. I just felt like, "This is our deal. We're gonna win this game. It doesn't matter who our opponent is."

Corbett was referring to the Georgia players who had shaved their heads following their Southeastern Conference championship. Coach Vince Dooley told his players he would do the same if the team won that title and, true to his word, spent the week at official Sugar Bowl functions sporting a toupee. He wore a Georgia cap atop his shaved head during the Sugar Bowl game.

The night before the game, Georgia fans staged a combination pep rally-New Year's Eve party in the Marriott lobby. Early that evening, some Pitt players were jostled by Georgia fans while trying to reach the elevators.

"The Georgia fans were pretty bold," said Tony Dorsett. "They were all over the place. No sooner would you step off the elevator and one of them would be in your face, calling you, 'Dog Food! Dog Food!'"

This writer was a senior in high school at the time, and traveled to New Orleans with his family for the game. He sat alone in a corner of the Marriott lobby observing the Georgia rally, the last time Georgia's fans had any reason to be happy during their visit.

The Forty-Third Annual Sugar Bowl game was not much of a contest. Pitt took control early, and won convincingly, 27-3. "In a way, the game was somewhat anti-climactic," said Al Romano. "We dominated Georgia from the start, and it wasn't as if we surprised ourselves by what we did. We just knew we were going to win."

ABC sent its chief broadcast crew of Keith Jackson and Ara Parseghian to work the game. Pitt stalled on its first offensive series, and after Dorsett was stopped on a play on the second drive, Parseghian suggested that "it could be that Pittsburgh has not seen a defense quite as quick as this Georgia Bulldog defense is."

Several plays later, following a 36-yard pass play from Cavanaugh to Elliott Walker, and a short run by Dorsett, Cavanaugh rolled to his left, cut inside and raced 6 yards untouched into the end zone and the embrace of Dorsett and Willie Taylor. The iconic *Sports Illustrated* Pitt football cover shot, "Pitt Is It!" was born.

The telecast itself is an interesting time capsule. There was no panel of former players and coaches back at the studio ready to give their analysis.

During the game, Georgia defensive coordinator Erk Russell was the only aide identified, and almost in passing. There were no shots of the assistant coaches upstairs in the booth, plotting strategy. Things were much simpler. Jim Lampley, sporting a bulky headset complete with side antennae, did a quick sideline interview with Jackie Sherrill, Pitt's coach in waiting. ("We have to have a good recruiting year, but we have a lot of good kids coming back.")

Dave Wannstedt, a former Pitt lineman, then a graduate assistant and later Pitt head coach, was on the sideline, along with Robert Haygood, who dressed for the game in honor of the occasion. Actor Lee Majors, TV's "Six Million Dollar Man," who adopted his screen name from good friend John Majors, was there, wearing a Pitt cap.

But the telecast lacked drama as the first half continued, with Pitt building a 21-0 lead by halftime. The Panthers intercepted four Georgia passes in the first half, and limited the Bulldogs to a single first down and zero passing yards in the first quarter. Georgia completed only three of twenty-two passes in the game.

"They [Pitt] did cause some disorganization in our running game," Georgia coach Vince Dooley said at his press conference following the game. "When they forced us to throw, that got us away from our game, which is running. That's not the position we like to be in."

Cavanaugh hit Gordon Jones for a 59-yard scoring pass to boost Pitt's lead to 14-0. "Gordon Jones was one of the most talented people I've ever coached," Majors said many years later.

Dorsett capped the first half scoring with an 11-yard burst, and the Panthers coasted from there. Pitt won, 27-3. Majors stated: "We did [coast]. We didn't really open it up in the second half against Georgia. I've never believed in getting hoggish. The few times I did, a lot of times it didn't pay off. It's like my tax man tells me, 'Pigs get fat; hogs get slaughtered.'"

Tom Yewcic entered the game for the final series, stating:

Majors wanted us to run out the clock. He was going to Tennessee, and he knew he had to play Georgia. He didn't want to score again, but the guys out there with me wanted to score a touchdown. We were driving, and I called a timeout because one of our players had been poked in the eye, and nobody saw it. I couldn't run a play if one of the guys couldn't see. Majors was yelling at me because he just wanted to run it out.

The final play of The Major Change In Pitt Football era ended with Yewcic taking a nasty hit from a frustrated Georgia Bulldog defender. "I ran the last play," Yewcic remembered. "The whistle blew and a guy came in low and hit me with his helmet right in the small of my back. The guy really speared me in the back. The ump[ire] just looked at me. What could he do? The game was over."

In his final game in a Pitt uniform, Dorsett ran for a Sugar Bowl record 202 yards, but it was Cavanaugh who earned the game's Most Valuable Player trophy.

"One thing about this Pittsburgh club," Ara Parseghian said, "it's not a one man club."

"We came out on a high for that game," said Cavanaugh. "We were very ready to play."

But that one man (Dorsett) made sure Pitt would not lose its final game, and a rare opportunity at a perfect season and national championship. "I had tears in my eyes when I went our for the coin toss," Dorsett said after the game. "I had tears in my eyes when I went into the locker room. I was never ready to play as I was today."

"Pitt would not have won the national championship without Tony Dorsett," Jackie Sherrill later remarked.

John Majors received a victory ride from seniors Pelusi and Romano following the game. (Another Pitt football coach would receive the same treatment five years later after defeating Georgia in the Sugar Bowl in his last game at Pitt). For the first time, Majors stuck his forefinger in the air, denoting Pitt's ranking.

"Johnny Majors didn't have to stick his finger in the air to signify his Pitt team was No. 1 in the nation yesterday," Russ Franke wrote in *The Pittsburgh Press*. "His Pitt team stuck its offense and defense right up where a national television audience and a Super Dome full of people [76,117] could see what a champion is made of."[7]

"My hat is off to Pittsburgh," Vince Dooley said in the press conference after the game. "They are the best defensive team we have seen. I think that is obvious. They also are the best offensive team we've faced. They have no weaknesses."

After the game, while Pitt fans were racing to the French Quarter to celebrate, Georgia fans were setting records for fastest checkouts at the Marriott. Bill Hillgrove recalled:

I was on the sideline for that game, so I heard all the crap from the Georgia fans about "Dog Meat" and "How 'Bout Them 'Dawgs." But it was pretty obvious that the Dogs were outclassed by about the second quarter. Our players were giving it to their fans. The whole experience of being in New Orleans and being part of that was great fun.

The men who got it done on the field developed lifelong friendships and relationships while coming together for a relatively brief period.

"The Sugar Bowl was the perfect finish to our college careers," said John Pelusi. "There was great camaraderie with that group of players, and we really felt like family."

"That 1976 season was the culmination of a four year period in which a lot of guys came together to work hard for a common goal," said Al Romano, who finished a close second to Notre Dame's Ross Browner in voting for the Outland Trophy.

"We all knew what our roles were and what was expected of us, and it all came together to make a great season," added Bob Jury. "That has to be the highlight and biggest thrill of my playing career."

Alex Kramer, who had been watching Pitt football for most of his life, appreciated what Majors meant to Pitt's program at a dire time in its history.

"He [Majors] was the right person at the right time," said Kramer, "not only because of his coaching skills, but for his personality. He was very gregarious, very outgoing, extroverted; the kind of person and coach that we needed."

John Pelusi said:

One of the main things I'll always remember about Coach Majors was that, if you behaved like men, he treated you like men. He could be as tough a disciplinarian as you could find, if the circumstances warranted it, but if you got the job done and did what was expected of you, then that was fine.

To those for whom it was a professional responsibility, it was only until later that they were able to appreciate the full extent of what Pitt accomplished in those four years, as Dean Billick recalled:

Now, it's easy for me to look back and have great joy about what happened, and almost amazement at what transpired. But at the time, it was such a whirl, and there was so much work being done, both for me and the players and coaches, that I don't remember sitting back and enjoying it, because there was no time to enjoy it.

In the afterglow of the marvelous job he, his staff, and players had accomplished, Majors was left to wonder what he might do for an encore. "Maybe I should just quit while I'm ahead," he remarked after the Sugar Bowl. "I don't know how four years like this can be repeated." Many years later, Majors admitted how difficult it had been for him to leave Pittsburgh for Tennessee:

> The first two or three years after I left Pittsburgh, when I'd come back through that Fort Pitt Tunnel for recruiting or to visit friends, my heart hurt because I knew what we left here, and I knew what we had to get done at Tennessee. I also missed the city of Pittsburgh very much. I've enjoyed living everywhere I've coached, but going from Pittsburgh to Tennessee was the toughest move I ever had to make.

But for Pitt and its followers after the championship season, the winning was only beginning.

4

JACKIE COMES BACK
(1977–1978)

There was a good feeling between the players and Sherrill, and we feel his appointment will be a continuation of the success we have had.

Cas Myslinski

The most successful, powerful people in any walk of life are usually the most hated.

Jackie Sherrill

The winter of 1976–77 was a harsh one for Pittsburgh, its coldest on record. The average temperature in January was 11 degrees. School closings were commonplace during the first two months of the new year. Tragedy struck too close to home when, on January 20, 1977, a gas leak explosion at Pitt's Langley Hall killed three students and injured more than twenty.

The Pitt football program, however, was glowing. Giddy from its first national championship since 1937, there was brief pause for reflection, to revel in the accomplishment. Dean Billick said:

I'm not sure many of us truly understood the significance of the high mountain we had climbed. It was not easy. It was a different time than it is now [2019]. We did it with no money, and with very inadequate facilities. You look back on it now, and it's absolutely amazing what was accomplished.

While Pitt's 1976 team captured the attention of the college football nation, its impact at home was, notably, something less. Despite the championship season, there was no city or (Allegheny) County sanctioned parade or mass assembly to honor the team. Pitt honored itself, scheduling the presentation of the MacArthur Bowl, given to the top team in the nation, for halftime of the Pitt-Cincinnati basketball game at Fitzgerald Field House on February 2, 1977. The 3-14 Panthers did their part to make it a festive occasion, defeating the nationally ranked Bearcats, 65-64, on a buzzer shot by Larry Harris.

Membership in the Golden Panthers Booster Club increased along with the victory total during John Majors' four years in Pittsburgh. When the group formed in 1970, fifteen members contributed $2 each. By early 1977, its membership totaled 3,500, while raising $287,602. Local chapters also were formed, and would customarily hold weekly gatherings throughout football season. Many years later, internet and other social media bloggers would suggest that the Golden Panthers were doing more than conducting happy get-togethers, that maybe its actual purpose was to enrich the football players who were helping Pitt win so many games.

"In their dreams," said Dean Billick. "These bloggers have built the Golden Panthers into something they weren't. There was a core group of Golden Panthers who wanted to win, and gave some money to some degree, but it was never significant. Never!"

"I read that all the time, and I just laugh about it, because they think that we, the Golden Panthers, were shelling out money to individual players," said Ed Ifft, who was president of the organization during the 1976 season. "That was not true at all."

There was direct university oversight of the Golden Panthers. The administration kept tabs on its activities and practices, with Ed Ifft stating:

> The Golden Panthers were an arm of the athletic department, organized by Cas Myslinski originally. What it was about was trying to bring people into the program and to raise money for the university. Events that were held, the money was used for that. For the spring game—it was given back to the university. The athletic director always sat in on our meetings.

"It's just something that, as the years have gone by, the whopper has become bigger," added Dean Billick. "The Golden Panthers were not a force that drove any administrative decisions. Our fundraising was way below what was going on down South with those schools."

But while Pitt could not match the financial record of those schools in the South, two coaches with southern roots, John Majors and Jackie Sherrill, had built a winning football program at Pitt. "Johnny Majors and Jackie Sherrill were recruiting size and speed," said Lloyd Weston. "They were recruiting kids from winning backgrounds. They saved Pitt football."

With Majors back in his native Tennessee, the coaching mantle had been passed to Sherrill, his former top aide at both Iowa State and Pitt. Fresh from a national title, Pitt became an attractive destination.

"Good coaches wanted to come to Pitt to put Pitt on their resumes," said Dean Billick. "Good players wanted to play there because we had good coaches and we won. It kind of fed on itself."

"At that time, Pitt's name kind of sold itself, and when you walked in, they [recruits] listened," said Sherrill. "It was kind of like a Notre Dame or Nebraska. I mean, you're going to get in the front door."

Jackie Wayne Sherrill was born November 28, 1943 in Duncan, Oklahoma. He was the youngest of eight children—four boys and four girls—born to William and Dovie Sherrill. Dovie was aged forty at the time of Jackie's birth. Both parents were native Oklahomans. William Sherrill had been a machinist for Halliburton in Duncan, but when he and Dovie separated, William moved to Richmond, California, in early 1944 where he worked in a shipbuilding plant during World War II. The other Sherrill children were either off on their own or had moved to California with their father. That left Jackie alone with his mother in Duncan.

"Where I come from, there were lots of Billy Joes and Bobby Genes," said Jackie, who noted that, from the time he was in elementary school through his undergraduate years at Alabama, his name would occasionally appear on female student rosters by mistake.

Jackie Sherrill never really knew his father. Once, when he was aged thirteen or fourteen, he took a bus to California to visit his dad, but cut the visit short, returning to Oklahoma days before the end of the scheduled trip. The elder Sherrill never attended any of Jackie's sporting events, even when he was a member of national championship teams at Alabama in 1964 and 1965. Still, Sherrill never harbored any animosity toward his father.

That left Jackie at home, alone with his mother, who worked a number of odd jobs—domestic work, clerk at a department store, night classes for nursing—to support herself and her son. "There were days when lunch was two pieces of bread with mayonnaise in between," admits Jackie Sherrill.

The circumstances made Jackie Sherrill become especially close to his mother. He developed a strong protective instinct, of wanting to take care of her. At the age of three, however, he gave his mother a good scare when he wandered from their house and ended up about eleven blocks away. The radio reported a missing child in the neighborhood. He was found by a woman, and Jackie rode home in a patrol car. It was the first time he was in the news. It would not be the last.

Always big for his age, Sherrill ran with an older crowd and did a variety of jobs, earning money for himself while growing up. He sold newspapers on a street corner; he stocked shelves at Delbert's Grocery Store; and he set pins at a bowling alley when that particular job was done manually. An older boy took to picking on him. "I picked up a crowbar and whacked him good," Sherrill remembered. "He didn't bother me after that."

A Baptist minister named Jess Kirkley was an early influence. "He [Kirkley] always made time for people," said Sherrill. "There wasn't an ounce of prejudice in his body. To him, everybody was equal."

Kirkley even managed to talk young Jackie Sherrill into joining the church choir.

But, of course, what really attracted Jackie Sherrill were athletics endeavors. He loved competition. At first, Dovie Sherrill did not want her son getting involved in sports, thinking that work was a more productive, practical pursuit.

Sherrill's life took a dramatic turn when, at the end of ninth grade, his mother informed him of her plans to remarry. Jackie did not take the news well. Until then, he had enjoyed an uncommon amount of freedom and independence for someone his age, and the prospect of a bossy stepfather telling him what to do was not very appealing. He called his brother, John, who was fifteen years older than he and living in Biloxi, Mississippi, where he, his wife, and three children, owned and operated a chicken farm. It was a difficult decision, but with his mother's blessing, Jackie Sherrill moved in with his brother, who put him to work immediately.

Biloxi is located on the coast of the Gulf of Mexico, about 80 miles east of New Orleans. It is where Jackie Sherrill established himself on the football field. To this day, he claims Mississippi, not Oklahoma, as his place of origin.

"Biloxi was a tough town," said Bruce Sokol, a college friend of Sherrill's. "It had the Keesler Air Force Base, and there was a lot of illegal gambling going on in Biloxi."

Sokol first met Sherrill when the two were standing in line next to each other as part of some campus activity.

"Jackie looked like he was about twenty-five years old when he was a freshman," said Sokol. "He had an intimidating air about him. But he's a survivor. Jackie has always seemed to land on his feet."

John Sherrill worked his brother hard on the farm, pushing him to the limit. Jackie recalled: "I had to go spread the feed, go to football practice, come back, gather the eggs and start grading them and then go back to practice and then come back that night. Before I'd go to practice I'd spread the feed again and then come back that night and finish grading the eggs."

John Sherrill was making it hard on his younger brother with the idea that it would convince him to return to Duncan, Oklahoma. The strategy did not work.

Sports were popular in Biloxi. It had an excellent youth baseball program. Sherrill's football coach, W. D. Wiles, was a great believer in the importance of a strong defense. He also thought it enlightening to bring together young men from different social and economic backgrounds.

Sherrill was elected "Mr. Biloxi High School" during his senior year. He was being recruited by both Oklahoma and Georgia Tech, but figured he would probably end up a Sooner. He visited Atlanta, where four Georgia Tech players escorted him and some other prospects to an all-black nightclub on Peachtree Street, which impressed Sherrill. Still, he was leaning toward Oklahoma, until a two-hour meeting with Alabama coach Paul "Bear" Bryant and one of his assistants, Sam Bailey. Bryant was scouting around for a place to have his team practice before going to New Orleans to meet Arkansas in the 1962 Sugar Bowl.

The meeting took place at Biloxi Stadium, and Sherrill was impressed by the fact that Bryant never once tried to persuade him to come to Alabama. Assistant coaches Gene Stallings and Dude Hennessey recruited Sherrill, and he decided to play for the Crimson Tide.

The summer before enrolling at Alabama, Sherrill borrowed $100 from one of his sisters and took a bus to Farmington, New Mexico, where he netted $1,038 working eight-hour shifts on an oil field for six weeks. "I'd get home, get in the bathtub and fall asleep because I was so damn tired," Sherrill recalled. "I'd leave a ring about four inches thick around the bathtub."

Sherrill enrolled at Alabama as a freshman in 1962. There were sixty-seven freshman football players on campus. Sherrill was enrolled in Alabama's School of Business. On the gridiron, he lettered three times, playing fullback and linebacker. He was impressed by the Tide's sophomore quarterback, Beaver Falls, Pa.'s Joe Namath:

I remember seeing Namath at practice for the first time. Watching him throw the ball, I was in awe. He's the best athlete I've ever been around. He was so quick. In basketball, he could jump or go to the baseline. He could dunk backwards. He could do some things with a football that other people couldn't do.

By his senior year, Sherrill was one of Alabama's starters. The Tide defeated Nebraska in the 1966 Orange Bowl. Sherrill spent once season working for Bryant before moving to Arkansas, where he was a defensive assistant under Frank Broyles. He joined John Majors at Iowa State in 1968 and the two worked together until Sherrill left Pitt for Washington State after the 1975 season.

Pullman, Washington, was a long way from Duncan, Biloxi, and Pittsburgh. Soon after accepting the WSU job, Sherrill was taken to an automobile dealership where he received his courtesy car—a pickup truck. When Sherrill was hired, he told university officials that Pitt and Alabama were the only schools he would leave Washington State for. One year later, Pitt came calling, and Sherrill was back as head coach of the Panthers.

His first order of business was to assemble a coaching staff. Gone to Tennessee with John Majors were assistants Joe Madden, Joe Avezzano, Bobby Roper, Bill Cox, and Jim Dyar, as well as trainer Tim Kerin and assistant Kevin O'Neill. Academic advisor Alan Beals also left Pittsburgh for Knoxville.

Larry Holton remained at Pitt, where he would coach the secondary. Dave Wannstedt, who had been a graduate assistant in 1976, joined the staff as strength coach. Bob Leahy, who had left Pitt to go to Washington State with Sherrill, returned to Pittsburgh as offensive coordinator. Bob Matey, a holdover from Majors' Pitt staff, coached the defensive line for Sherrill.

During the period between the 1976 victory against Penn State and the playing of the Sugar Bowl, Sherrill had hired Jimmy Johnson to be his assistant head coach and defensive coordinator at Pitt. Sherrill and Johnson observed Pitt's practices leading up to the 1977 Sugar Bowl game. The idea was for Johnson to familiarize himself with the returning players he would be instructing a few months later. According to Sherrill, the arrangement did not sit well with some of Pitt's outgoing assistant coaches who had wanted to be the successor to Majors at Pitt.

"I get the same feeling in bringing Jimmy to Pitt that I get when I sign a great prospective recruit," said Sherrill. Johnson had thought he was in line to be the successor to the retiring Frank Broyles at Arkansas following the 1976 season. But when that job went to Lou Holtz, Johnson went looking for an out. He found it in the opportunity at Pitt, entering a program coming off the national championship. From the start, Johnson impressed Pitt's players with his boundless energy.

"Here's Jimmy Johnson running around the huddle, clapping his hands, trying to pep us up," Jeff Delaney recalled. "I used to think to myself, 'God, I wish I had that much energy.' And his hair was never out of place."

Don Boyce, who had worked with Johnson at Arkansas as offensive line coach, accepted Sherrill's offer to do the same at Pitt. Otto Stowe, who had played wide receiver at Iowa State and then several years in the NFL, had coached the receivers under Sherrill at WSU, and would serve in that capacity at Pitt.

Sherrill tapped the local high school ranks for Joe Moore, who had been head coach at Upper St. Clair (Pa.) the previous four seasons. Moore would come to be recognized as one of football's premier offensive line coaches, but he actually coached the backs at Pitt during his first two seasons, and for part of a third. Sherrill explained his reasoning for adding a local high school coach to his staff during a preseason interview with Bill Hillgrove. Sherrill said: "He (Joe Moore) is the old man on the staff. It's important to have a coach on the staff who's been around a long time. His relationships with the high school coaches has turned out to be a great benefit for us."

Sherrill rounded out the staff by bringing back another coach with strong ties to Pitt and the local high school scene. Foge Fazio, who played at Pitt and was an assistant under Carl DePasqua, had been the defensive coordinator at the University of Cincinnati in 1976.

With the coaching staff in place, Sherrill and his assistants set out on the recruiting trail. In retrospect, it may be the best class in Pitt history. Although John Majors' first class produced so many key members (seniors) from the 1976 championship team, Sherrill's initial class is more impressive when looking at what many of those players achieved, not only at Pitt, but in the professional ranks. Recruiting was different then, with Sherrill noting:

Back then, as a head coach, you could go and see kids as much as you wanted to. We got lucky in recruiting some outstanding players; I mean some big time players. At the time, some of them were not big time players, but they had the potential. I just got on the phone and asked who the kids were being recruited by, and if they weren't being recruited by the top guys, I went on to the next one.

Alex Kramer, who joined the Pitt football staff in 1978 as administrative aide to Sherrill, remembers the staff meetings Sherrill conducted to go over recruiting. "Jackie would go around the room and ask each coach who he was recruiting, and how it was going," said Kramer. "He would inevitably ask, 'Who else is recruiting him?' Obviously, he put some stock in who our competition was."

North Natchez and Pascagoula were two of the better high school programs in Mississippi. Pascagoula had a star running back named Ray Charles "Rooster" Jones, while North Natchez boasted the state's top defensive player, end Hugh Green. The teams played each other twice that year, once in the regular season and once in the state playoffs. Pitt's coaches had plenty of film with which to evaluate Jones, but another player caught their eye.

"They [Pitt coaches] were watching film, but I kept popping up," said Green. "They had to be wondering, 'Who is this guy who keeps going from one side of the field to the other making plays?'"

Pitt's coaches were interested in both players, but there was a potential snag; both Jones and Green had signed non-binding Southeastern Conference Letters of Intent with Mississippi State in December. "I had basically talked Rooster into going to Mississippi State," Green later admitted. "Eventually, I had to decide if I wanted to stay in the state [Mississippi] or go somewhere else."

The two Mississippi prospects visited Pittsburgh, where they were hosted by departing players Tony Dorsett, Cecil Johnson, Don Parrish, and a holdover, J. C. Wilson, from the 1976 team. "I really liked J. C. Wilson," said Green. "We went to some parties, and it was a really good visit."

Another player to visit was a large offensive line prospect from Oneonta, New York, Mark May. Much of his recruitment was done by graduate assistant Tony Wise who, like May, was from a town (Newtonville) in upstate New York. May said:

Every place when I made my trips, they told me, "You're gonna start. You're gonna play right away." I was like, "How do they know that? I'm from a small town in upstate New York." One thing about Jackie [Sherrill]; he said, "You'll have a fair opportunity to start and play when you come here."

May remembers the treatment he received from his hosts. "Tony [Dorsett], Cecil [Johnson] and Jake [Don] Parrish were all at Tony's apartment," he said. They told us, 'We don't usually take recruits around, so you guys better come here.' Little did we know that that recruiting trip would end up meaning the three of us would go to Pitt and end up doing what we've done since."

Green remembers Jackie Sherrill's closing recruiting speech:

At the end of the visit, before going home, I met with Jackie Sherrill. He told me something that I still dream about to this day. "You will get more publicity in one year at Pittsburgh than you will in four years at Mississippi State." He understood the growth in college football and the advantages Pitt had with the media in this part of the country.

Some of Pitt's recruits that year were not as heralded as others. Southmoreland High School's Russ Grimm did a little bit of everything, including scoring forty-one points in a basketball game and also playing in the Big 33 football game, but was not considered a top level recruit by some services.

Defensive lineman Jerry Boyarsky (Scott, Pa.) was told by some college coaches he was not good enough to play Division I football.

Then there was a lanky defensive end from Pahokee, Florida, named Ricky Jackson who, while in high school, changed his first name to "Rickey." His recruitment to Pitt was almost an afterthought. "One of our coaches said, 'Hey, this kid is a pretty good athlete," Sherrill recalled. "'He might be worth taking a chance on.'"

Jackson, who played tight end as well as defensive end, also possessed a unique talent—the ability to catch a rabbit with his bare hands, a claim usually met with skepticism. "I didn't believe it either," said Hugh Green. "But I went down to Pahokee and saw him do it, with my own eyes. Now, I'm a believer."

Both Russ Grimm and Rickey Jackson are now enshrined in the Pro Football Hall of Fame. Hugh Green would win the Lombardi, Maxwell, and Walter Camp Awards during his senior season (1980) at Pitt. He and Rickey Jackson would come to be known as the "bookends" on Pitt's great defensive teams from that era.

Aside from terrorizing opposing quarterbacks and running backs, Green and Jackson displayed a kinder, gentler side; they often babysat for Bill Hillgrove, Jr., Dean Conomikes, son of WTAE executive John Conomikes, and Jimmy Johnson's two boys, Brent and Chad.

Green had no qualms about leaving home for Pittsburgh and its harsh winters. He had sisters living in Michigan and Indiana, and visited them frequently at different times of the year, long before he chose to attend Pitt. He also had plenty of company in the Pitt locker room, as the program had been adding players from the South since John Majors started that trend at Pitt four years earlier.

"We called ourselves 'The Southern Boys,'" said Green. "It wasn't as if I had to go through it alone. We were all of the same experience. You weren't there by yourself."

"[Assistant coach] Don Boyce did a great job in finding Hugh," said Sherrill. "There wasn't any question about Hugh."

By the end of the recruiting season, one national publication named eight Pitt signees—Benjie Pryor, Lindsay Delaney, Mike Christ, Artrell Hawkins, Rooster Jones, Walter "Skip" Sylvester, Rick Trocano, and Carlton Williamson—"can't miss" prospects. Ranking recruits, then, as now, is an inexact science.

Pitt moved its August preseason training camp from Johnstown to West Liberty State College in West Virginia in preparation for the 1977 season and defense of the national championship. The team's personnel losses were significant, the biggest hole, of course, at tailback, where Tony Dorsett was about to begin his rookie season with the Dallas Cowboys.

From the offensive line, Pitt lost regulars John Pelusi, John Hanhauser, George Messich, Joe Stone, and tight end Jim Corbett. Fullback Bobby Hutton also had gone.

Defensively, Pitt lost six of its front seven, four linemen, and linebackers Arnie Weatherington and Jimbo Cramer. Linemen Al Romano, Cecil Johnson, Ed Wilamowski, and Don Parrish were no longer there, nor were both kickers, punter Larry Swider and placekicker Carson Long. Some of the incoming freshmen made the coaches take notice early at camp. Mark May said:

> We were just a young bunch of kids. I was sixteen turning seventeen. Hugh [Green] and I met for the first time in the dorm rooms at Tower A during our recruiting trip. All the guys were in Tower A the night before we went to camp. At camp we were doing our thing, and we were doing it against a lot of juniors and seniors, and beating those guys. Hugh was getting after the quarterbacks, and so was Rickey [Jackson]. I'm blocking guys older than I was, and the coaches were looking at each other and thinking, "Where'd these guys come from?"

Not only did Mark May become one of the greatest offensive linemen in Pitt history, he evolved into one of the team's most approachable, eloquent speakers. It was not surprising that he found a career in broadcasting following his playing career. Smizik noted: "Mark was a very thoughtful person, more so than most players. Mark was a smart guy, a real gentleman. He could take you into the game and give you some technical stuff, talk about his hometown. I liked Mark a lot."

When May was a freshman, there was no question at quarterback, where Matt Cavanaugh, coming off an MVP performance against Georgia in the Sugar Bowl, was back for his senior season. In fact, one of the main objectives in training camp was to find a capable backup. Tom Yewcic, 1976's substitute hero, had another season of eligibility, and was on the roster. Wayne Adams, a tall, lanky sophomore from nearby McKeesport, appeared to have the inside track throughout camp. Pitt had a pair of freshman quarterbacks in Rick Trocano and Lindsay Delaney.

"[Wayne] Adams looked good," said Sherrill. "He had excellent scrimmages. During camp, there weren't any exchange problems."

To prepare his starting quarterback for the season, Sherrill had Matt Cavanaugh study film from his 1976 Washington State team and quarterback Jack Thompson, who had a prolific season and was nicknamed "The Throwin' Samoan."

During an interview with Bill Hillgrove at the outset of training camp, Sherrill made a telling statement about Cavanaugh's value to the team:

If you had a lot of Number Twelves [Cavanaugh], you could win a lot of games. Matt's become more mature. He's solid. Every day he's improving. His throwing game, his leadership—you can't say enough adjectives about Matt. If Matt stays healthy, which I'm sure he will, he's gonna give us that plus you need in that spot.

Cavanaugh later explained that he was held out of excessive scrimmage action in order to develop a backup quarterback. Tom Brzoza, who had played guard prior to 1977, was moved to center, a switch he was unhappy with at first, but adapted to well, earning All-America honors as a center that year.

"Wayne Adams, who had a lot of talent, had an extremely good camp," said Rick Trocano. "He performed well. [Tom] Yewcic got some play as well, but usually the first and second quarterbacks get all the reps with the first team. I would say Yewcic did not get a lot of time with Brzoza. Yewcic would be in the second team huddle with the backups."

Bill Hillgrove was at camp, and he remembered it this way:

It was a scrimmage, and Wayne Adams had a great scrimmage. He threw a bomb to Willie Taylor. I can't recall the other one. I remember later, John Conomikes, Dean Billick, myself and Jimmy Johnson had gone to a diner for a sandwich, and that's when Jimmy said, "The one thing we can't afford is for Number Twelve [Cavanaugh] not to play."

At his introductory press conference, Sherrill made it clear that he planned to devise ways for his quarterback to get the ball in the hands of wide receiver Gordon Jones, who had a disappointing sophomore season in Pitt's championship year.

"He [Jones] is a young man blessed with a lot of talent," said Sherrill. "He's like a racehorse. A two million dollar racehorse is a lot different than a nickel plug."

There were no questions about Pitt's defensive secondary entering the 1977 season. It returned all four starters, cornerbacks J. C. Wilson and LeRoy Felder along with strong safety Jeff Delaney and free safety Bob Jury. Delaney, who had played for Joe Moore at Upper St. Clair, was happy that Sherrill was the new head coach, stating:

We were all familiar with Jackie. There was a lot of respect for him. He helped build a lot of good things before he left that one year for Washington State. There's always the unknown when a new coaching staff comes in. Having Jackie back, there was that knowledge of what the expectations were. You wouldn't have to worry about a new coach coming in and changing the system entirely. Jackie knew the players, so we knew what we were getting. And he knew what we could do.

But a short time after Sherrill returned to Pitt as head coach, and the players had been around him, Delaney seemed to notice a subtle change. "When he was an assistant, he was a guy you respected, but also feared," said Delaney. "He was the disciplinarian on the staff. I wouldn't say that he was the players' friend. He wasn't close to the players as far as being buddy buddy."

Not sure what to make of the situation, Delaney found himself sitting face to face with Sherrill in the coach's office:

After he became head coach, there was sort of an aloofness about him. He had a nickname amongst some of the players who called him "King Jackie" because it was almost like he didn't want to listen to or even relate to what was going on. In some of our eyes, there was a certain aloofness. He didn't get that "King Jackie" nickname for nothing. To this day, I can't believe I had the nerve to go in and say that to him.

"I said, 'Jeff, I haven't changed," Sherrill recalled. "My roles and responsibilities have changed, but I haven't changed.' He looked at me and he said, 'I guess you're right.'" Dean Billick said:

He [Sherrill] had his own way of doing things. He had played under the Bear [Bryant], and he tried to emulate the Bear. He wanted people to be in fear of him, in awe of him. That was not Johnny Majors' style, but both styles were very successful. They went about doing their jobs in different ways, but both were very successful.

Many years after leaving Pitt, Sherrill was asked about his reputation for being cold and arrogant; he said:

I don't do things for political reasons. I do things for the right reasons. The biggest thing is that people think I'm unapproachable. The media have said I'm aloof, "out here." That's absolutely incorrect. I don't go approach people. And that's the difference. I'm not out trying to get votes. People who really know me, know I'm not gonna put my arm around 'em and make 'em smile and laugh. My philosophy has always been that it's not my place or responsibility to give people false impressions. What you see is what you get.

"He [Sherrill] had an air about him," Matt Cavanaugh said.

Sam Sciullo, Sr. represented Sherrill in legal matters and was privy to some of his private affairs, and came to accept and understand the Pitt coach:

A lot of people didn't like Sherrill because he didn't cater to them. He catered to them in a different way. Even when he and I talked on the phone, he would be very matter of fact, straight to the point. He didn't make a fuss over you. John Majors was much more outgoing and, I dare say, more charming. That's the kind of stuff people in the media fall for.

Bill Hillgrove came to know both coaches well, and his description of the two was consistent with the attorney's: "He [Sherrill] is a personable guy, and easy to talk to. John [Majors] had a game plan, and John's game plan was to 'sell, sell, sell.' He's great at it. Jackie's much more quiet. In a setting where you're going one on one, he's much more personal in that regard."

Personalities aside, Majors was gone and Sherrill had plenty to think about preparing for Pitt's season opening game September 10 against Notre Dame at Pitt Stadium. Similar to 1976, the game originally was scheduled for later in the season, but ABC TV asked both schools to move it to the first game for each team. Kickoff was set for 3:50 p.m. The Irish were ranked third going into the season; Pitt was seventh. Notre Dame returned its entire defense from 1976.

Sherrill liked his team as the Notre Dame game approached. Despite the personnel losses from the championship team, he understood how that could work to Pitt's advantage.

"When you lose as many players as we have from last year, sometimes players work a little harder," he said. "They don't get to ride the shirttails of Tony Dorsett and Al Romano and people like that. They have to work."

Several days before the season opener, and with the start of the NFL season still more than a week away, Tony Dorsett placed a phone call to Robert Haygood, who had become something of a forgotten man since his 1976 season ended with a knee injury at Georgia Tech a year earlier. Dorsett would be coming to Pittsburgh for the game, and asked if Haygood would be interested in standing on the sideline with him. Haygood accepted Dorsett's offer.

Since his surgery, Haygood thought he might be able to return for the Sugar Bowl game, and later claimed that he was "about seventy-five to eighty percent" by the end of the season. He did dress for the game, but there was no chance that he would play.

Following the Sugar Bowl, Haygood spent the next few months rehabilitating the knee, hoping he could show that he was fit to play football or basketball competitively. He met with Sherrill, noting:

> We spoke a couple times. At that time, Matt [Cavanaugh] was playing pretty good football. Our conversations were to make Pitt the best we could, and he [Sherrill] just felt that it was time for Matt to have the opportunity. I said, "That's fine. I'll play basketball. I'll put my efforts toward getting ready to play basketball."

Following the 1977–78 basketball season, Haygood was invited to training camp with the New Orleans Jazz of the NBA, but did not make the team. In 2019, he has no regrets:

> I think I would have been able to do it [play football], but I was focused on basketball. There are totally different muscles you have to get ready to use in basketball, opposed to football. I hadn't been hit since that [1976] Georgia Tech game, so I wasn't real sure if the knee would hold up."

On the eve of the Pitt-Notre Dame opener, Hugh Green and the rest of the Pitt team spent the night at a Monroeville hotel, as was customary. Green was walking down a hallway when he observed several coaches emerge from a meeting room. They were talking animatedly, but became silent when they spotted the freshman.

"It was Jackie [Sherrill], Jimmy Johnson and [Dave] Wannstedt." said Green. "One of them said, 'Oh, by the way, Hugh, you're starting tomorrow.' I ran to my room, took out my playbook and studied it for most of the night."

Jeff Delaney recalled:

> You could see he [Green] could do some things on the field that normal people couldn't do. Being a freshman, you could tell a lot of it was raw talent because he still didn't know the system yet. People like Hugh Green had a way of making the players around him look good, too.

Green was confident that he was ready to play at the top level of the collegiate game. "I was just a wild and wooly freshman, but I had a great camp," said Green. "I knew I could play."

The Irish, who had their own designs on a national championship, were a slight favorite. Pat Livingston of *The Pittsburgh Press* thought otherwise, giving the Panthers the nod in his weekly forecast. "Strictly on the hunch that quarterback Matt Cavanaugh will be a more viable threat than anyone the Irish can offer," he wrote.[1]

On the day of the opener, Pitt fans were treated to one impressive aesthetic addition to Pitt Stadium—a new scoreboard. Sponsored by Westinghouse and Equibank, it featured a message board capable of producing limited cartoon-like special images. By 2020 standards, it would be pedestrian, but in 1977, it signified Pitt's upward trend in college football.

Following an exchange of punts, Pitt made its first break when J. C. Wilson intercepted a Rusty Lisch pass. Several plays later, with the ball at the Notre Dame twelve, Cavanaugh dropped back, rolled to his right, stopped and planted his feet, spotting a wide open Gordon Jones across the field in the back of the end zone. Notre Dame defensive end Willie Fry closed in on Cavanaugh, but not before the pass was on its way to Jones for a touchdown. While Pitt fans and players were celebrating, Cavanugh was on the Pitt Stadium turf. He landed awkwardly, and painfully, when Fry leveled him as he was releasing the ball.

From his broadcast position, Keith Jackson, noting how Cavanaugh was holding his arm, and left wrist, might have been the first person to recognize the severity of the problem for Pitt. "Hold on," said Jackson. "Disaster may have struck Pittsburgh."

It had. It was a broken wrist. As Cavanaugh walked to the locker room with team physician Dr. James McMaster, he took with him Pitt's hopes for repeating as national champion. While Pitt has suffered its share of heartbreaking and devastating losses in its long football history, it is doubtful that any was as frustrating as the 19-9 loss to Notre Dame at Pitt Stadium on September 10, 1977.

Wayne Adams, then Tom Yewcic, tried their hands—literally—at replacing Cavanaugh, but the rest of the game was disastrous for the Panthers, who had a number of fumbled exchanges between Tom Brzoza and the quarterbacks. Pitt fumbled the ball eight times, losing five. Following the Cavanaugh injury, Pitt's total offense for the rest of the game was minus 11 yards. The Panthers turned the ball over on six of their last seven possessions. Sherrill offered this explanation in his talk with the press after the game.

"What hurt us were the cadences in the voices of the quarterbacks," said Jackie Sherrill. "Tom [Brzoza] also had a tendency to ride forward as he was snapping the ball, and the quarterback has to adjust to that."

What made the loss more disheartening was the brilliance of the Pitt defense. The Panthers increased their lead to 9-0 on a safety resulting from a blocked punt early in the second quarter. Hugh Green blocked the Irish extra point attempt following Notre Dame's only touchdown. Green, linebacker Al Chesley and nose guard Dave Logan were dominant. Chesley had fifteen tackles, while Logan was named ABC Defensive Player of the Game. All three were making their first collegiate starts.

"That performance by the Pitt defense was one of the best I've ever seen," Notre Dame coach Dan Devine remarked afterward.

From his vantage point on the Pitt sideline, Robert Haygood could only ponder what might have been. "It hurt me to see him [Cavanaugh] go down," said Haygood. "I said to myself, 'Wow, this is gonna be tough right here.'"

Could Haygood have played quarterback for Pitt in 1977? When asked if he had been discouraged in his earlier discussions with Sherrill, he did not deny the notion:

> To some degree, that is correct. But I didn't want to risk it. I was fearful of if the leg would hold up when the licks came. But, if during the summer, when we had conversations, if I had heard, "Hey, I need you to get in here. Gotta have you on the team," that may have made a difference in my thinking.

Instead, Jackie Sherrill, in his first game as Pitt's head coach, was left to explain how and why Pitt's backup quarterbacks were not better prepared, if not able, to handle their responsibilities after Cavanaugh was injured.

"With Matt, we are a great football team, one of the best in the country," Sherrill said following the game. "Without him, we are in trouble."

Center Tom Brzoza later said that the quarterbacks had been adequately prepared during training camp. Cavanaugh offered his opinion. "Any time you bring in a new quarterback, the exchange between center and quarterback can be a problem.... Fumbled exchanges can happen. It doesn't matter how many times you practice it, it's still a different game."

Sherrill stated: "What we had was the most complex offense in the country. There aren't many quarterbacks in the country who could run it. We built our offense around Matt. When you build an offense around a kid like Matt, it's tough to expect somebody to fill those shoes."[2]

The media covering the game were less than understanding in their stories about Pitt's misfortune. Russ Franke of *The Pittsburgh Press* noted: "What could have been another glorious season for Pitt may become simply a good one except someone dropped the basket and spilled eggs all over Pitt Stadium on Saturday. In the language of football coaches, eggs are fumbles."[3]

Sports Illustrated sent John Underwood, one of its top writers, to Pittsburgh to cover the game:

> Just when it appeared that the Panthers were going to get over the loss of a Coach of the Year [John Majors], and a Heisman Trophy winner

[Tony Dorsett] without missing a beat—just when it seemed they were on their way to an upset of Notre Dame—Pitt suffered a lulu. One that confirms the fact that nothing enhances bonfires, bowl trips and financial wellbeing like a healthy star quarterback.[4]

Two men close to Pitt's program remember the devastating effect of Cavanaugh's injury so many years ago.

"The pin hit the balloon, and the air came out of Pitt Stadium" said Bill Hillgrove. "Little did I know that we would have trouble even taking the snap from center."

"I thought, had that injury [to Cavanaugh] not occurred, that that team would have won the national championship," said Dean Billick. "We were gonna run Notre Dame out of the stadium. We would have beaten them pretty handily."

"Keith Jackson even said, maybe in retrospect Pitt should have punted on first down," said Hillgrove. "They might have had a better chance to win."

The initial prognosis was that Cavanaugh would miss four to six weeks. As soon as he was able, he began receiving snaps in his dorm room from John Takacs, a backup center who happened to be from Cavanaugh's hometown of Youngstown, Ohio. Meanwhile, Jackie Sherrill, Bob Leahy and the rest of Pitt's coaches had to prepare for William & Mary at home the following Saturday. By the middle of the week, freshman quarterback Rick Trocano was taking the majority of the snaps. Just three months removed from high school, Trocano would be asked to lead a program coming off a national championship.

"It was Jackie's responsibility, and it was his head on the line," said Trocano. "He made the decision to name me the starter."

Trocano, an upbeat redhead who never lacked for confidence, was unfazed by the magnitude of the situation. "I had a lot of experienced ballplayers around me," he said. "I spent the first three weeks meeting with the coaches and practicing and sharpening up my knowledge of the offense."

While Pitt's 1977 offensive line was inexperienced, it would not be accurate to label it young. Seniors Art Bortnick, George Link, and Jim Buoy had been in the program for several years, along with junior tight end Steve Gaustad. Running back Elliott Walker became Pitt's feature back; sophomore Larry Sims became the first fulltime replacement for Tony Dorsett, along with another sophomore, Fred Jacobs.

Pitt had little trouble dispatching William & Mary, 28-6. Walker ran for three touchdowns and Jacobs scored another. Jacobs ran for 98 yards in his first collegiate start. Pitt passed for 164 yards.

Seven different players scored the following week when Pitt easily defeated Temple, 76-0, at Veterans Stadium in Philadelphia before a crowd of 13,199. It was Pitt's highest point total in a game since a 96-0 defeat of Dickinson at Forbes Field in 1914. Trocano ran for a pair of touchdowns and tossed his first collegiate pass for a score, a 10-yard strike to Gordon Jones. Another freshman quarterback, Lindsay Delaney, threw a 31-yard scoring toss to Randy Reutershan.

Pitt won its third straight game the following week by defeating Boston College, 45-7, at Chestnut Hill. Earlier in the week, Matt Cavanaugh pronounced himself ready to play. In fact, Cavanaugh had his father discuss the situation by telephone with Jackie Sherrill. The elder Cavanaugh instructed Sherrill to play his son, if needed, but Sherrill had decided that was out of the question.

Sherrill did, however, play a little gamesmanship prior to the contest. Cavanaugh was in uniform, taking snaps from the shotgun formation during pregame, sending the Boston College coaches into a tizzy. It did not matter. Pitt raised its record to 3-1—and Trocano to 3-0 as a starter—in an easy 45-7 defeat of the Eagles. Elliott Walker ran for 112 yards and a touchdown. Jacobs gained 90 yards on only eleven carries, and Trocano scored a pair of rushing touchdowns. JoJo Heath returned a punt 59 yards for a touchdown as Pitt built a 24-0 halftime lead, then scored three touchdowns in the final quarter.

Trocano would relinquish the quarterback position to Cavanaugh for the remainder of the 1977 season, but the experience of working with All-America center Tom Brzoza was both pleasurable and enlightening. Trocano recalled:

> Of all the years I played football, Tom Brzoza was one of the best centers I played with. He would try to cut off the nose guard or the backside linebacker. Brzoza was very good at that, almost like a wrestler because he could scramble. It was impressive. Not all centers could do what he was doing. He had that ability to get into that second level and block.

Matt Cavanaugh returned after missing only three games, when Pitt traveled to Gainesville to meet Florida in a night game on October 8. Cavanaugh, wearing a soft cast on his left wrist, led the Panthers to close to almost 400 yards of total offense, but the game ended in a 17-17 tie. He ran for one touchdown and Willie Taylor caught a pass from JoJo Heath in the third quarter to put Pitt ahead, 14-7. The Panthers had a chance to add to that lead, but a fumble deep in Florida territory stopped that drive. The Gators tied the game by recovering a blocked punt in the end zone. Mark Schubert's field goal gave Pitt a 17-14 lead in the fourth quarter, but Berj Yepremian (younger brother of Miami Dolphins kicker Garo Yepremian) kicked a 28-yard field goal late in the game for the final score. Pitt fumbled eleven times in the game, losing six of them.

At 3-1-1, Pitt won its next five games by defeating Navy, Syracuse, Tulane, West Virginia and Army. Against Navy, Pitt compiled 532 yards of offense, led by Elliott Walker (169 yards) and Fred Jacobs (109) to down the Midshipmen, 34-17. Mark Schubert added a pair of field goals.

Old nemesis Bill Hurley returned to Pitt Stadium—Pitt had played at Syracuse in 1974 and 1975—and again gave the Panthers all they could handle. Pitt won, 28-21, but Hurley passed for 203 yards. Matt Cavanaugh was even better, passing for 332 yards, including a 45-yard completion to Gordon Jones with less than two minutes to play, setting up Cavanaugh's 1-yard keeper to provide the margin of difference. Pitt had trailed, 21-14, entering the fourth quarter.

Freshman defensive end Rickey Jackson gave a preview of great things to come when he returned an interception 48 yards to match Pitt's point total in a 48-0 whitewashing of the Tulane Green Wave at Pitt Stadium. Four freshmen—Greg Meisner, Bill Neill, Jerry Boyarsky, and Mark May—started for Pitt that day. Cavanaugh played only one half, directing the Panthers to a 34-0 lead at intermission. He threw two touchdown passes. Safety Mike Balzer also returned an interception for a score, and senior safety Bob Jury became Pitt's all-time leader in interceptions when he made his fifteenth career pick. He had two in the game. Elliott Walker ran for 119 yards and two touchdowns.

A sellout crowd at old Mountaineer Field was giddy when West Virginia took an early 3-0 lead on November 5, but Pitt won the game, 44-3, its most lopsided victory against West Virginia in Morgantown in the long history of the series. Pitt had 234 yards rushing and 217 yards passing. Robert Alexander, WVU's prized freshman running back who was Pitt's guest at the Backyard Brawl in Pittsburgh the previous season, was limited to 36 yards rushing.

"Pitt is by far the best team we've faced all year, and one of the best I've ever seen," West Virginia coach Frank Cignetti remarked after the game.

Pitt traveled to East Rutherford, New Jersey to meet Army on November 12, and left with a 52-26 victory. The Panthers raced to a 38-0 halftime lead, then coasted in the second half. Cavanaugh passed for 197 yards and three touchdowns, and also ran for 52 yards playing only a short time into the third quarter. Rick Trocano entered the game in the second half and tossed a touchdown pass to freshman tight end Benjie Pryor. Pitt's final score came on a 93-yard kickoff return by Gordon Jones.

The win at Giants Stadium improved Pitt's record to 8-1-1 with a scheduled week off before hosting 9-1 Penn State at Pitt Stadium on November 26, 1977. The Nittany Lions and Panthers were jumbled together in the national rankings with Penn State eighth and ninth in the UPI and AP Polls while Pitt was ninth and tenth. Penn State's only loss was a 24-20 road defeat at Kentucky in its fourth game. Bowl bids were to be extended after games on November 19, when Penn State also had an open date.

According to Jackie Sherrill, there were people in Pitt's administration who believed Pitt had a bid to one of the major bowls in its pocket. Sherrill thought otherwise. "It doesn't make any difference what you did last year," he tried to explain to school officials. "They're going to take the best team and the best scenario for them. They're in the business to make money."

The bowl bids came and were extended on November 19. Pitt accepted an invitation to play Clemson in the Gator Bowl on December 30. Penn State secured an offer to the Fiesta Bowl, where it would meet Arizona State on Christmas Day.

Pitt conducted its weekly football press luncheon at the Crossgates Inn on Forbes Avenue four days before the Penn State game. Penn State coach Joe Paterno answered questions from the media via an amplified telephone hookup, a procedure rarely practiced anymore by college media relations departments. Most of the questions were related to the apparent bowl snub against both Pitt and Penn State. Paterno had heard enough. "I don't want to get into that other nonsense," he announced. "I don't know enough about it to blame anybody."

Matt Cavanaugh injected a little levity into the luncheon when he was asked his impressions of the Ohio State-Michigan game three days earlier. Both the Buckeyes and Wolverines were ranked ahead of Pitt and Penn State. "I fell asleep watching it," Cavanaugh admitted. Michigan won the Big Ten heavyweight bout, 14-6.

Many years later, when asked about the late season drama, Jackie Sherrill had no difficulty assigning responsibility for the bowl slight.

"The Orange Bowl wanted to make a deal where it would take the winner of our game with Penn State," said Sherrill. "But [Joe] Paterno wouldn't go for it. He didn't think he needed us."

"If Paterno hinted at it, and Jackie said it, then what Jackie said was probably true," Dean Billick said in 2019.

In any event, Pitt was pleased and excited to be going to play Clemson in Jacksonville. The invitation came from George R. Olsen, executive vice president and general manager of the Gator Bowl Association, during a party at the home of Cas Myslinski. Chancellor Wesley Posvar also was in attendance. The payout from the Gator Bowl was approximately $350,000.

"The Gator Bowl committee feels that, without the injury to Matt Cavanaugh, Pitt would be undefeated and ranked number one in the country," said Olsen.

That left the Pitt-Penn State game. The Lions were making their first visit to Pitt Stadium since 1971. If historians want to pinpoint a certain time when Pitt-Penn State became not just a football game, but a bitter battle of egos and arrogance between two respective fans bases, simply follow the chronology. Penn State became a force in college football in 1966 when it hired Joe Paterno. Six years later, Pitt hired Johnny Majors, who presided over Pitt's football renaissance. By 1975, Pitt had caught up to Penn State, and surpassed the Lions in 1976. Even though Joe Paterno had produced three undefeated, untied teams (1968, 1969, and 1973) during his first eight years in Happy Valley, the subjective manner (polls) in which a national champion was selected, had kept Penn State from claiming that title.

To make it more distasteful, along came Pitt, a punching bag and doormat program for so many years. For a *nouveau riche* program from the same state to capture the top spot in college football had to grate on Penn State supporters, not to mention its players and coaches.

A sellout crowd assembled on a snowy, blustery, cold Saturday, November 26 to see if Pitt could defeat Penn State in consecutive seasons for the first time since 1948 and 1949. The game was telecast nationally by ABC.

Penn State opened the scoring on a 34-yard field goal by Matt Bahr, but Pitt took a 7-3 lead later in the quarter on a 1-yard keeper by Cavanaugh. The Panthers appeared poised to make it 14-3 toward the end of the quarter when it had the ball at the Penn State one, but a procedure penalty (it was called offside in 1977) pushed Pitt back to the six. Cavanaugh's pass into the end zone was intercepted by Gary Petercuskie.

Bahr added another field goal in the second quarter to bring the Lions to within a point at 7-6. Then came what Jackie Sherrill later called "the play that decided the game." Penn State's Jimmy Cefalo fielded a Joe Gasparovic punt, then reversed his field and handed off to Mike Guman, who raced 52 yards for Penn State's only touchdown of the afternoon. The Lions led, 12-7, at halftime.

With the temperature dropping and snow beginning to fall, neither team scored during the third quarter, but that did not deter the quarterbacks, Pitt's Cavanaugh and Penn State sophomore Chuck Fusina, from throwing the ball. Cavanaugh threw it twenty-nine times to Fusina's twenty-seven. Both teams were somewhat successful on the ground. Pitt and Penn State rushed for 204 and 150 yards, respectively.

Matt Bahr's third field goal of the afternoon, this time from 20 yards, gave Penn State a seemingly safe 15-7 lead, considering the conditions. But Cavanaugh led Pitt on a dramatic 48-yard drive while completing three passes in only twenty-nine seconds. He hit Gordon Jones on a crossing route from 17 yards out with only twelve seconds remaining on the field. Penn State led, 15-13, with a two-point conversion attempt to follow.

With the turf covered by snow, Cavanaugh handed off to Elliott Walker, who was stopped short of the end zone by Matt Millen. Photographs of the play show Cavanaugh extending both arms upward, while several Penn State defenders make the "no good" crossing of the arms sign. Walker later claimed that the whistle had blown prematurely, that he had crossed the plane. But without any replay in 1977, and snow muddling the playing field, the game was over.

Chuck Fusina, the Penn State quarterback, had an interesting perspective. From nearby McKees Rocks, he grew up following Pitt, and used to ride a bus from his hometown to watch the Panthers play at Pitt Stadium. In the days before cable television, computers, and ESPN, it took some searching to gain access to the area teams.

"I actually knew nothing about Penn State," Fusina admitted in a 2019 interview. "Actually, you didn't know much about the local teams, either. When you live in the [McKees] Rocks, there's always something else to do! I was always a Pitt fan. A couple of the quarterbacks from McKees Rocks went on to play at Pitt, so I followed them, especially Bobby Medwid."

Fusina holds a unique distinction—he is Penn State's only quarterback to have played in four games against Pitt. His indoctrination came as a freshman in 1975 when he replaced a struggling John Andress and directed the Lions' only score in the unforgettable 7-6 contest at Three

Rivers Stadium. "We were lucky to get out of there with a win that night," he later admitted.

Speaking of Joe Paterno, Chuck Fusina said:

> Joe [Paterno] was as old school as old school could be, so he stressed that it's just your next opponent. We knew when Thanksgiving was coming. We knew that Pitt was always good. We were usually pretty good, too. It got a lot of attention locally, and I think people around the country came to know about the rivalry, especially when you have Top 10 teams playing against each other most of the time.

Having played four seasons at Penn State, Fusina was no stranger to nasty weather conditions, but he will not soon forget the 1977 clash at Pitt Stadium. "It was cold, it was rough," he said. "I'm no tough guy. When you played at Penn State, the vast majority of my games were very windy or raining. Nobody said anything about global warming then."

The weather was reasonably warmer when the Pitt team traveled to Jacksonville for the Gator Bowl date with Clemson, coached by Charley Pell. Both Pitt and Clemson had identical 8-2-1 records. Each team had suffered disappointing losses to Notre Dame. The Irish had rallied in the fourth quarter for a 21-17 win at Death Valley on November 12. There was a familiarity between Sherrill and Pell. Pell had been a senior at Alabama during Sherrill's freshman year. At a Gator Bowl press conference, Sherrill reminded Pell of their time together in Tuscaloosa.

"I told him, 'Coach Charley, you remember all those knots you put on my head at practice?'" said Sherrill. "'Well, they're about to be repaid. I'm not going to do it, but these players of mine are.'"

The 1977 Gator Bowl was the only game Pitt played on natural grass that season. The surface agreed with the Panthers, who won easily, 34-3, in their most complete performance. Matt Cavanaugh passed for 387 yards and four touchdowns in his final collegiate game for Pitt. Three of the touchdown passes went to Elliott Walker, while the fourth went to Gordon Jones. Jones had ten receptions for 163 yards. Pitt's offense gained 566 net yards while collecting thirty first downs.

"I was shocked in the difference in the ball clubs," Charley Pell told reporters after the game. "Pitt is the best football team we've played all year."

Cavanaugh, who earned his second bowl game Most Valuable Player trophy in as many seasons, was asked to compare his senior season with the 1976 team that won the national championship. "Last year we had a lot of seniors," Cavanaugh remarked. "This year it was more exciting, in a way, because we used a lot of young players."

Pitt ended the year ranked seventh nationally. Including the bowl game, Elliott Walker rushed for 1,025 yards, making him the only player in school history, other than Tony Dorsett, to gain at least 1,000 yards in a single season. Cavanaugh, Randy Holloway, Tom Brzoza, and Bob Jury earned first team All-America honors.

Pitt held six opponents—Temple, Florida, Tulane, West Virginia, Penn State, and Clemson—without an offensive touchdown.

For Jackie Sherrill, the youngest coach in college football history put in the position of having to defend a national championship, it was a trying first season. He had to live with the stinging losses to Notre Dame and Penn State. Sherrill said: "This [Gator Bowl] was a must win for me. This season has not been nice for me, with all the pressure and all the adversity our team has had. Tonight, I feel I'm a very fortunate young man."[5]

Preparing for the 1978 season, Sherrill and his staff had more big shoes to fill. Twelve starters were gone from the 1977 team, including eight players who had been selected in the NFL Draft. Only Notre Dame had as many.

All-Americans Tom Brzoza, Randy Holloway, and Bob Jury needed to be replaced, along with two-time bowl MVP quarterback Matt Cavanaugh. Among the returnees, safety Jeff Delaney, guard Matt Carroll, and receiver Gordon Jones were the three remaining players who had started for Pitt in the 1977 Sugar Bowl win to claim the national championship.

Sherrill and his staff went to work assembling what became a solid recruiting class. Linemen Emil Boures, Jimbo Covert, and Paul Dunn became major players for the Panthers. Running back Bryan Thomas was a late bloomer who made significant contributions to the program, while cornerback Wallace "Pappy" Thomas became a fixture on defense.

Veteran *Pittsburgh Press* sportswriter Bob Smizik was another new face on the Pitt football front. Having covered some very successful Pittsburgh Pirates teams earlier in the decade, but a follower of Pitt athletics for many years, he had some preconceived ideas about his new beat, but discovered they were wrong. "The thing that surprised me was the quality of the [Pitt] kids, the players," said Smizik. "I expected a lot less. I had heard stories."

One involved a white freshman, new to the team, who, at first, was afraid of some of his teammates in the locker room. "He'd never been around blacks before," said Smizik.

Smizik soon came to realize that perception and reality are two very different things. "They were just a nice bunch of kids, very respectful," he said. "I was shocked, really. There were a lot of smart kids, absolutely.... I'd come from the Pirates, and I had a reputation for being a very tough reporter. I was very flattered. They [Pitt] were thrilled to have me covering the team. Jackie [Sherrill] was, and I know Dean [Billick] was."

Covering a Pitt football team in 2020 is quite different from what it was like in the late 1970s. Today, reporters have very strict restrictions and limitations as to how and when they can watch practice and interview players. Locker rooms have become off limits to the media. No players are brought to the weekly press conferences. Players and coaches are brought to a designated interview room following games. Pitt coach Pat Narduzzi instituted a policy forbidding players to do any interviews leading up to the Penn State games. During Sherrill's tenure at Pitt, it was more relaxed, as recalled by Bob Smizik:

Everything was completely wide open to the media, during training camp and during the season. We had the run of training camp. I was up there with [Pittsburgh reporters] Ed Bouchette and Tom McMillan. It was a lot of fun. I treated the Pitt locker room as I treated the Pirates locker room. Before practice, I'd be in there—go to this guy, go to that guy, interview whoever you had to. Jackie was tremendous. This is unheard of now, but I had one on one access to him all the time, every day.

Smizik knows all about Jackie Sherrill's reputation—then and now. "I really liked Jackie," he said. "I think if you asked a lot of people around Pittsburgh, they would not have a high opinion of him. He was just great for us [media]. I appreciated how much he helped us in the media to do our jobs."

Acquiring proper information about player injuries is another aspect of the job that has changed dramatically since Pitt's great run in the 1970s. "This is unbelievable," said Smizik. "The trainers controlled the injury reports. "We would meet with him [Pitt trainer Kip Smith] and find out about the injuries. I think that's because the doctors wanted it that way. That didn't last much longer."

Dean Billick helped accommodate the media and their accessibility to Pitt's football players:

We wanted them [players] to talk to the media. We had the weekly luncheon down at the old Crossgates Inn on Forbes Avenue. We'd bring a couple players. That was part of the educational experience for them. Once in a while a player might say something that wouldn't look too good in the papers the next day, but that was all part of it. We tried to help them deal with the media.

Smizik also came to know and respect Pitt's assistant coaches, including the one in charge of the defense. "Jimmy Johnson was a pretty open guy," said Smizik. "I was unaware of what a hot assistant coach he was. Dean [Billick] had clued me in on that. He told me Jimmy wouldn't be here very long."

As Pitt's coaches reviewed the depth charts for 1978, it was apparent that the sophomore class, the players brought in following the national championship, would form the nucleus not only for that season, but for subsequent years. Rick Trocano earned the role as starting quarterback, and started all twelve games, and directed a more inexperienced offense than he and Matt Cavanaugh had worked with in 1977. "The team had a new running game," said Trocano. "We had gone to the Veer. Tony Dorsett had been in the I for much of his career."

Trocano explained that what football fans see from so many teams today is not radically different from what teams were running in the 1970s. "The Veer is similar to the spread offense which you're seeing now. The main difference is, now, the quarterback is in the shotgun, where back then he was directly under center."

One of the most versatile quarterbacks in Pitt history, Trocano was capable of running the option, along with the occasional naked bootleg play. Running backs Fred Jacobs, Larry Sims, and Rooster Jones gave Pitt a stable of similarly skilled runners. Tight end Steve Gaustad returned for his second season at that position, while senior Gordon Jones was Pitt's most dangerous offensive weapon.

A newcomer, but a familiar face around Pitt football, joined the staff in 1978. Alex Kramer left his job as director of curriculum for the Moon Area School District to become Jackie Sherrill's administrative assistant, a relatively new position at Pitt. One of his duties would be coordinating travel arrangements for the football team, selecting hotels and arranging bus transportation, among other responsibilities. "I became like his [Sherrill's] alter ego," said Kramer. "I always appreciated the trust Jackie had in me."

Routinely, Kramer would travel the day before to the hotel where Pitt's team would be staying. When the team would arrive at the site, Kramer would be standing behind a small table that had been set up the lobby. Before him would be envelopes containing room keys for the names of the players, coaches and staff members.

Kramer's first official road trip was a memorable one. Pitt was scheduled to play Tulane at the Super Dome on September 15, 1978. The night before, at the same venue, Muhammad Ali and Leon Spinks staged a rematch to see if Ali could reclaim the heavyweight title belt Spinks had taken from him seven months earlier. All the pretty people were in New Orleans, most of whom assembled in the lobby of the New Orleans Hilton, where both Pitt and Ali were headquartered. Pitt's travel itinerary came off without a hitch, considering the carnival atmosphere, and the Panthers, like Ali, came up winners in the Big Easy.

The folks back home were able to watch the Panthers' opener on WTAE Channel 4, a local production with Steve Zabriskie as lead announcer. The teams traded field goals in the first quarter before Larry Sims scored on touchdown runs of 35 and 4 yards in the second period to give Pitt a 17-6 halftime lead.

Pitt's young defense was strong throughout the game, yielding only 140 total yards, and Trocano tossed a 37-yard touchdown pass to Gordon Jones in the third quarter and Pitt defeated the Green Wave, 24-6.

Pitt struggled in its home opener the following week. Lindsay Delaney replaced Trocano at quarterback for a spell during the first half, which ended with Pitt trailing the Owls, 6-3. The Panthers came to life in the third quarter on touchdown runs by Trocano and Fred Jacobs., while holding Temple to a late touchdown. Pitt won, 20-12.

A regional ABC TV audience watched Pitt rally from a late deficit to defeat North Carolina, 20-16, at Pitt Stadium on September 30, 1978. It was a memorable sports weekend in Pittsburgh.

The Pittsburgh Pirates entered the final week of the regular season trailing the Philadelphia Phillies by three and one half games in the National League Eastern Division. The Pirates needed to sweep the four game series to force a one-game playoff the following Monday. Pittsburgh swept a doubleheader on Friday night, and jumped to an early 4-0 lead when Willie Stargell hit a grand slam home run in the bottom of the first inning. Pittsburgh fans, many of whom brought transistor radios to Pitt Stadium, erupted following Stargell's dramatic hit. Public address announcer Roger Huston then gave the baseball score, evoking more applause.

This went back and forth throughout the football game. Phillies fans, and there were many among Pitt's student body, let Pirates fans know when their team had done something significant. The Phillies eventually won the game, 10-8, clinching the division title. A crowd of 28,095 saw the baseball game. More than 50,000 were at Pitt Stadium at the same time.

Neither team scored a touchdown in the first half, which ended with North Carolina leading, 3-0. The Panthers hurt themselves by losing four of six fumbles, but Fred Jacobs and Trocano made enough big plays in the second half to offset the mistakes. Jacobs scored on short touchdown runs in both the third and fourth quarters, but Pitt trailed 16-13 with time running out. Trocano engineered a game winning drive, aided by a clutch reception by tight end Steve Gaustad. With 1:34 remaining and the ball at the UNC thirteen, Jacobs took a short pass from Trocano and raced into the end zone to give the Panthers a thrilling 20-16 victory.

Matt Cavanaugh, then in his rookie season with the New England Patriots, watched from the sideline as Pitt won 32-15 at Boston College on October 7. Pitt scored on its first four possessions—two touchdowns and two field goals—to take a 19-0 lead early in the second quarter. Trocano and Rooster Jones ran for touchdowns in the first half and Mark Schubert kicked a pair of field goals.

Trocano hit Gordon Jones with a 29-yard touchdown pass and Rooster Jones added another rushing touchdown from 2 yards out, to improve Pitt's record to 4-0, and national rankings of ninth in both wire service polls.

Notre Dame was 2-2 and unranked when the Panthers traveled to South Bend on October 14. The Irish, defending national champions, had lost to Missouri and Michigan, both at home, to open the season before rebounding with a home victory and a road win at Michigan State.

The Pitt-Notre Dame game was telecast nationally by ABC, and when Trocano scored his second touchdown of the afternoon on a 4-yard run, the Panthers appeared to be in good shape with a 17-7 lead. Trocano had scored on a 3-yard scamper in the second quarter.

But Notre Dame, led by quarterback and Ringgold High School graduate Joe Montana, rallied to score nineteen unanswered points in the final eleven minutes to hand Pitt a harsh 26-17 loss. A pair of fumbles led to two Notre Dame scores. Pitt's defense, which had been strong for three quarters, was unable to make a stop once Montana found his rhythm.

"We got Montanad before a lot of people knew who Joe Montana was," said Trocano. "He led a great comeback. But that wasn't the only time he did that during his career."

But Pitt's defense bounced back the following week with a 7-3 home victory against Florida State. "I didn't think any team in the country could hold us to only three points," said Seminoles' coach Bobby Bowden, who was making his first appearance against Pitt at Florida State. His West Virginia teams were 3-3 against Pitt from 1970 through 1975. "Pitt proved something to me today."

Florida State had 331 yards of total offense, but could not reach the end zone. The only touchdown of the game was a 13-yard run by Fred Jacobs in the second quarter. Neither team scored in the second half.

The Panthers traveled to Annapolis to meet 6-0 Navy the following week. None of Navy's six opponents had reached double figures on the scoreboard. The Middies had registered three shutouts; each of the other teams scored eight points, a scoreboard oddity. A Navy-Marine Corps Memorial Stadium record crowd of 32,909 watched as Navy soundly defeated Pitt, 28-11. Despite beginning four drives in Navy territory in the first quarter, the Panthers came away with zero points. Unable to move the ball on the ground, Rick Trocano threw for 275 yards on fifty-two pass attempts, but Pitt did not score a touchdown until Fred Jacobs ran for 2 yards in the fourth quarter.

Pitt had a defection from the team at midseason in senior nose guard Dave Logan. A powerful, yet sensitive type, Logan had been bothered by an ankle injury during the season. One of Logan's former teammates understood.

"Dave was a lot like [former Pitt nose guard] Gary Burley," said Al Romano. "Big guys with skinny little ankles. Ankle injuries can be the worst. You could probably get away playing easier with a knee injury than if your ankle is sore."

During his nightly radio sports talk show, WTAE's Myron Cope put out a plea for Logan to reconsider his decision, and to return to the team. Logan did come back, and played throughout the rest of the 1978 season.

Syracuse coach Frank Maloney, whatever his whim, tried a little trickery when Pitt visited Archbold Stadium for the last time on November 4, 1978. Maloney had his team warm up on an adjacent field prior to the start of the game. Syracuse did not appear at the game venue until shortly before kickoff.

If the tactic had any effect on the game is open to debate, but Pitt found itself trailing 17-7 entering the fourth quarter. Trocano marched the Panthers 76 yards, helped by a 20-yard completion to Steve Gaustad. Trocano scored a touchdown on a 5-yard run, and Fred Jacobs added the two-point conversion to make the score 17-15. With three minutes remaining, Mark Schubert kicked a 28-yard field goal and Pitt escaped with an 18-17 victory.

Pitt had its most impressive performance of the 1978 season in a convincing 52-7 defeat of West Virginia at Pitt Stadium on November 11. The Panthers rushed for 283 yards, led by Rooster Jones, who had a career high 169 yards and two touchdowns. Larry Sims scored on two touchdown runs of 1 yard and Trocano added another from the same distance to give Pitt a comfortable 21-0 halftime lead. A 32-yard touchdown pass from Lindsay Delaney to Gordon Jones, along with the touchdown runs by Rooster Jones, put the Panthers ahead 42-7 by the end of the third quarter. Sophomore Dave Trout booted a 51-yard field goal to account for the team's final points.

With bowl bids to be extended later that day, Pitt found itself trailing Army, 7-0, with the Cadets perched at Pitt's one, threatening to go ahead by two touchdowns. Jeff Delaney, however, made the play of the game when he caught an Army fumble and raced 99 yards in the other direction to tie the score. Rick Trocano added a 6-yard touchdown run to give the Panthers a 14-7 halftime lead.

Trocano hit Willie Collier for a 31-yard scoring strike, then Jacobs and Rooster Jones scored on short touchdown runs in the final quarter to close Pitt's scoring. After the game, Pitt accepted an invitation to play North Carolina State in the Tangerine Bowl on December 23 in Orlando, Florida.

But first there was the annual grudge match with Penn State. In 1978, Pitt would be visiting Beaver Stadium for the first time since 1973, when Tony Dorsett was a freshman and John Majors was in his first season as coach.

Pitt was a prohibitive underdog entering the game. The Lions had won eighteen consecutive games, were 10-0, and ranked first in the nation. They boasted a senior quarterback (Fusina) and a standout pair of defensive tackles in Bruce Clark and Matt Millen. Penn State had secured a bid to meet Southeastern Conference champion Alabama in the Sugar Bowl.

The Panthers were 8-2, but less experienced across the board. "A majority of our players were sophomores," recalled Rick Trocano. "We were very capable, athletically, but we still had a lot to learn."

And what would a Pitt-Penn State game be without a peripheral controversy? The game was scheduled for Friday afternoon, November

24. The Pitt team arrived in Happy Valley the day before and held a light workout at Beaver Stadium. Penn State public works personnel who had witnessed the practice thought something amiss; the cleats worn by Pitt's players, in their belief, were not legal. Joe Paterno received word of this.

The morning of the game, Emil Narick, a former Pitt football player under Jock Sutherland and Charles Bowser, was preparing for the day in his room at the Nittany Lion Inn on the Penn State campus. It was around 7 a.m. when his phone rang. It was Ed Czekaj, Penn State's director of athletics. "I need to see you," Czekaj informed Narick. Narick, then a senior commonwealth judge, moonlighted as a supervisor of officials. In fact, he and Jackie Sherrill spoke by telephone each Sunday during football season. Narick had once officiated games himself.

Narick, Czekaj, Pitt AD Cas Myslinski, and game official Bill Parkinson convened at Beaver Stadium. By 2020, all four men, and Paterno, were deceased. At the meeting (Paterno was not present), Narick was informed that Paterno was not happy with the situation, and demanded that Pitt's cleats be examined.

Narick and Parkinson visited the Pitt locker room and conferred with Sherrill. "There's no problem with our cleats," Sherrill told them, and there wasn't. Sherrill claimed that Narick, at the behest of Paterno, then took one of Pitt's shoes to Penn State's locker room for Paterno to inspect. "By you taking a pair of shoes over to show them, that shows you're putting Paterno above you," Sherrill told Narick, "Why should he be the one to decide if our cleats aren't legal?'

Narick, who died in 2007, told the author in a 1998 interview that he had no recollection of taking a shoe to Penn State's locker room, but "if that's what Jackie says, I have no problem with that."

The matter of the cleats settled, the two teams engaged in a defensive struggle over the next several hours on a cold, windy afternoon. Pitt held Penn State's veteran offense to 230 total yards, but had difficulty moving the ball itself. "We ran into a tough, crusty defense," Trocano remembers. "[Bruce] Clark and [Matt] Millen were some of their better players. Especially Matt Millen. He was a force."

Rick Trocano said:

Our offensive running attack was the Veer. The most effective way to disrupt it is to have the defensive tackles crashing in. It's called Veer stunts. What they do is blow up the entire play by stunting. Our scheme did not match up well against Penn State's talent that day. We had a hard time running the ball.

But Pitt's defense was stout for most of the game. Veteran sportscaster Ray Scott, calling the game for Penn State's delayed telecast production, throughout the game noted that Pitt's defense was the best Penn State had faced all season. The score validated Scott's claim.

The Lions took a 7-0 lead on a 3-yard run by Mike Guman in the first quarter, but would not score again until late in the fourth quarter. Pitt tied the game in the second quarter when Trocano hit tight end Steve Gaustad alone in the back of the end zone from 16 yards out. Mark Schubert's 27-yard field goal were the only points scored by either team in the third quarter. Pitt led 10-7 entering the final quarter, but Penn State enjoyed the wind at its back for the last fifteen minutes.

The Lions missed a chance to tie the game when a bad snap from center disrupted a Matt Bahr field goal attempt. Pitt took over on downs, but could not generate a first down.

Penn State mounted what would be its winning drive, aided by a roughing the passer penalty against Dave Logan following Fusina's clutch third down completion to tight end Brad Scovill. Ironically, Fusina and Logan would spend the next four seasons as teammates with the NFL's Tampa Bay Buccaneers. "Dave [Logan] came to be one of my best friends," Fusina later said. "And he was one of the nicest guys you'll ever meet." Logan, who went on to do football color commentary for CBS, died in 1999.

The penalty against Logan placed the ball at the Pitt 12. Three plays later, the Lions faced a fourth down and 2 yards to go from the Pitt 4. Initially, Matt Bahr and the field goal unit trotted out for an apparent attempt. Penn State called time out. With a perfect season in the balance, Joe Paterno had a decision to make.

"Everyone who was looking at him [Paterno] from the huddle had the feeling that, 'C'mon, this is the time to go for it,'" said Fusina. "We had a really good offensive line, and two good running backs [Matt Suhey and Mike Guman], who would go on to play in the NFL."

A legend grew that Fusina lied to Paterno about how much yardage Penn State needed to gain on fourth down. Fusina dispelled it. "I remember going to the sideline, and we talked about it," he said. "I think Coach Paterno made the decision for probably ninety-eight percent of what we did, both offensively and defensively. Joe was really on top of things like that."

Penn State went for it, making not only the first down, but a touchdown. Mike Guman ran left, then inside, racing virtually untouched into the end zone to put Penn State in the lead at 14-10.

Pitt's offense was unable to move the ball, and Matt Bahr added a 38-yard field goal to make the final score 17-10.

Pitt's valiant effort against an undefeated top ranked Penn State team may have been the team's proudest moment during the 1978 season. Part of the credit for the team's showing that day went to Jimmy Johnson, whose defense played well enough to put Pitt in position to win the game. And in the aftermath, Johnson, then in his fourteenth season as an assistant coach, finally received the call he had been waiting for when Oklahoma State reached out and named him its new head football coach. He would coach Pitt through the Tangerine Bowl before departing for Stillwater, taking with him fellow Pitt assistants Dave Wannstedt, Pat Jones, Larry Holton, and graduate assistant Tony Wise.

Feelings were strained in the Pitt camp during the week leading up to Pitt's Tangerine Bowl game against North Carolina State, coached by Bo Rein, who died a year later in a mysterious plane crash into the Atlantic Ocean before ever coaching a game at his new outpost, LSU. The Wolfpack roster included a linebacker from the Pittsburgh area named Bill Cowher.

There were hints of trouble even before the team arrived in Orlando, with Jeff Delaney noting:

> There were a lot of things that went on before that last game, and they started back in Pittsburgh when we started practicing for that bowl game. There were some people who were missing practice, and Jackie [Sherrill] finally got to the point where he said he was gonna make some rules. "Okay, if you're a starter and you miss a practice, you're not starting. If you're not a starter and you miss a practice, you're not making the trip." He put down that law.

Delaney, a two time Academic All-American at Pitt, later claimed that Sherrill did not stick to his policy. "There was a little rift there," Delaney said. "People weren't being treated equally."

Later, in Orlando, factions had developed between the coaches who were staying at Pitt and those who would be following Johnson to Oklahoma State. "It was pretty obvious that it was a staff divided," said Bill Hillgrove. "The guys who were gonna go to Oklahoma State with Jimmy would go in one car, and everybody else would go in the other car."

"They [coaches] all left in different cars after practice," said Bob Smizik. "A lot of people thought that had a lot to do with the performance of the team in that game."

Pitt's performance in that game was disheartening. North Carolina State jumped out to a 17-0 lead and was never seriously threatened, defeating the Panthers, 30-17. In a 2019 interview, Mark May did not mince words when asked to talk about the disappointing experience in Orlando:

> Jimmy Johnson and all those assistants knew they were going to Oklahoma State, so they goofed off all week. They got to practice late, they didn't care about meetings. At the game they were up in the press box screwin' around, eating hot dogs. At halftime, Jackie (Sherrill) went off in the locker room. Not in front of us [players], but in the coaches' room. He fired those guys at halftime.

Quarterback Rick Trocano, who had an interception returned for a touchdown in the game, had his own perspective of the events that week:

> As a coach, your heart is in the right place, but that is a disruptive process. You've just been named head coach at a different school. You have a new responsibility. You have to recruit, you have to hire assistant coaches. All this while you're trying to coach in a bowl game at the same time? If one, maybe two coaches go, maybe it's not so disruptive. But we had more than that who were going to be leaving. That handicapped Jackie [Sherrill] tremendously.

The Tangerine Bowl was a sad way for Jeff Delaney and Pitt's other seniors—who were members of a national championship team two years earlier—to end their college careers. "I always look back at that last game, and it bothers me a lot, because that was not indicative of the team we were," said Delaney. "There were a lot of things going on behind the scenes."

Bob Smizik remembers interviewing Jimmy Johnson after the Tangerine Bowl game. He said: "The defense was terrible in the game. "Oh, nobody is more upset about this than I am," he said. "All those people at Oklahoma State must be thinking, We're getting this guy to be our coach?" When he [Johnson] left, there was a real division within Pitt's program."

The mass exodus from Pittsburgh to Stillwater almost claimed Pitt's most celebrated defensive player. "I was very close to Jimmy Johnson," admitted

Hugh Green. "I told him, 'Hey, I want to go with you to Oklahoma State.' I visited him out there, but he told me that I'd established myself at Pitt, and that I should stay there."

Jackie Sherrill acted quickly to turn the disappointing end to the 1978 season into a positive, as a springboard for future success. Mark May recalled:

Later that night, Jackie brought all of us sophomores up to his suite. He had it catered. He told us, "Guys, this is your team. You guys are sophomores. It doesn't matter. It's your team. Take it in which direction you want to go. You can be great if you want to be great. I'll do everything I can to help you. It's up to you guys if you want to have success."

5

33 AND 3
(1979–1981)

The National Football League conducted an early preview of next spring's draft up in the Carrier Dome here yesterday afternoon as the Men of Pittsburgh buried the Boys from Syracuse, 43-6.[1]

Arnie Burdick (*Syracuse Herald-American*, November 1, 1980)

There was no color barrier on our teams. My freshman year, Hugh Green was my roommate before home and away games. We'd stay up late and talk. There was no prejudice. We all loved each other. There was no black or white; only Pitt blue and gold.

Greg Meisner

During the late 1970s, the city of Pittsburgh, under the stewardship of Mayor Richard Caliguiri, was undergoing what was known as Renaissance II, a building project that dramatically enhanced the city's skyline.

Pittsburgh's sports teams were doing their part to contribute to the town's growing reputation. Through the 1978 season, the Steelers had won three Super Bowls during the decade, and were about to claim a fourth. The Pirates had captured six National League East Division titles and a pair of World Series titles in 1971 and 1979. Pitt football was enjoying its most successful stretch since the 1930s. Pittsburgh became known as "The City of Champions."

"Everybody knew each other," said Jackie Sherrill, who received a belt buckle as a gift from Pirates slugger Willie Stargell during that period.

"The Pirates knew the Steelers. The Pirates knew the Panthers. The Steelers knew us, and they actually came and worked out and interacted with our players."

The 1979 season was a new beginning of sorts for Sherrill and Pitt's football program. Gone were the assistant coaches who had decided to accompany Jimmy Johnson to Oklahoma State, and the team's disappointing loss to North Carolina State in the Tangerine Bowl was simply an unpleasant memory.

No starters remained from the Panthers' 1976 national championship team. Heretofore, the majority of the players would be those who had been recruited by Sherrill as head coach, with the great 1977 class comprising the heart and soul of the team for at least the next two seasons.

Five new assistant coaches—Wally English (offensive coordinator), Ron Dickerson (secondary), Joe Pendry (quarterbacks), Ray Zingler (defensive ends), and Joe Naunchik (receivers)—joined the Pitt staff following the 1978 campaign. English, who was a teammate of Paul Hornung at Flaget High School in Louisville, Ky, served as offensive coordinator at Brigham Young before arriving at Pitt. Dickerson, from nearby Coraopolis, Pa., had coached the secondary at Louisville. Pendry, a West Virginia graduate, had been offensive coordinator for Frank Cignetti at WVU in 1978, while Zingler was a Utah State graduate who had had extensive experience as a high school coach in New Jersey. Naunchik had been a longtime high school coach in Western Pennsylvania and had played running back in college for Frank Kush at Arizona State.

The revised coaching staff got down to business, stockpiling another strong recruiting class. Key signees in early 1979 included wide receivers Julius Dawkins and John Brown, offensive linemen Ron Sams and Rob Fada, defensive linemen J. C. Pelusi, Dave Puzzuoli, Al Wenglikowski, and Michael Woods, and safety Dan "Peep" Short. Before leaving Pittsburgh for Stillwater, assistant coach Dave Wannstedt left a key recruit for Pitt, bruising running back Randy McMillan, from North Harford Junior College in Maryland.

But no signee received as much hype or created excitement for Pitt fans as Central Catholic High School quarterback Dan Marino, who had grown up just a few blocks from the Pitt campus in Oakland. Marino was probably the most heralded football recruit from Western Pennsylvania since Tony Dorsett six years earlier. He earned virtually every honor possible in high school, where he also starred as a pitcher and shortstop for Central Catholic's baseball team. In fact, Pitt's coaches were more concerned that Marino would turn to baseball as his career path. Following his senior year at Central Catholic, and in the heat of football recruiting, the Kansas City Royals selected Marino in the fourth round of the Major League Baseball Draft. Later, in that same draft, the Royals picked another outstanding senior quarterback, John Elway from Granada Hills High School in California.

Marino signed a letter of intent with Pitt on February 9, 1979, but the Royals were determined to make a pitch of their own. Jackie Sherrill, Marino's parents (Dan and Veronica Marino), Dan, and a representative from the Royals' organization gathered around the kitchen table to discuss the situation. Sherrill explained that if Marino signed with Kansas City, he would not be eligible for a football scholarship. The Kansas City scout explained that the club was looking to move George Brett away from third base to make room for Marino. Fortunately for Pitt, Dan Marino chose not to accept the Kansas City offer.

"Deep down, I always felt like Danny was coming to Pitt," said Foge Fazio, adding that, in his opinion, baseball powers Arizona State, Clemson and UCLA presented a more serious challenge for his talents. "Lots of times, kids who are good at baseball and football will think, 'Why should I get my head beat in playing football?'"

Along with visiting Marino at his home, Fazio and new assistant coach Joe Pendry invited Marino and his Central Catholic teammate and future Panther, Lou Lamanna, to Fitzgerald Field House, where the two coaches would play the high school seniors in basketball on the main court. "That was probably an NCAA violation," Fazio later joked, adding that he attended many of Marino's high school baseball games as well.

Throughout the process, Marino received valuable information and advice from Pirates' manager Chuck Tanner and infielders Phil Garner and Bill Madlock, but Marino had decided to represent his hometown team in college. Along with his enormous talent, Marino received an abundance of hype and expectations from Pittsburgh fans and media before he even reported to campus.

"His [Marino's] dad was very, very smart and streetwise," said Jackie Sherrill. "His dad told me, 'You don't worry about telling him things to make him happy.' He said, 'you just tell him what you're going to do, and that's it.'"

With the 1979 team assembled, the coaches and media were able to preview the newcomers during three days of light workouts before leaving for training camp. At least one Pitt beat writer remembers being at Pitt Stadium during those sessions in August 1979. Bob Smizik said:

Jackie [Sherrill] was amazing at analyzing talent. During the workouts he would come over to us [media] on the sideline and say, "Keep an eye on that kid and that kid. He's gonna be a good one." He was almost always right. I remember he singled out Michael Woods. Who knew anything about Michael Woods? But he turned out to be an excellent player.

And how did junior quarterback Rick Trocano, who had started all twelve games as a sophomore in 1978, and had won eleven of his fifteen collegiate starts, feel about the arrival of Dan Marino? Trocano said:

> From an upperclassman's standpoint, I realized Danny was very talented, and that was good for the team. We always wanted as much talent as possible. Everybody's press releases and statistics from high school are impressive going into college. I always took a wait and see approach. That's the attitude I had, but I was glad that Pitt was continuing to get great players.

One Pittsburgh daily newspaper, feeding the Marino hype and capitalizing on the City of Champions label, staged a photo of Marino—who had yet to play a game in college—along with Steelers quarterback Terry Bradshaw, cigars in mouth, on the cover of its August football tabloid beneath the heading "Pittsburgh's Classy Quarterbacks."

As for another prominent young player, defensive tackle Jimbo Covert was discouraged about his role after the 1978 season. He believed he should be playing more, but felt stuck behind linemen Greg Meisner, Bill Neill, and Jerry Boyarsky. Jackie Sherrill stated:

> Jimbo and his dad [John Covert] came into my office and said Jimbo wanted to transfer. How do you handle that? What I explained to Jimbo and his dad was that it was everybody in the mill where his dad was working was saying, "Why isn't Jimbo playing?" So the pressure on the parents, and from the parents on the kid—sometimes it's overwhelming. And I told that to Jimbo's dad. "Jimbo's gonna be fine. You're the one who has to deal with it."

Jimbo Covert had been dealing with an injured shoulder since his high school days, but was hesitant to tell anyone about it. "How do you get an operation when you're sixteen years old?" he said. "How do you tell your dad about it?"

Instead, Covert played hurt, but decided he was not playing enough. He recalled the meeting with his father and Jackie Sherrill: "My dad and I went in there. It got kind of intense. But Jackie did say that to my dad. 'Don't worry about Jimbo. He's going to be fine. I know you got people coming up to you at the mill wondering why Jimbo's not playing. Tell those guys Jimbo's gonna be a great player for us here.'"

Jimbo Covert did see action at defensive tackle in Pitt's 1979 season opener against Kansas at Pitt Stadium, but the shoulder became so bad he had to have surgery immediately. He missed the rest of the season, was redshirted, and was moved to offensive tackle in 1980.

Pitt's 1979 season began on a sunny September 15, the same day Dan Marino turned eighteen, but junior Rick Trocano was the Panthers' starting quarterback that day. Randy McMillan carried the ball twenty-one times for 141 yards in his Pitt debut, while Ralph Still—who came to Pitt as a quarterback but was moved to wide receiver—caught three touchdown passes, two from Trocano.

Marino entered the game in the second quarter with Pitt leading 10-0. His first collegiate pass was intercepted and his second attempt fell incomplete. Marino's third pass was charmed, a 23-yard catch and run for a touchdown by Still to give Pitt a 17-0 lead at halftime. The only score in the second half was Trocano's touchdown pass to Still, also from 23 yards.

Pitt's defense suffocated the Jayhawks the entire afternoon, limiting Kansas to minus 17 yards rushing.

Pitt traveled to hot, humid Chapel Hill to meet North Carolina the following week. The Tar Heels' lineup featured a pair of standout players in running back Amos Lawrence and linebacker Lawrence Taylor. Decades later, North Carolina would come to be known as a place where Pitt football teams went to lose, and September 22, 1979 was no different. After a scoreless first quarter, the Tar Heels scored a pair of touchdown to take a 14-0 lead at halftime. Pitt's only score of the day came in the third quarter when Trocano found Kenny Bowles in the end zone to make the score 14-7. North Carolina added a field goal in the final period to make the final score 17-7. Randy McMillan, who had a big debut against Kansas the week before, carried the ball eleven times for 34 yards. It would be Pitt's only loss in 1979, and left one of its star players devastated.

"After the game, Hugh Green was on the table getting dripped because he got dehydrated," Jackie Sherrill remembered. "He was crying, and he said, 'Why did we lose this game?' That really affected him."

The Temple Owls, Pitt's next opponent, finished the season 10-2, its only losses coming to Pitt and Penn State. Pitt and Temple met under the lights at Philadelphia's Veterans Stadium on September 29. The Pitt offense struggled throughout the evening, managing only a 7-yard touchdown run by McMillan in the second quarter. The Pitt defense kept the Owls out of the end zone, but three field goals by Ron Fioravanti had the Owls clinging to a 9-7 lead late in the game. Pitt special teams whiz Glenn "Bulldog" Meyer blocked a Temple punt, and Mark Schubert booted a field goal from 47 yards out with four minutes remaining to give Pitt a narrow 10-9 victory. Rick Trocano played the entire game at quarterback for the Panthers.

Trocano and Marino each played at Pitt Stadium the following week in the Panthers' 28-7 victory against Boston College, and both quarterbacks completed eight of twelve passes in the game. Randy McMillan scored on three short touchdown runs while Marino rolled out and cut back and scored from the two late in the second quarter. The Pitt defense, led by its strong junior class, held the Eagles to 191 yards of total offense while forcing five turnovers.

With the Pittsburgh Pirates set to meet the Baltimore Orioles in Game Four of the 1979 World Series at Three Rivers Stadium on Saturday afternoon, October 13, Pitt decided to push up the starting time of its Homecoming game with Cincinnati to 10 a.m. The early start did not faze the Panthers, even with a pronounced glare making the yard markers difficult to discern throughout most of the first half. Pitt amassed 502 yards of total offense in routing the Bearcats, 35-0. Five different Pitt players scored touchdowns while Trocano and Marino each threw a touchdown pass. Randy McMillan carried the ball eighteen times for 119 yards as Pitt raised its season record to 4-1.

While most of Pittsburgh was still recovering from the celebration of the Pirates' World Series triumph in Baltimore the night before, the Pitt football team was boarding a charter aircraft bound for Seattle, Washington, on the morning of October 18, 1979. It was Pitt's first visit to the West Coast since defeating UCLA in the 1971 season opener, and Jackie Sherrill decided to have the team leave two days before the game in order for everyone to become acclimated to the time difference. In 2020, it is virtually unheard of for a college team to spend three nights on the road for a regular season game, but that is what Pitt did in 1979. The Panthers would fly back from Seattle to Pittsburgh on Sunday, one day after the game.

In between, Alex Kramer had to make arrangements with the Washington Plaza Hotel to have an extra-large bed supplied for Mark May.

The Pitt defense carried the day for the Panthers in their important 26-14 win against the Huskies on a glorious afternoon overlooking Puget Sound. The Panthers forced six turnovers—three fumbles and three interceptions—and twenty-three of Pitt's twenty-six points were direct results of defensive takeaways. Defensive linemen Hugh Green and Jerry Boyarsky picked off passes and cornerback Terry White another. Randy McMillan ran for a pair of touchdowns while Artrell Hawkins added one. Mark Schubert kicked a pair of field goals for Pitt's other points.

"The victory over the Washington Huskies in Seattle was a key game during those years," said Alex Kramer. "That's when you could see that group of players really coming together."

Pitt had revenge on its mind when Navy visited Pitt Stadium on October 27. The Midshipmen had dominated the Panthers in Annapolis the year before. The Panthers sustained a key loss when Trocano, while rolling right, suffered a severe pull of his left hamstring during the first quarter.

"I was running at top speed when it happened, and that's never good," said Trocano. "I left the field in a wheelchair. I couldn't even walk."

Trocano missed the rest of the 1979 season. He could not play any more football that year, but still had to attend classes and get to Pitt Stadium for regular treatments to his injured leg. "I had a tough time getting around campus on crutches," he said. "You know what that [Cardiac] hill is like going up to the stadium. Sometimes the [Pitt] campus cops would recognize me and give me a ride."

Dan Marino's time had come. He entered the Navy game as Pitt faced a 7-3 halftime deficit. He directed Pitt's offense to three touchdowns, one on a run by Rooster Jones, and touchdown passes to Fred Jacobs and Ralph Still. Pitt's defense was superb, holding Navy to 116 yards of total offense, but the freshman quarterback was the story of Pitt's 24-7 win. Mark May stated: "When Danny [Marino] first got there, he was a lot younger than most of us, so he was a little timid in the huddle. He started maturing in the process and taking charge. We just followed him. He was the quarterback calling the plays. There weren't any issues in the huddle."

ABC TV was in town to televise freshman Dan Marino's first collegiate start when Pitt hosted Syracuse on November 1, 1979. His opposite number was Bill Hurley, back for a fifth season with the Orange following a redshirt year in 1978. In fact, it was the third time Hurley started a game at quarterback against Pitt at Pitt Stadium.

Terry White turned in a stellar performance for Pitt, returning a punt 85 yards for a touchdown and recovering a Syracuse fumble, while Marino completed eighteen of twenty-six passes for 170 yards and two touchdowns. While Marino was throwing for scores, Hurley ran for his, crossing the goal line twice in the second half to keep the game close, but a touchdown run by Rooster Jones late in the third quarter helped secure the 28-21 victory, Pitt's sixth straight win.

In their long and colorful sports histories, Pitt and West Virginia had already shut down two sporting venues. In 1951, Pitt defeated the Mountaineers 74-72 in the final college basketball game played at Pitt Pavilion, the basketball facility inside Pitt Stadium. In March 1970, the Panthers rallied from nineteen points down in the first half to beat WVU, 92-87, in the last game at the old WVU Field House. Pitt later defeated WVU in the final college football game at Three Rivers Stadium in 2000, and later downed the Mountaineers in the last basketball game at Fitzgerald Field House in 2002.

Pitt traveled to Morgantown on Friday, November 9, 1979 and set up headquarters at the Holiday Inn adjacent to the WVU Coliseum. The Panthers and Mountaineers would meet in the final game at old Mountaineer Field the following day, and Morgantown was in a festive mood. The Mountaineers, in what would also be Frank Cignetti's last home game as head coach, were prohibitive underdogs against Pitt, but that did not discourage the locals from raising a little hell leading up to the game. Jackie Sherrill got in the act, sporting a "Beat Pitt" button" on the lapel of his sport coat while moving through the hotel the afternoon before the game. Mark May said: "Their [West Virginia] fans hated us with a passion. The night before the game, out in the parking lot at the hotel, people were making noise until four in the morning. They were partying, yelling, anything they could do to try to disturb us."

The rowdiness and emotion carried into Saturday at the dilapidated, dated football stadium in what was Dan Marino's first road start. In the West Virginia radio booth, adjacent to and visible from the booth where Bill Hillgrove and Johnny Sauer would be calling the game for Pitt fans, Sandy Yakim, who served as spotter for her father, WVU announcer Jack Fleming, was sobbing uncontrollably as the West Virginia band conducted its pregame show. Fleming, who grew up in Morgantown and graduated from WVU, had a lifetime hatred of Pitt, even when he eventually moved to Pittsburgh and served many years as radio voice of the Steelers.

Following a scoreless first quarter, Pitt took a 10-0 lead on a field goal by Mark Schubert and a short touchdown plunge by Rooster Jones. At halftime, WVU officials decided to open the gates to everyone, allowing fans mingling outside the stadium to enter and fend for themselves as far as seating or standing room. During the second half, rows of people crammed the sidelines to view the action.

In the third quarter, WVU closed the gap to 10-3 on a field goal by Steve Sinclair, whose father had played for Pitt in the late 1930s. Pitt extended the lead to 17-7 when Marino hit Benjie Pryor from eight yards out. Shifty Mountaineer quarterback Oliver Luck, who gave Pitt trouble all afternoon with his running ability, threw a touchdown pass to Cedric Thomas, but a short scoring run by Fred Jacobs in the fourth quarter gave the Panthers a comfortable 24-10 lead. JoJo Heath made a key interception of a Luck pass to thwart another WVU drive. The final score was 24-17. After the game, fans went to work scavenging for whatever souvenirs they could detach from their moorings of the historic facility.

"It was an exciting game," Jackie Sherrill told the assembled press. "Probably a little more exciting than I would have liked."

Pitt raised its record to 9-1 with a convincing 40-0 victory against Army the following week at West Point. Pitt's defense held the Cadets to a scant 67 yards of total offense. Marino passed for 272 yards and a touchdown strike to Ralph Still. Running back Fred Jacobs showed off his throwing arm by hitting Kenny Bowles from 33 yards as Pitt stormed to a 28-0 lead at halftime. Rooster Jones ran for a pair of touchdowns and Randy McMillan added another. Mark Schubert kicked two field goals and freshman J. C. Pelusi registered a quarterback sack for a safety.

After the game, the 9-1 Panthers accepted a bid to play Arizona in the Fiesta Bowl on Christmas Day. The team had an open date before its December 1 game at Penn State.

The 1979 Pitt-Penn State game, played on a cold, sunny day at Beaver Stadium, lacked the national implications of the most recent games in the series. The Nittany Lions entered the contest with a 7-3 record and a No. 19 national ranking. The Panthers were No. 11. Penn State had lost to Texas A&M, Nebraska, and Miami, and had been playing without injured star defensive linemen Bruce Clark and Matt Millen, an advantage Pitt would exploit. But the game, as usual, was not without some controversy, this time because of an earlier comment Joe Paterno made that he thought had been off the record.

During his heyday as coach of the NFL's Green Bay Packers, Vince Lombardi customarily hosted a social gathering of media members, both from Green Bay and any visiting writers or broadcasters who had come to town to cover the game. The confab was held a night or two before that weekend's games, and it provided an opportunity for the media to engage Lombardi in conversation in a relaxed atmosphere away from the strict guidelines around the practice field and locker room.

Joe Paterno instituted a similar party during his time as Penn State's coach, the function usually taking place at the stately Nittany Lion Inn on campus. At one such gathering in 1979, a media member asked Paterno if and when he might retire from coaching. Thinking his response was strictly confidential, Paterno emphasized he had no such plans, especially because he did not want to leave the collegiate coaching profession "to the Barry Switzers and Jackie Sherrills" of the world.

A Pittsburgh writer told Sherrill what Paterno had said, and Sherrill decided to bring it up with Paterno on the field prior to the game at Beaver Stadium.

"Joe came up to me and said something to the effect that he wasn't aware of how young our team was," Sherrill recalled. "As he was walking away, I said, 'Joe, it's too bad you're not going to retire and leave college football to the Barry Switzers and Jackie Sherrills.' He turned around and said, 'Where'd you hear that?' I said, 'You said it last night, Joe.' He said, 'You'd probably like for me to retire, wouldn't you?' I said, 'It'd make things a whole lot easier for me if you did.'"

Pitt's 29-14 victory was not as close as the score indicated. The Panthers made twenty-two first downs to Penn State's eleven. The Nittany Lions' two touchdowns came on a 54-yard run by Matt Suhey and a 95-yard kickoff return by Curt Warner. They had no sustained scoring drive. Pitt dominated the line of scrimmage.

"And no one would dare suggest the Panther lines, on offense and defense, did not simply beat up on Penn State," Bob Smizik wrote for *The Pittsburgh Press*.

"They knocked us off the ball," said Joe Paterno. "They blocked us very well. They were obviously ready to play."

Dan Marino, playing in his first Pitt-Penn State game, passed for 279 yards and one touchdown. With Pitt leading 23-14 in the fourth quarter and the ball at midfield, Randy McMillan took a short pass in the flat and raced across the field for a touchdown. McMillan, Pitt's leading rusher in 1979, also gained 114 yards on twenty-six carries, bearing the bulk of Pitt's attack in the victory. His teammates had come to expect that level of excellence. Mark May said:

Randy had a great sense of humor. He was always joking a little bit, but when he was on the field, you could tell how good he was. When he started running over people and running through people, you knew he was something special. We knew once we had him, we had no issues when we had short yardage and goal line situations. When we needed a tough yard, he was gonna get it, but he also had the speed to pick up first downs. He was a special back.

McMillan scored Pitt's three touchdowns, and Mark Schubert kicked three field goals as Pitt defeated Penn State for the first time in Happy Valley since 1955. Sherrill could not resist taking a dig when asked after the game if Penn State had been Pitt's toughest opponent. "Penn State has a lot of good players and we were very impressed with them" said Sherrill. "But I would think that Washington might have better overall personnel."

At least two Pitt players shared Sherrill's belief while talking to reporters.

"Washington was our biggest win," said Greg Mesiner. "This one was nice, but Washington proved we were a good team. People were saying we couldn't beat a good team, but when we beat Washington we beat a good team."

"When we beat Washington, we showed another section of the country how good we are," said Hugh Green. "We beat a Pac Ten team, and that was something."

Pitt was about to face another Pac Ten team, Arizona, in the Fiesta Bowl in Tempe. The Wildcats were coached by Farrell, Pa. native and Clarion University graduate Tony Mason. In later years, Mason would work as a sideline reporter during Pitt's football radio broadcasts. In 1979, Mason was in his third, and final, season as coach at Arizona.

The Wildcats finished the regular season with a 6-4-1 record that included a three-game losing streak. Prior to the Fiesta Bowl, Arizona had defeated rival Arizona State in its most recent game.

The Pitt offense struggled in the Fiesta Bowl. The Panthers could generate only three Mark Schubert field goals and a touchdown pass from Marino to Benjie Pryor, but they were enough to defeat Arizona, 16-10. Pitt never trailed in the game.

The 1979 Panthers finished the season with an 11-1 record. Only the 1976 national champions (12-0) had won as many games. Hugh Green was named a first team All-American, and the Panthers ended the season ranked No. 6 and No. 7 by Associated Press and United Press International.

Pitt found itself closer to the top, ranked No. 3 (AP) and No. 4 (UPI) prior to the 1980 season. Before that, however, came a whirlwind of offseason activity. The Pirates and Steelers were coming off championships, and with sixteen starters returning, the Panthers were positioned to make a strong push toward another national championship.

Dan Marino appeared on the cover of *Pittsburgh Magazine*. And *Sports Illustrated*, selecting Pitt as its preseason No. 1 team, flew Hugh Green to Los Angeles for a cover shoot. "People think you walk in, sit down and they take a picture," Green remembered. "That's not how it works."

The memorable cover shot has Green in his blue Pitt game jersey with arms folded, with a live black panther appearing over his right shoulder. The title read "BADDEST CAT IN THE GAME: Hugh Green of the No. 1 Pitt Panthers."

"Orpheus was a female cat," said Green. "She was a very mature cat, but also a pain in the butt. She tore two of my jerseys. At one point I told the handlers that if she kept acting up, I was gonna put my helmet on. I actually walked off the set two or three times."

After five tedious hours of shooting, *Sports Illustrated* had its shot. Green flew back to Pittsburgh.

"I wasn't there for the shoot, but Hugh told me it scared the heck out of him," said Dean Billick, who made the arrangements for the session with the magazine. "Hugh was really unsure of that whole situation."

That was not the only plane trip Green made to help stir interest in Pitt prior to the 1980 season. He and Mark May flew with Jackie Sherrill in a small plane to a Golden Panthers function in the eastern part of the state. They were not aware that Sherrill, a licensed pilot, was going to fly them back. Mark May said: "Not a lot was said during the flight. It was a white-knuckle trip, and we were happy as hell when that thing landed. I think we damn near clapped. That was the first—and last—time that I flew with Coach Sherrill as the pilot."

"A Potential Powerhouse" was the title of Pitt's 1980 outlook in the team's media guide. With a veteran nucleus back, including a pair of experienced quarterbacks in Rick Trocano and Dan Marino, and the entire starting front five of its defensive line, the optimism was warranted. "We will obviously be a senior-dominated football team," said Sherrill. "Our fellows have been together for four years. They've played well together; they've molded together."

The defensive line of Green, Jackson, Meisner, Boyarsky, and Neill received special praise from Pitt's coaches. "Up front, the down five people have been together for a long time, and they are a great group of players," said Sherrill.

"They all have great passion for football," said Foge Fazio many years later. "They were tough guys—mentally and physically. Nothing bothered them. If they were in a situation where their backs were to the wall, it didn't faze them."

Jimbo Covert made the move from defense to offensive tackle. Mark May was set on the opposite side and senior Russ Grimm was a future pro at center. Emil Boures, Ron Sams, and Rob Fada alternated at the guard positions.

Pitt's coaching staff was largely unchanged in 1980. Joe Pendry had left Pitt for a position at Michigan State, and was replaced by Joe Daniels, who, like Pendry, had been coaching at West Virginia. Joe Moore was finally coaching the offensive line from the start of the season. A pair of young, aspiring coaches—Bob Davie and Kirk Ferentz—joined the staff for the 1980 season.

Highlighting Pitt's crop of freshman recruits for 1980 was running back, basketball standout and track star Dwight Collins from Beaver Falls High School. Other key freshmen from the Pittsburgh area were quarterback/safety Tom Flynn (Penn Hills) and Seton LaSalle High School offensive lineman Jim Sweeney. Bill Maas was a rugged defensive lineman from Newtown Square, Pa., and Pitt went to Miami, Fla., to sign running back Joe McCall.

With the personnel in place, Rick Trocano wondered what his role would be in his senior season. Wanting to play quarterback, but realizing that Dan Marino was going to be the starter, Trocano paid a visit to Sherrill's office. "I asked if I could be moved to defense," Trocano recalled. "He [Sherrill] asked if I had ever played there. I lied. I told him I'd been All State as a safety in high school. I'd never played any position but quarterback."

Sherrill had a fib of his own for Trocano, and he would use it at a crucial point in the season.

ABC broadcast Pitt's 1980 season opener against Boston College at Pitt Stadium on September 13. Marino threw a pair of touchdown passes to Benjie Pryor in Pitt's 14-6 victory. Pryor caught ten passes, while linebacker Steve Fedell made eleven tackles and cornerback Terry White intercepted two passes. Adversity struck as Pitt lost two offensive playmakers, flanker Barry Compton and running back Larry Sims to knee injuries. Both would be lost for the season. The injuries forced Pitt's coaches to move Dwight Collins to flanker, where he had an outstanding season.

The Pitt defense was dominant in an 18-3 win against Kansas on a hot, windy day in Lawrence. The Jayhawks could garner only 86 yards of total offense while Pitt rolled up 456. In his first collegiate start, Collins caught a 43-yard halfback pass from Artrell Hawkins. Marino added touchdown passes to tight ends Pryor and Mike Dombrowski. Steve Fedell registered Pitt's final points when he tackled Kansas quarterback Larry Kemp for a safety in the fourth quarter.

The Panthers stretched their overall winning streak to thirteen games with a 36-2 victory against Temple at Pitt Stadium. Dan Marino threw three touchdown passes in the first half before leaving the game in the second quarter because of a twisted knee. Danny Daniels and Rick Trocano finished the game. Pitt's coaches understood they had an insurance policy in Rick Trocano at quarterback; Trocano said:

> I was a senior, so I was experienced already. We had the same offense, so there wasn't a big learning curve. The coaches were smart enough to keep me sharp enough that just in case I was needed, I could come back and play quarterback. The defenses really couldn't do anything to confuse me. I'd seen it all by then.

Throughout training camp and the first few weeks of the 1980 season, Trocano had been taking snaps at quarterback, usually before the start of practice. "I was taking some snaps, but not many because I was the starting free safety," Trocano remembered. "I had to practice on defense because the free safety had to make the calls to change the secondary as teams shifted or went into motion."

After limiting Temple to 65 yards rushing, Pitt's next opponent was expected to provide a more formidable challenge. Maryland came to Pitt Stadium featuring star running back Charlie Wysocki, but he gained only 38 yards on nineteen carries. Pitt played its best game to date, winning 38-9. Marino threw touchdown passes to Collins and Willie Collier in the first quarter for an early 14-0 lead. Randy McMillan then ran for a score and Marino hit Collins for another touchdown in the fourth quarter.

Pitt traveled to Tallahassee to play Florida State in a night game on October 11, 1980. It was a homecoming for many of Pitt's players from the South. It was an opportunity for their family and friends to visit with them at the Holiday Inn where the team was staying. The mood around the swimming pool was content and casual, and Jackie Sherrill was left wondering if his team was ready to play the Seminoles, who had upset

Nebraska on the road the week before. "There were too many distractions when we got down there for that game," Sherrill said. "I should have had the team stay out of town, isolated from everything that was going on. We were not ready to play that night. I could sense it before that game."

Before a Doak Campbell Stadium record crowd of 52,894, the Panthers seemed very ready to play at the outset. Hugh Green sacked Seminole quarterback Rick Stockstill deep inside FSU territory on the first series. A few plays later, Marino hit Collins from 39 yards out to give Pitt a 7-0 lead, but the Panthers trailed 23-7 at halftime. Strong safety Carlton Williamson and cornerback Terry White missed the game with injuries, and Seminole running back Sam Platt gained 123 yards on the ground, the only player to top 100 yards against Pitt in the regular season.

The rowdy Florida State crowd had an effect on Marino. "Early in the game, Danny asked the one official for help with the crowd," Sherrill recalled, "which he [official] did. But he told Danny, 'you will run the play the next time.'"

Bill Capece kicked five field goals and punter Rohn Stark kept Pitt backed up by averaging 48 yards on seven punts. "Talk about the importance of special teams," noted Bob Smizik, who covered the game for *The Pittsburgh Press*. "Pitt found out the hard way that night."

The Seminoles began only one of their seven scoring drives in Florida State territory. The bitter 36-22 loss snapped Pitt's fourteen-game winning streak and dealt a severe blow to its hopes for a national championship.

Pitt celebrated Homecoming the following week by welcoming West Virginia to Pitt Stadium. The Mountaineers had a new coach in 1980. Don Nehlen had been an assistant coach at Michigan before accepting the job at WVU, replacing Frank Cignetti who had been let go after the 1979 season.

The Mountaineers took an early 7-0 lead on a touchdown pass from Oliver Luck to Cedric Thomas. Pitt fans had to be concerned about another upset loss, especially when Dan Marino had to leave the game with a knee injury in the first quarter. With Danny Daniels at quarterback, Pitt tied the game on a touchdown run by Joe McCall. The second quarter was all Rick Trocano. The free safety jumped from defense to offense and directed the Panthers to four touchdowns in five minutes to give Pitt a 35-7 halftime lead. The Panthers won, 42-14. Rick Trocano recalled a conversation with the coaches:

> The coaches turned to me and said, "Can you help?" And I was ready to
> go. Playing free safety I learned about defensive backs and where they

were supposed to be. I could recognize better when a defensive back was out of position. That was one of the nice things I was able to glean from having played defense.

The player Trocano replaced at quarterback had special words for the senior after the game. "Ricky [Trocano] does things that no one else in the country could do," Dan Marino told reporters. "He just amazes me. No one in the country knows more about our offense and defense than Rick Trocano."

Mark May said:

It was fun, because we kind of missed Rick and his attitude because he was a free flowing guy who liked to have a lot of fun. We knew that, in his heart, he loved to play quarterback. But the bottom line was that he wanted to win, to contribute, and that's why he went to defense.

Rick Trocano's career as a defensive back was over. He returned as Pitt's starting quarterback for the remainder of the 1980 season.

Jackie Sherrill took his fourth Pitt team to Knoxville to face John Majors' fourth University of Tennessee edition. It would be the first time Sherrill and Majors would compete against each other as head coaches. In 1991, Majors and Tennessee defeated Sherrill's first Mississippi State team, 26-24, in Knoxville. But the 1980 matchup was especially intriguing to Pitt fans—and to Rick Trocano, who had been recruited by Majors and Tennessee. In fact, when Trocano was in Pittsburgh in 2019 for Pitt's Hall of Fame Induction ceremony on September 20 at Petersen Events Center, he was shocked when Majors—one of that year's inductees—recognized and addressed him at the event. Majors knew Trocano as a quarterback from (Brooklyn) Ohio. Majors' quarterback at Tennessee in 1980 was another Ohioan, Jeff Olszewski from Parma.

Minutes before kickoff at Neyland Stadium, Sherrill approached Trocano on the sideline and told him that, during the recruiting season in 1977, Majors had remarked that Olszewski was a better prospect than Trocano. Sherrill turned and walked away. The story was not true, but Trocano had no way of knowing. To him, it was vintage Jackie Sherrill. "He would say things to challenge you," said Trocano. "But his bark was always worse than his bite."

In his first start at quarterback in more than a year, Trocano led the Panthers to a convincing 30-6 win against the Volunteers. He directed Pitt to 489 total yards, with 252 rushing, and 237 passing. Joe McCall and Randy McMillan scored rushing touchdowns to give Pitt a 16-6 halftime lead. Tennessee's only score came on a 100-yard kickoff return by track star Willie Gault. Trocano turned a broken play into a 31-yard touchdown run in the third quarter and McMillan finished the scoring with his second touchdown of the day in the final period.

Majors praised Trocano along with Pitt's backs and receivers, during his postgame meeting with the press, but was more disappointed in how his team had played. "It was a game of many mistakes and breaks, and we outmistaked them," said Majors. "We continue to have problems with continuity. We cannot move the ball with any consistency, but can only get some bits and pieces."

Pitt visited Syracuse's new Carrier Dome for the first time on November 1, 1980 and dominated the Orange 43-6 in their finest performance to date. Syracuse coach Frank Maloney had a surprise for the Panthers, having his offense start the game using no huddle, an uncommon strategy at the time. But the trickery made no difference, as Pitt beat Syracuse for the eighth consecutive time. "A good many of these eye filling Panthers should be playing on *The NFL Today*, rather than wasting their Saturdays just earning block letters," according to Arnie Burdick in the *Syracuse Herald-American*.[2]

Pitt's defense was superb, holding running back Joe Morris to 15 yards on twelve carries. Offensively, Randy McMillan scored on runs of 39 and 45 yards to help Pitt build a 26-6 halftime lead. Trocano threw a pair of touchdown passes to Dwight Collins, and a third to Joe McCall. Pitt totaled 500 yards in total offense in raising its record to 7-1. After the win, Pitt was ranked No. 8 by AP and No. 9 by UPI.

Hugh Green, Mark May, Rick Trocano, and the rest of Pitt's senior class hosted Louisville on November 8 for the final home game of their careers. The Panthers were undefeated at Pitt Stadium during the 1978, 1979, and 1980 seasons.

It did not start well. The Cardinals took an early 9-0 lead, but the Panthers overpowered Louisville afterward, leading 20-9 at halftime and extending it to 41-9 before the visitors scored a pair of late, meaningless touchdowns. Louisville could take some consolation in knowing it was one of only two teams—Florida State was the other—that scored at least twenty points against Pitt in 1980. In fact, in its twelve games, the Panthers held nine of their opponents to single digits.

Julius Dawkins returned seven punts for 105 yards, while Trocano threw two touchdown passes to Dwight Collins. But the real story of the day was the halftime ceremony in which Hugh Green's jersey No. 99 was retired. Cas Myslinski and Jackie Sherrill presided over the ceremony, which provided public address announcer Roger Huston a special opportunity to give a special rendition of his signature "HUUUUGGHH" Green call:

> I liked to have fun with names, exaggerate them where appropriate. Names such as Ed Wilamowski. Sal Sunseri, Hugh Green. I remembered the baseball player, [Baltimore Oriole] Boog Powell. Fans would be calling out, Boog! Boog! So it got to where whenever Hugh Green made a tackle, I'd say, "Stop made by number ninety-nine, and the fans would say, Hugh!" And I'd finish just by saying, "Green!"

Green's teammates and those associated with the program developed a special appreciation for Green, his playing ability, and his personality.

"Hugh was a dominating player, but very humble," said Alex Kramer. "He received a lot of publicity, but he carried it very well. He was never arrogant, self-assured, and got along very well with his teammates."

"His motor was unbelievable," said Bill Hillgrove. "He had the great natural strength to keep the blockers off his legs, and that was one of his keys to success."

"Hugh was a little different," said Mark May. "He was really quiet off the field. He didn't say a lot. When he did say something, he was like one of those E. F. Hutton commercials; you listened."

Greg Meisner noted: "Beside his speed and quickness, to this day I have never seen anybody engage in a block, get off a block as quickly as he could. He had great lateral and open field speed, and he was just naturally strong. His instincts were relentless, and he practiced like he played."

"The fame that he earned never caused him to be an egotist, or to think of himself first, or to promote himself," said Alex Kramer. "He was so good, consistently, that the extraordinary would have been ordinary for him."

Green's football excellence had Dean Billick and his sports information staff working hard to bring Pitt its second Heisman Trophy winner in four years. It would not be easy. A defensive player had not won the Heisman since a two-way player, Turtle Creek, Pa.'s Leon Hart at Notre Dame in 1949. Promoting Green would be different from the campaign in Dorsett's behalf. Billick said: "In Hugh's case, we knew it was an uphill battle because he was a defensive player. He wasn't a quarterback or running back with glaring statistics. He wasn't in a position of high visibility. We actually had to work a lot harder, and spend more resources, spend more time, working for Hugh."

Billick and his staff produced a huge promotional poster endorsing Green's candidacy. It featured Green, posed in uniform holding his helmet, along with quotes about him from opposing coaches, a long list of Green's honors and a message about why a defensive player could and should win the Heisman. The sports information staff then used green felt tip pens to write a short note to be included in the envelopes in which the posters were to be sent around the country. Billick stated:

> It culminated to me on a Sunday on one of the NFL pregame shows when one of the announcers rolled this poster out for everyone to see, and the person said, "This Hugh Green guy should win the Heisman just because of the creativity of the people at Pitt." That made me feel good. I felt a lot of pride in that. That poster got a lot of attention.

Before the Heisman balloting was complete, Pitt had road games at Army and Penn State on the schedule. The Panthers easily dispatched Army, 40-0, scoring four touchdown in the first quarter. Dwight Collins and Willie Collier caught touchdown passes from Trocano, while Wayne DiBartola and Artrell Hawkins ran for touchdowns. Dan Marino, seeing his first action since being injured in the West Virginia game four weeks earlier, threw for a personal high 292 yards and two touchdowns. Rickey Jackson blocked a punt and had an interception, earning *Sports Illustrated* Defensive Player of the Week honors.

Both Pitt and Penn State were 9-1 heading into a showdown on November 28 at Beaver Stadium, Pitt's third consecutive visit to Happy Valley. The Panthers and Nittany Lions were third and fourth, respectively, in AP's poll, and each team still had hopes of winning the national championship, but they needed outside help. Georgia sat atop the ranking at No. 1 with a 10-0 record. The Bulldogs, champions of the Southeastern Conference, had their invitation to the Sugar Bowl secured, where they would face Notre Dame. After bowl invitations were extended, Georgia defeated Georgia Tech, and Notre Dame lost at Southern California, something that would grate on Pitt for many years.

ABC's top announcing crew of Keith Jackson and Ara Parseghian were at Penn State to call the action on a cold, dark day. Jackson was prophetic when he was previewing the game just minutes before kickoff. "We might wind up in one of those kind of games where the last team to make a mistake loses the ballgame."

Parseghian, the former Notre Dame coach, recognized the strength of Pitt's defense. "As far as defense is concerned, it's rare to see as many good football players as Pittsburgh has on its team," said Parseghian.

Pitt went into the game leading the nation in both total and rushing defense, and had not allowed a touchdown on the ground until the eighth game (Syracuse) of the season. Penn State's defense also was stellar, but Pitt's unit, with its back to the wall throughout much of the second half, saved the 14-9 victory for the Panthers on a day when the offense, particularly in the second half, had trouble moving the ball.

Penn State scored first on a 27-yard field goal by Herb Menhardt, but in the second quarter, facing third and fourteen from the Penn State forty-eight, Trocano was able to loft a short pass just over the hand of defensive tackle Frank Case and into the waiting arms of Randy McMillan, who galloped to the 16. Trocano said:

That was one of those plays where everything slowed down. I remember thinking to myself, "I gotta get this ball over his hand and into McMillan's hands." If you can, you just caught the defensive player out of position, and you have a fantastic play. That was inches away from being a disaster.

On the next play, Trocano found Benjie Pryor backing into the end zone for the game's first touchdown. Pitt led 7-3, and that is how the half ended.

Pitt caught a break on the first play of the second half when Tom Flynn recovered Curt Warner's fumble at the Lions' 36. The drive stalled, and Dave Trout came in to attempt a field goal. The kick was good, but Penn State's Rich D'Amico was called for roughing the kicker. Jackie Sherrill took the penalty, taking the three points off the board. Two plays later, Trocano crossed everybody up, calling his own number from the Penn State 9. "It was a naked bootleg play," said Trocano. "The only person who knew I was gonna keep the ball was me. We had some plays up our sleeve."

With Pitt leading 14-3 late in the third quarter, Penn State faced a fourth and one at Pitt's fourteen. Joe Paterno sent Joel Coles into the game. Coles took a pitch right from quarterback Todd Blackledge, and appeared to want to throw an option pass. Coles hesitated, which was a fatal mistake; Hugh Green wrapped him up along the sideline for a loss on the play and Pitt took over on downs.

With a light snow beginning to fall, and darkness descending over Beaver Stadium, Trocano was intercepted on Pitt's ensuing possession.

Blackledge found Kenny Jackson in the end zone for a touchdown. The Lions' two-point conversion attempt failed, and the quarter ended with Pitt leading 14-9.

Jackie Sherrill replaced Trocano with Dan Marino early in the fourth quarter, but Marino could produce only one first down, on a crucial completion to Benjie Pryor from Pitt's 1-yard line. A long pass by Marino downfield was intercepted by Penn State's Pete Harris, which might have been advantageous for Pitt, considering the difficult time punter Dave Hepler had been having all afternoon.

With four minutes remaining, Penn State faced another fourth and one, this time at the Pitt 36. A blitzing Sal Sunseri forced Todd Blackledge to pitch the ball prematurely to Curt Warner. With the timing of the play disrupted, Carlton Williamson caught Warner in the backfield for a loss of three yards. Pitt took over on downs, but again failed to move the sticks. Penn State regained possession with time for one final drive. After scrambling for a first down on a fourth down play, and with fifty-eight seconds remaining, Blackledge hurried to the line of scrimmage and tossed a quick out pass toward the sideline. Carlton Williamson made the interception, sealing one of Pitt's most satisfying wins in the history of the Penn State series.

After the game, Blackledge explained that he was simply trying to throw the ball out of bounds. Williamson thought otherwise. "I think Blackledge was trying to make the completion," he said. "He didn't see me break out there. He never saw me."

"They weren't intimidated by us," said Jackie Sherrill. "But we were able to hang in there where a younger team might not."

"It was a double Excedrin game," remarked Hugh Green. "Lot of pounding, lot of limping and headaches afterward."

"It was hard-hitting, rock 'em, sock 'em football," Jerry Boyarsky added.

"I thought both defenses played great football," said Joe Paterno. "They attacked all day."

The defensive struggle, played in less than ideal conditions, produced some colorful descriptions from the writers who had witnessed it; Bob Smizik of *The Pittsburgh Press* noted:

Jock Sutherland would have loved it. Woody Hayes, wherever he is, is smiling. It was their kind of football game.

   On a day that Mother Nature would like to disown, Pitt and Penn State got together for a classic.[3]

"One of those great and gritty football games that mostly resemble two mean kids fighting in a mud puddle," Phil Musick wrote in *The Pittsburgh Post-Gazette*.[4]

"Pitt won it, 14-9, on a chill, grim day on which the weather matched the tempo of play, sullen and savage," Bill Lyon penned for *The Philadelphia Inquirer*.[5]

Douglas S. Looney of *Sports Illustrated* noted on December 8, 1980: "When the brutal hitting ceased, the No. 4-ranked Panthers had defeated the No. 5-ranked Nittany Lions on the strength of a defense that halted Penn State's running game and left the losers viewing the world through the ear holes of their helmets."[6]

"It was a classic Pitt-Penn State, slug it out," said Bill Hillgrove. "The Panthers prevailed. Of course, there was some ill will between Jackie and Joe, obviously."

Bob Smizik said:

> That was the greatest era in the history of the Pitt-Penn State rivalry. It was just fantastic. Some time prior to that, people would ridicule Eastern football, but back then Pitt and Penn State were equal to anybody. They were both nationally elite programs, and Pitt was actually better than Penn State for a good period of that time. The recruiting that Jackie and his staff did then was utterly remarkable. You talk about putting a wall around Allegheny County!

The win was Pitt's second straight against Penn State, the first time Pitt had beaten the Nittany Lions in consecutive seasons since 1948 and 1949. Pitt's seniors also could take pride in knowing—then and forever—that they were the only teams to beat Penn State in back to back seasons at Beaver Stadium during Joe Paterno's long term as head coach. Decades later, Penn State, as a member of the Big Ten Conference, would assume a posture of being unrivaled. But, by 2019, the men who comprised Pitt's football teams in the Jackie Sherrill years had no trouble explaining the significance of beating Penn State. Mark May recalled:

> It was very special to beat them because we heard about it all the time from people like Eddie Ifft and [Golden Panthers Director] Bob Heddleston. They were close to the team, and we knew how important it was to them for us to beat Penn State. Paterno and Jackie had a little

thing going. They [Penn State] thought they were better than we were for some reason.

Rick Trocano said:

To this day I consider Penn State our rival, and I'm sure every one of my teammates does. It's a shame we don't play them. Back then, you had similar talent on both sides of the ball. It's a tougher game at the line of scrimmage, for both teams, just because of the talent. Penn State was a great atmosphere for a game.

Greg Meisner said:

There was not a greater feeling in the world than beating Penn State at Penn State. To go into their house and beat them, if you talk to any of the guys, they would probably tell you the same thing. Playing them up there with all those people on a dark, dreary day after Thanksgiving. In fact, if I had it my way, we would play them up there every year. We didn't like Penn State. We still don't like 'em.

Meisner's hard feelings for the Lions continued during his career in the National Football League. "They [Penn State] had a lot of great players on that offensive line," he said. "Even in the pros, it was extra motivation for me to line up against a Penn State guy, because I didn't like 'em."

As the 1980 bowl season approached, Pitt needed three things to happen to win the national championship. First, it had beat South Carolina in the Gator Bowl. Second, it needed Florida State to lose to Oklahoma in the Orange Bowl. Finally, unbeaten Georgia had to fall to Notre Dame in the Sugar Bowl. The Panthers' stinging loss to Florida State lingered, but Pitt people still believed they, not Notre Dame, should have been in the Sugar Bowl. When both Pitt and Penn State were 9-1, bowl officials were reluctant to pick one, and end up with the loser in its game.

"The politics of the selection process worked against us," Hugh Green stated in 2019. "The bowls panicked and chose other teams. We were the best team in the country, but we didn't get a chance to show it."

Hugh Green received additional disappointing news when it was announced that South Carolina running back George Rogers had been voted recipient of the Heisman Trophy. Green said: "I knew what it was about. It was about paying your dues. I'd been an All-American for three years. Our team was known nationally. I had a heck of a senior year. When you've paid your dues, you feel like maybe your school [Pitt] is next in line to get it."

"He [Green] did come in second, and I thought that was a pretty good showing," said Dean Billick. "I felt good about the efforts that we made for Hugh."

Hugh Green and George Rogers traveled together as part of ABC's College Football Tour prior to the season. "That was about getting to know each other on a personal basis rather than just as football players," said Green.

Green, Rogers, and their respective teams would meet at the Gator Bowl in Jacksonville, Fla. On December 29, 1980. The Gamecocks entered the game with an 8-3 record, and were coached by Jim Carlen, who had been the head coach at West Virginia before Bobby Bowden.

Rogers, who rushed for 1,781 yards and fourteen touchdowns in the regular season, fumbled on the first play of the game, and Pitt recovered. Rick Trocano scored from a yard out and the rout was on. Pitt put on an impressive display of offensive and defensive football in beating South Carolina, 37-9. A Dave Trout field goal extended the lead to 10-0 after one quarter. Trocano and Marino split duty at quarterback. Trocano threw a pair of touchdown passes and Marino added one. Randy McMillan, playing in his final game for Pitt, ran for 59 yards and two touchdowns. Another running back in his last collegiate game, senior Artrell Hawkins carried the ball nine times for 50 yards.

George Rogers rushed for 113 yards on twenty-seven carries, but did much of his damage after the game had been decided, and he failed to reach the end zone.

A few days later, Oklahoma defeated Florida State, handing the Seminoles their second loss, but Georgia got past Notre Dame 17-10 in the Sugar Bowl to complete a 12-0 season and finish the season ranked No. 1. Pitt was second in both wire service polls. *The New York Times*, however, in its inaugural computer rankings of college football, selected Pitt as the No. 1 team in the nation.

"They lost to Florida State," Bob Smizik said in 2019. "You can't say they were the best team in the country. You can look back now and say it, but they had no complaints then. They had no ground to stand on."

Mark May, the big offensive tackle from the small town in upstate New York, was named an All-American, and won the prestigious Outland Trophy as the nation's outstanding interior lineman.

"He [May] is a bright, articulate young man whose head has not been turned by success, who says thank you and please, who respects his parents and who, on Saturday afternoons, blows away defensive linemen," wrote Bob Smizik in *The Pittsburgh Press*.

But Pitt's final position in the national rankings irked May, who said:

I'm still bitter about that. If we had the BCS or playoff system, obviously, we would have been there. We knew that we could play with any team in the country. We had that one blip [Florida State]. To win a national championship you have to have a little bit of luck. That season we felt we had the best team.

"I don't think enough has been made of the fact that *The New York Times* selected Pitt as the national champion," said Alex Kramer. "I think that is unappreciated."

Three Pitt players—Green, May, and Randy McMillan—were chosen in the first round of the NFL Draft. A total of twelve Panthers were selected overall, including eleven in the first five rounds, the greatest draft class in school history. Especially impressive was that all five members of the defensive line were taken, and each made his NFL team in 1981. It was a special group of players.

"The common denominator was football," said May. "We knew we had to work hard together, and everything just fell into place for us. We were one big family."

"We never had, and I would have noticed it, any animosity among the members of the team," said Alex Kramer. "That goes back to Jackie and the chemistry on the team. They melded into several powerful teams."

"When you win, you win because of the players, and the chemistry with our players was very good," said Sherrill.

Greg Meisner was especially close to his line mates. He can remember Jerry Boyarsky's parents bringing platters and trays of Polish food to their hotel suite for the players to enjoy after home games. Meisner's parents hosted players at their home for meals, as did Sal Sunseri's mother.

"We never wanted to let our teammates, the guys next to us, down," explained Meisner. "Jerry Boyarsky was as tough as they come. He would create a new line of scrimmage backward." He continued:

If you wanted to make a clinic reel on how to play the defensive tackle position, Bill Neill was that guy. He never gambled. He did everything he was supposed to do. Rickey Jackson was like having a defensive tackle at a standup position. He was athletic enough to drop into pass coverage or rush the passer. He could play head up on a tackle, if needed.

The camaraderie extended well beyond the playing field. Following the end of the 1979 regular season and before Pitt's trip to Arizona for the Fiesta Bowl, Meisner took several of his teammates to his family's hunting cabin in Emporium, Pa. It was bear season. Pitt's coaches did not know that the players had gone. Jackie Sherrill, of course, got wind of it, and sent assistant coach Bob Matey in search of the hunters. Meisner recalled:

> There was no GPS navigation system or cell phones or anything like that back then. Matey had no idea where our camp was. He was driving all through the mountains looking for us. He eventually found us. We didn't have any practices scheduled, so we decided to go. And I got a bear.

Meisner and fellow nature lover Boyarsky kept the line of scrimmage lively by making bear calls to each other during the games. "It would echo inside Pitt Stadium," said Meisner. "Our opponents thought we were nuts."

Their own teammates knew it when, one night at a party at Jackie Sherrill's house, Meisner, on a bet, swallowed a large worm ('night crawler" as Meisner identified it). "The crazy part was I could feel it moving around inside my stomach for a little while." Not to be upstaged, Boyarsky did the same thing a few minutes later.

Meisner also liked to hunt for rattlesnakes, but he was not all fun and games. He earned Academic All-America honors during his time at Pitt.

Hugh Green was not too keen on the hijinks. He likes to remember his teammates for how they performed on the football field, rather than the wilds of Pennsylvania. He said: "Boyarsky was all muscle and meat. Meisner was about speed and quickness. Bill Neill was Mr. Technique. Rickey Jackson was like me; the Southern Force. That was our defense—Northern Strength and Southern Speed."

The five linemen understood their opponents' strategy. "We usually knew what the other team wanted to do," said Green, "and that was to run away from me." Green continued:

> We had very good linebackers in Sal [Sunseri] and [Steve] Fedell. We called Carlton Williamson "The Hammer." Lynn Thomas and Terry White were very good on the corners. We called [safety] Tom Flynn or

Miracle Boy because he started as a freshman when Trocano went back to quarterback.

"We had a good reputation," said Meisner. "We had the best defense in the country, and that just added to it. All the personalities you had on that defensive line made it what it was."

"I used to kid Carlton Williamson, telling him he'd be the next mayor of Atlanta [his hometown]," said Alex Kramer. "He ended up being an executive in the Waffle House chain."

Kramer also was fond of wide receiver Willie Collier, who, along with kicker Snuffy Everett, led Pitt's teams of that era in Pitt buttons, ribbons and paraphernalia worn on a daily basis.

Bob Smizik took special pleasure in seeing how Rick Trocano's Pitt career ended:

You kind of rooted for him. Guys would transfer today [2019] if they lost their job to Dan Marino. Rick was a good athlete. His dad was around a lot. I remember talking to his dad after the Gator Bowl, how pleased and happy his dad was that it worked out for him, and how proud he was.

Rick Trocano and the rest of the superb 1980 senior class were gone. It was generally conceded that 1981 would be a transitional year for Pitt. Jackie Sherrill even remarked that the Panthers were probably a year away from competing for the national championship.

Sherrill hired two new assistant coaches for 1981. George Pugh, who had played at Alabama, had been an assistant coach at New Mexico. Pugh would coach Pitt's tight ends. Andy Urbanic, most recently the head coach at Penn Hills High School in suburban Pittsburgh, joined Sherrill's staff, and coached the running backs.

Then there was the new football player, also from Penn Hills, who signed up to be a member of Pitt's program after the 1980 season. At 6 feet, 5 inches and 265 pounds, Bill Fralic was one of the area's most decorated scholastic athletes. The Dial Male National Athlete of the Year, Fralic also was a heavyweight wrestling champion. He lettered in football as a sophomore at Penn Hills, the first player ever to do so. He developed a passion for weightlifting at an early age, and became the subject of an intensive recruiting battle between Pitt and Penn State.

The summer before Fralic entered Penn Hills, he had caddied for Jackie Sherrill at Alcoma Country Club, where Fralic's mother worked as a waitress. Not familiar with Fralic, and thinking he was a college player, Sherrill asked the youngster when he had to report for training camp.

Years after leaving Pitt, Fralic admitted that, as a kid, he rooted for Penn State ("I had an affinity for Lions") in its annual grudge match with Pitt. But Fralic signed with Pitt, and was the cornerstone of its strong offensive lines for four years, although there was some debate initially as to where he would play.

Jackie Sherrill once stated that, in all his years of coaching, Bill Fralic was the only offensive lineman he had coached who was good enough to be a starter from the first day of practice as a freshman. "He [Fralic] had so much strength, and when he locked out on you, you're dead," said Sherrill. "He was groomed all the way up. His dad did a great job with him."

Fralic came to appreciate Sherrill, too. "There was no bullshit with him [Sherrill]," Fralic said in a 1998 interview. "He was very straightforward. He wasn't a rah-rah kind of coach. He let the assistants do their jobs. He was good at delegating."

Having lost its entire defensive line from 1980, Pitt's coaches considered having Fralic play there as a collegiate. It was decided he would play offensive tackle, replacing the departed Mark May. Jimbo Covert was set at the other tackle. Emil Boures moved from guard to center, while Ron Sams and Rob Fada were back at the guard positions, along with Paul Dunn.

Pitt's many lopsided wins in 1980 afforded the coaches an opportunity to play many players from the second defensive unit. Linemen Michael Woods, Bill Maas J. C. Pelusi, and Dave Puzzuoli stepped into starting roles in 1981, and were joined by a converted defensive back, Al Wenglikowski. An intriguing freshman prospect, York, Pa.'s Chris Doleman became a major contributor as a freshman. Junior linebacker Rick Kraynak moved in at linebacker opposite Sunseri, while secondary men Dan "Peep" Short and cornerbacks Tim Lewis and Wallace "Pappy" Thomas joined the starting lineup.

Senior linebacker Sal Sunseri and sophomore free safety Tom Flynn were the only starters returning from 1980.

"Before the season, Jackie Sherrill told us we were probably an eight and three team," said fullback Wayne DiBartola.

Most of the talk entering 1981 was about the offense, where Dan Marino was poised to have a record-setting season. A pair of juniors, wide receiver Julius Dawkins and tight end John Brown, also had breakout years.

As an established national power, Pitt was ranked No. 9 by AP and No. 8 by UPI as it hosted Illinois in the opening game. The Illini featured transfer quarterback Tony Eason, who was making his first start, but the day belonged to Dan Marino and Pitt. Collins and Dawkins each caught touchdown passes as Marino passed for 204 yards in Pitt's 26-6 win. Wayne DiBartola scored Pitt's first touchdown of the season on a 4-yard run set up by Tom Flynn's recovery of an Illinois fumble. Pitt's rebuilt defense was outstanding, limiting Illinois to 48 yards on thirty-three rushing attempts.

Following an off week, Mike Gottfried brought his Cincinnati Bearcats to Pitt Stadium on September 19. Pitt won easily, 38-7, as Marino threw five touchdown passes, including four to Dawkins, a Pitt record for touchdown receptions in a single game. Marino's five scoring passes tied a Pitt record. Pitt's surprisingly stout, young defense was dominant, holding the Bearcats to minus 28 yards rushing on forty-three attempts.

Pitt's October 3 game at South Carolina was selected as a regional telecast by ABC TV Keith Jackson and Frank Broyles called the game, and they witnessed a spectacular performance by Marino, Pitt's receivers, and the Panther defense. Marino completed twenty-four of thirty-nine passes for 346 yards and six touchdowns, breaking the record he had tied seven days earlier. John Brown and Julius Dawkins each caught a pair of touchdown passes and Barry Compton grabbed another. The Pitt defense registered eleven sacks of Gamecock quarterback Gordon Beckham,

With Pitt leading 28-0 at halftime, ABC officials made the decision to cut away from the telecast to a more competitive game. The Gamecocks mounted a comeback in the second half, testing the nerves of Pitt fans forced to listen to the game on the radio, but the network did not have the capability of returning to the game in Columbia, SC. The Panthers won, 42-28, without a rushing touchdown. After the game, South Carolina coach Jim Carlen remarked that Pitt's lack of a running game would prove costly later in the season. Broyles, the ABC analyst and former Arkansas coach, did not think so. "When you put Compton on one side, Brown at tight end and Dawkins on the other side, Marino throwing the football," said Broyles, "why run it?"

But the Gamecocks' comeback forced Pitt to pay a price. Marino sprained his right shoulder late in the fourth quarter. His status was questionable for the next week's game at West Virginia.

By that point in his career, Marino had considerable pull in running Pitt's offense. Sherrill stated: "At that time, Danny called all the plays at the line of scrimmage. He had the ability to do things that other people could not do.

He was very, very intelligent and knew where the ball was going. He could get rid of the ball, and he was, mentally and physically, a tough kid."

Pitt's coaches and players knew early in the week that Marino would not be able to play against West Virginia in Pitt's first game at the new Mountaineer Field. That meant preparing junior quarterback Danny Daniels for his first start—in a hostile environment against an undefeated opponent that was improving under coach Don Nehlen.

As Daniels prepared for his assignment, his roommate and fellow quarterback, D. J. Cavanaugh (Matt's younger brother), tried to relax Daniels. "He [Cavanaugh] just tortured me," said Daniels. "He told me I had nothing to worry about. 'It's just your first start in front of 50,000 people. Don't worry about it.'"

Jim Carlen would have been impressed by Pitt's 17-0 shutout of the Mountaineers. Danny Daniels played the entire game without completing a pass, and was intercepted once. Wayne DiBartola and Bryan Thomas ran for 103 and 99 yards, respectively as Pitt was content to play it conservatively while relying on its defense to shut down WVU. "We knew we weren't gonna throw the ball forty times, but in no way did we feel that we would throw it only six times," said Daniels.

"It was a big, big test in adversity, and we passed it," Jackie Sherrill remarked afterward.

"That was great," said Wayne DiBartola. "That was my first hundred-yard game at Pitt. Of course, I carried the ball a lot, and we had a nice offensive line."

West Virginia and senior quarterback Oliver Luck were held to 92 passing yards and the Mountaineers gained only 46 yards rushing on twenty attempts.

"I don't know where or how you can run on that [Pitt] defense," Don Nehlen said in postgame remarks. "I hope somebody writes me a letter if they know the secret. That defense is just murder."

The first quarter was scoreless. The Mountaineers threatened to take the lead in the second quarter when Curlin Beck was about to reach the end zone before a hit by Tom Flynn forced a fumble recovery in the end zone for a touchback. Late in the first quarter, Bryan Thomas broke loss for a 43-yard touchdown, even more impressive because he had to adjust his helmet that had come down over his eyes during the run; he remembered:

It was a sprint draw. As I took the ball and went through the line, one of the down linemen had grabbed my helmet or facemask, and I felt my head swivel. I was able to continue my momentum, trying to pull the facemask across my eyes so I could see. I was able to keep my balance enough where I was able to break into the secondary and just sprint to the end zone.

One of the most unusual, spectacular touchdown runs in Pitt history has never been seen by many Pitt fans. The game was not on live television.

The following night, a Sunday, Wayne and MaryLou DiBartola, Wayne's parents, invited Pitt's entire offensive line to their home in Whitehall, a suburban community in the South Hills area. "My mom made seven pans of lasagna, and it was all gone," said Pitt's fullback.

Up to No. 3 in both wire service polls, and trailing only Texas (No. 1) and Penn State (No. 2), the Panthers returned home looking to avenge their 1980 loss to Florida State. The Seminoles entered the game 3-1, and were coming off a 19-13 win against Notre Dame.

On a beautiful, sunny day, the Pitt offense put on an impressive display of balanced football. With Dan Marino healthy, the Panthers ran for 252 yards and passed for 251. Marino threw three touchdown passes, two to Julius Dawkins and one to Wayne DiBartola. Bryan Thomas rushed for 217 yards and a touchdown. Sal Sunseri scored on an interception return and Tom Flynn brought a punt back 63 yards in Pitt's 42-14 victory. Seminoles' coach Bobby Bowden, whose Florida State teams were 1-4 against Pitt during his time in Tallahassee, was especially impressed by Pitt's junior quarterback. "He [Marino] is a pro quarterback in college, really," said Bowden.

A big part of Marino's success during those years was the protection he received from his offensive line. The unit provided him with ample time to find an open receiver. And the man in charge of instructing that unit was Joe Moore, who in 1981 was in his second full season as offensive line coach. His unique personality and approach to football resonated with his players.

"When I first met Joe Moore, I thought he was crazy," said Mark May. "He was always chain smoking. He'd be trying to hide it from Coach Sherrill on the practice field. We all knew he was smoking off in the corner."

Bill Fralic noted: "I owe a lot to him [Moore]. He affected a lot of guys in a great way that went beyond football. He was very rough around the edges, but he had a heart of gold, and he really made guys want to be the best they could be."

Mark May said: "The thing about Joe was that it was always about continuity, about guys staying together and hanging together. You guys are a group together. He used to take us to The Pleasure Bar where we would all have fried mozzarella."

Moore recognized what he had in Bill Fralic. "Bill Fralic is the best," he said. "If you can find somebody better, bring him to me."

"He [Moore] was a great motivator, and he wasn't afraid to get up into your grille if you messed up," said May. "He was one of the guys who was instrumental in my career."

Bill Hillgrove recalls an early incident involving both Fralic and Joe Moore:

> When he [Fralic] was a freshman I tried to interview him, and I think Joe Moore jumped in and interceded and didn't want that to happen. I got him aside and said, "Look, Billy; this microphone and this camera? They're gonna end up making you a lot of money. So the sooner you give in to this process, the better off you're gonna be." He understood.

Penn State was No. 1 and Pitt No. 2 when Syracuse, a traditional thorn in Pitt's side at Pitt Stadium, came to Pittsburgh on October 24. The trend continued as the Orange took a 10-0 lead by the end of the first quarter. Pitt answered with a Snuffy Everett field goal and two touchdown passes from Marino to Brown and Dawkins for a 17-10 halftime lead. The only score by either team in the second half was a touchdown pass from Marino to Dwight Collins late in the game. Pitt won, 23-10, and maintained its national rankings.

An unknown freshman quarterback named Doug Flutie nearly upstaged Dan Marino and the undefeated Panthers when Pitt visited Boston College on October 31. Flutie passed for 347 yards and a pair of touchdowns and fell just short of spoiling Pitt's season. The Panthers won, 29-24, but had to hold off the pesky Flutie, who rallied the Eagles from a 29-10 deficit in the second half. Foge Fazio, Pitt's defensive coordinator, left his position in the coaches' booth and went down to the field to better assess the situation in the fourth quarter. BC had the ball with a chance to take the lead in the final minutes before Sal Sunseri put a stop to the comeback by intercepting a Flutie pass. Years later, Jackie Sherrill admitted that, if the game had lasted another few minutes, the Panthers likely would have lost.

The lead changed hands three times in the first half, which ended with Pitt leading 20-10. The Panthers scored on passes from Marino to John Brown and Dwight Collins, and an 11-yard run by Bryan Thomas. Pitt extended its lead to 29-10 on a safety and a short touchdown run to seemingly put the game away before Flutie passed for two touchdowns to produce the final score. Bryan Thomas was a workhorse for Pitt, carrying the ball twenty-seven times for 149 yards.

Meanwhile, at the Orange Bowl in Miami, No. 1 Penn State staged a second half rally of its own before falling to the Hurricanes, 17-14, in a driving rain. The loss, coupled with Pitt's win, put the Panthers atop the college football rankings seven weeks into the 1981 season.

Pitt won its fifteenth consecutive game the following week by defeating Rutgers, 47-3, on a cold, windy day at Giants Stadium in New Jersey. The Panthers' offense produced 544 total yards, including 315 on the ground. Bryan Thomas and Wayne DiBartola gained 168 and 105 yards, respectively and Dan Marino passed for two touchdowns and ran for a third. Pitt's defense held Rutgers to 161 total yards and only twelve first downs.

The Panthers held another opponent without a touchdown by blanking Army, 48-0, at Pitt Stadium a week later. Dan Marino passed for 282 yards and four touchdowns in becoming Pitt's all-time passing yardage leader. The Panthers scored seven touchdowns on the afternoon, including another four touchdown receptions by Julius Dawkins. Marino also set a school record for completions in a season. Pitt gained 566 yards in total offense to Army's 174.

That same day, Penn State lost to Alabama, 31-16, and fell to No. 13 and No. 14 in the next week's AP and UPI rankings.

Pitt recorded its third shutout of the season—and second straight—by defeating Temple 35-0 at Veterans Stadium. Barry Compton caught two passes from Marino in the first quarter to give Pitt a 14-0 lead. Bryan Thomas ran 19 yards for Pitt's third touchdown. Following a scoreless second quarter, the Panthers added single touchdowns in each of the final two periods when Marino hit Julius Dawkins and Keith Williams to produce the final score. It was Pitt's seventeenth consecutive win. More impressively, the Panthers were 31-1 in their last thirty-two games and, unlike the previous year, this time Pitt would get to meet Georgia at the Sugar Bowl in New Orleans. Only one game stood between the Panthers and an 11-0 record.

Pitt was 10-0, No. 1 in the nation and had won twenty consecutive games at Pitt Stadium when the Nittany Lions came to Pittsburgh for the November 28—Jackie Sherrill's thirty-eighth birthday—regular season finale. The Panthers were supremely confident entering the game.

"We felt that we were that much better than everybody else," said Wayne DiBartola. "We were the Number One team in the nation. We were feeling pretty good about ourselves. We were at our peak performance."

Portable bleachers had been set up on the running track to accommodate the overflow crowd of 60,260. It was a cold, blustery day, similar to the conditions the last time (1977) Penn State visited Pitt—and the last time Pitt had been defeated at home. Penn State crashed Pitt's party in a stunning 48-14 rout, not so surprising that Pitt lost the game, but by the manner in which it happened.

Pitt's defense held the Lions without a first down on their first three possessions, and Dan Marino led the Panthers on touchdown drives, mixing short and long passes, culminating in a pair of scoring strikes to Dwight Collins.

"Some people in the press box were laughing at Penn State at that point," remembered Bob Smizik. "They were kind of making fun of Joe [Paterno]."

Pitt led 14-0 at the start of the second quarter, and was driving for a possible third touchdown when Marino's pass was intercepted by Roger Jackson in the back of the end zone. Providing color commentary on the broadcast, former Texas coach Darrell Royal thought Marino was simply trying to throw the ball beyond the end zone, but did not throw it far enough. Television replay seemed to indicate that Jackson was beyond the line when he came down, and did not get either foot down in the field of play, but with no replay available in 1981, Penn State took over and scored forty-eight unanswered points.

The game was tied 14-14 at halftime, but Todd Blackledge connected with Kenny Jackson for two touchdown passes in the third quarter and the Panthers were helpless to stop the onslaught. Pitt did not help its cause by committing seven turnovers and being called for thirteen penalties. Trailing 28-14, the Panthers seemed to lose their poise.

"You had to wonder where the leadership was on that Pitt team in that game," said Bob Smizik.

"On offense and defense, we started trying to do things just to win the game right then," said defensive coordinator Foge Fazio. "We panicked. In the secondary, we had some guys going the wrong way, playing the wrong coverages"

Wayne DiBartola said: "Afterward, we were all stunned. Why didn't we just go back to the basics? We kept throwing deep passes, deep passes, deep passes. There's film footage of me, standing on a little route as an outlet, with thirty yards in front of me, and nobody around me. Bryan Thomas, too."

The 48-14 loss will haunt Pitt fans forever. The fact that it came against the school's most bitter football rival made it especially difficult to understand. One fact is overlooked by many Pitt fans when recalling that game; Penn State had an excellent team that year, a battle tested group a year away from a national title of its own. It had played Nebraska, Miami and Alabama, a trio of opponents a younger Pitt team could not match in 1981.

"Their receivers that year were probably the best that they had ever had at Penn State" said Jackie Sherrill.

"Penn State had a pretty good team that year," said Fazio. "They had a lot better team than some people thought they were."

"I think we all felt the same way; we blew it," said DiBartola. "We should have run the ball a little bit, take what you can get in the passing game instead of going deep every time."

The crushing loss dropped Pitt all the way from No. 1 in both polls to No. 8 (AP) and No. 10 (UPI). Georgia, Pitt's opponent in the New Year's Night Sugar Bowl, was ranked second in each. Pelusi remembered:

> It was the saddest moment in my Pitt football career. It was devastating. It cost us a national championship. At the end of the game I remember being on one knee on the sideline in disbelief, with my head down. It was very disappointing, especially when you think of how the game started. It felt like everything was going in a good direction, then the snowball started going downhill.

Unlike the 1980 season, when a Sugar Bowl meeting with Georgia would have meant a national championship for either team, only Georgia entertained such thoughts in late 1981. That did not make the game any less important to Pitt.

"Pitt really had something to prove," said Bob Smizik. "A lot of these bowl games are meaningless. They really had something to prove after that loss to Penn State."

Jackie Sherrill, looking for a way to eliminate the hangover from the Penn State game, reached into his bag of motivational tricks to prepare his team for the Sugar Bowl. Wayne DiBartola recalled:

> Jackie Sherrill convinced us, masterfully, that we had no starting positions, and we had to earn our positions while we were down there

preparing for the Sugar Bowl. It was serious. He stripped us of our honors and awards. He put second-string guys, guys he knew weren't going to play in the game, in with the first team at practice. He got us fired up. It wasn't an option to lose.

DiBartola was not sure his fullback job was secure. During pregame warmups the night of the game, Bill Beach was working with the first offensive unit. "He [Sherrill] walks over to me and says, 'Do you really think I wasn't gonna start you? You're starting, but don't you make any mistakes,'" said DiBartola.

Georgia was the defending national champion, and brought a 10-1 record into the game against Pitt. The Bulldogs' only loss was a 13-3 defeat at Clemson in the third game of the season. Pitt was 2-0-1 against coach Vince Dooley's teams since Johnny Majors and Tony Dorsett made their debuts in the opening game of the 1973 season at Georgia.

The Bulldogs were led by superstar running back Herschel Walker, who was a freshman for the Bulldogs' national championship team the year before. Blessed with an abundance of speed, size and strength, Jackie Sherrill understood what his defense had to do to contain Walker.

"Herschel [Walker] was a great north-south runner, but he wasn't an east-west runner," said Sherrill. "We had to keep him going east to west. Whenever he turned north to south, he was tough to catch."

Georgia's quarterback was senior Benjamin Franklin "Buck" Belue, who, like Dan Marino, was an outstanding baseball player. Belue played all four years for the Georgia baseball team. Georgia was 27-2 in games Belue started at quarterback. The Sugar Bowl would be his final game. A student of college football history, Belue understood Pitt's frustration at not playing his Bulldogs the year before, stating:

That process [of picking teams] was frustrating, obviously. You needed the stars to align to really get the shot, not to have to rely on guys voting. Us getting that opportunity in 1980 was huge, and you treasure that. That [1980] Notre Dame team was challenged, offensively, and that was a big advantage for us.

Just as curious were the machinations of the Southeastern Conference, whose champion received the automatic spot in the Sugar Bowl. SEC teams played only six conference games at the time. To wit, during Belue's four seasons (1978–1981) at Georgia, the Bulldogs never played Alabama.

"That was the oddball thing," said Belue, "because they [Alabama] were kicking butt at the time." Belue continued:

> I grew up a college football fan. In 1980, I was tracking all the teams, especially the players. Pitt was on the radar. For whatever reason, Jackie Sherrill seemed to get the attention of a lot of the guys on our coaching staff. They were really excited about the chance to play Pitt in the Sugar Bowl the next year. That opened my eyes a little bit to, "Wow, they really want to beat these guys [Pitt]."

Belue was a junior in high school when the Panthers beat the Bulldogs to win the national championship in 1976. "I thought I had a pretty good education on Pitt football then," said Belue. "[Matt] Cavanaugh and [Tony] Dorsett were really impressive in that game, and they really put it on Georgia. Believe me, there was a healthy respect for Pitt football in Athens during those years."

As for the challenges the 1981 Panthers posed for Georgia, Belue was just as impressed. When asked about the prospect of playing quarterback opposite Dan Marino in a game, Belue showed a sense of humor. "That wasn't a very fair fight, was it?" he remarked during an interview in 2019. "With Dan, it was the gunslinger thing. He was fearless, and you knew he was gonna have some awesome protection. I remember Julius Dawkins was a playmaker for them."

Georgia's offensive and defensive coordinators were George Haffner and Bill Lewis, both of whom had been assistant coaches at Pitt. The Bulldogs enjoyed a pseudo home field advantage inside the Super Dome. The raucous crowd of 77,274 was alive with color—and noise—throughout the game. On Pitt's very first play from scrimmage, Bill Fralic moved prematurely. Pitt was penalized eight times in the first half, and Marino had to ask the referee for help with the noise more than once. Belue had no such problem. "I think most of the Georgia fans were coached up enough to calm down when we had the ball," he said.

J. C. Pelusi stated:

> That game was the highest moment of my career. The atmosphere of the whole week leading up to the game in New Orleans was so much fun. As the game wore on, you knew you were playing against a special team and a special player in Herschel Walker. I watched every film of every game he played as a freshman and sophomore because we had a month

to prepare for it. I've never seen, in those two years, a running back who was as good as Herschel Walker, college or pro. He was just that good.

One Pitt player, if not its fans, gave Belue fits throughout the game, with Belue recalling:

Sal Sunseri was calling most of our plays as we got to the line of scrimmage. He'd be saying, "Sweep Right, Sweep Right!" I don't know who he was reading, probably one of the offensive guards, or looking at tendencies, but he was hitting on a lot of them. I remember doing some dummy checks, and Coach Dooley was asking me what I was doing out there. I told him I had to do these dummy checks because Sunseri was calling our plays.

"Sal was a student of the game, so that would not surprise me," said J. C. Pelusi. "He was a coach on the field, essentially."

Following a scoreless first period, the Bulldogs took a 7-0 lead midway through the second quarter when Walker ran 8 yards for a touchdown. Snuffy Everett's 41-yard field goal made it 7-3 at halftime. Everett was Pitt's last conventional, straight ahead placekicker.

The second half went back and forth with each team scoring two touchdowns. Marino hit Julius Dawkins from 30 yards to give Pitt a 10-7 lead early in the third quarter, but Walker countered with a 10-yard run to put the Bulldogs ahead 13-10. The extra point attempt failed. Marino answered the Walker touchdown by tossing a soft pass to John Brown from six yards out to give Pitt a 17-13 lead with eleven minutes and thirty seconds left in the game.

Three minutes later, Belue found tight end Clarence Kay in the end zone, and Georgia was ahead 20-17 with eight minutes and thirty seconds left to play.

The score remained that way until Pitt faced a fourth and five at the Georgia 33 with only forty-two seconds remaining. Jackie Sherrill had a decision to make. "I called Danny over and he said, 'Coach, we didn't come here to tie the game,'" said Sherrill. "I knew then that he would get it done."

Due to Sugar Bowl radio contractual obligations, Pitt did not broadcast the game. Bill Hillgrove was standing on the Pitt sideline with Mark May, who had just completed his rookie season with the Washington Redskins. Hillgrove said:

Late in the game, one of our defensive players said, "Let's kick the field goal and get the hell out of here and go party on Bourbon Street." And Danny said to Jackie, "Give me the ball; I'll win the game." And Jackie went right up in his face and said, "Say that again." He said, "Give me the ball. I'll win the game." The rest is history.

Jackie Sherrill said:

They [Georgia] blitzed eight people, playing three-deep man coverage. Danny read the pre snap blitz. He actually dropped a little deeper than he normally did to give himself a little more time, and everybody had to pick up a defender. Everybody had a man. John [Brown] made a great play on it.

Wayne DiBartola said:

The play that was called was to pick up the first down. It was a crossing pattern, and Danny was supposed to hit Bryan Thomas or me across the middle. Georgia blitzed both linebackers, so Bryan and I had to stay in and block their linebackers. Danny didn't have many options. Danny Marino, The Ice Man, he just threw it down there, and what a catch John Brown made.

John Brown made the dramatic catch in the end zone, despite a solid hit from Georgia safety Ronnie Harris. "John Brown turned out to be a much better player than we thought he would be," Jackie Sherrill said, many years after the Sugar Bowl. John Brown continued:

I never felt a thing. Something happens to your concentration level that you're concentrating in such a way that's almost out of body. It's the power of the human mind. Those are hits that you feel the next day, maybe even that night, but you don't ever feel it as it's happening.

"John Brown was getting behind the secondary, and took a big lick," said Belue. "That was a great play. We lost in dramatic fashion. That stung a little bit."

Sherrill's strategy during Sugar Bowl preparations had paid off. "He [Sherrill] had us ready," said DiBartola. "We would have run through a wall for him at that point. It was serious business. It wasn't bowl fun. It was almost like going back to training camp."

Dan Marino concluded his stellar junior season by passing for 2,876 yards and thirty-seven touchdowns. Julius Dawkins set a school single season record with sixteen touchdown receptions. Sal Sunseri was a first team All American. Bryan Thomas ran for 1,132 yards, and Pitt's head coach was carried off the field in New Orleans, as John Majors had been exactly five years before. The thrilling 24-20 victory was No. 500 in Pitt's football history. Nobody—not even the coach—knew it then, but Jackie Sherrill had coached his last game at Pitt.

6

DISCORD, DEPARTURE, AND DISAPPOINTMENT (1982)

The guy who pushed me away was [Ed] Bozik. I knew what he was doing, and that wasn't going to change. It was gonna be a hell of a war between Bozik and me, and Pitt wasn't going to fire me. Pitt was more important to me than getting somebody fired.

Jackie Sherrill (2019)

There was jealousy, university wide, of some of the success that the football program was having during those years. You'll find that at any college or university. There's not a warm, fuzzy feeling by everybody all the time.

Dean Billick (2020)

Waves of white jerseys, gold helmets, and gold pants leapt upon each other, creating a mountain of happy Pitt football players beyond the end zone when Dan Marino's touchdown pass to John Brown gave Pitt an unforgettable victory against Georgia in the 1982 Sugar Bowl.

Later that night, back at the New Orleans Hilton where the Panthers were staying, not everyone was in a celebratory mood. Alex Kramer's phone rang. It was Jackie Sherrill.

"After that game, Jackie and I took a nice walk, at his invitation," Kramer recalled. "That was the first time he began to express doubts about whether he was going to stay on because of changes he saw coming in athletic administration, from Myslinski to Bozik."

Throughout the 1981 season, dissatisfaction between Sherrill and Pitt's administration had begun to fester. At the time, Bozik served as assistant chancellor, and maintained staff oversight of the athletic department. Sherrill remembered:

That's when Bozik started getting involved, and they started wanting to change the schedule and do some things. I went to Cas, and I said, "Cas, I want to be assistant A.D. in charge of football. I want to have a say in who we play, where, and those things." I said, "The monetary thing, the budget, that's yours," and he agreed. "That's no problem."

Sherrill and John Majors each understood the possibilities when they first arrived at Pitt in late 1972. Unlike the Big Eight, where they had to butt heads with Oklahoma, Nebraska, and Colorado on an annual basis, Pitt's independent status meant complete freedom in scheduling. Jackie Sherrill said:

We were in position to dictate our fate. I said, "You know, we need to play six teams we're going to beat. And then you schedule two teams that you know you're going to beat because you're going to outrecruit them. And you schedule two games that will be tossups. Then you schedule the last game that you'll have to play very well to win."

"Jackie wanted to have more control over the football program," said Dean Billick. "He wanted to report to the chancellor [Posvar]. That didn't happen."

"I was aware of what was going on, but because I had to keep a positive attitude, I kind of swept it to the back of my mind," said Bill Hillgrove. "I never really got into the whys and wherefores, but just knowing the people involved, I knew how the dominoes would fall."

As John Majors had done five years earlier, Sherrill took the team to Biloxi, where he spent his formative years, for the first round of practices before heading to New Orleans to prepare for the Sugar Bowl. Biloxi even staged a parade in Sherrill's honor, with Alex Kramer riding in the lead car with Pitt's head coach.

While in Biloxi, through a former classmate, Sherrill arranged for the players to go on a boat ride at no cost. A local merchant spent the entire overnight making Po' Boy sandwiches, at $2 each, for the players. Alex Kramer, looking to clear the expense, placed a call to John Blanton back in Pittsburgh. Blanton worked in the athletic department's business office. "Blanton was very reluctant to do that," said Kramer. "He opposed that. I told him, 'That's what Coach [Sherrill] wants.' He [Blanton] was very adamant."

The total bill for the sandwiches came to about $400. "I said, 'This is a lot less than any meal they're going to eat,'" said Sherrill. "They would spend a lot more than $400 for a meal for the chancellor's party."

Several weeks later, Bruce Keidan wrote a column for *The Pittsburgh Post-Gazette* in which he quoted an official from the NCAA who stated that buying the sandwiches would have constituted an "improper benefit." Money had already been allocated for the players' meal at that time of day.

"Nitpicking," was how Alex Kramer labeled the charge in 2019. "I don't buy that."

Several days before the Sugar Bowl game, Sherrill presented a list of demands to Myslinski and vice chancellor Jack Freeman, who said they would get back to him later. That did not happen, or not soon enough to suit Jackie Sherrill.

But Jackie Sherrill's angst was only beginning. While in New Orleans, Bill Fralic and several other players skipped a diner without paying their bill. Sherrill assigned them to their hotel rooms for the remaining evenings of the trip. Fralic, who passed away in late 2018, recalled the incident during an interview in 1998. "Looking back, I can laugh about it now," he said. "But it wasn't very funny at the time. Jackie Sherrill scared the shit out of me."

"Jackie's manner and disposition were generally more than sufficient to get his message across to the players, to make them understand what was expected of them," said Alex Kramer.

"I've always been a firm believer if a kid does something, then if you discipline him and he accepts it, then he's going to be okay," said Sherrill. "If he doesn't, then he's not."

Two officers from the Allegheny County Sheriff's office, Ray Goga and John Parker, also kept a close watch on the Pitt team during Sherrill's term as coach. In fact, the two lawmen and Alex Kramer probably were closer to the head coach than anyone else in the athletic department.

"Jackie had a close relationship with his two bodyguards, so to speak," said Kramer. The two lawmen were to witness another unfortunate episode, one which would hasten Sherrill's departure from Pittsburgh. More about that later.

Early in 1977, Sherrill approached John McNamara, an ardent Pitt football fan who happened to be the chief deputy in the sheriff's office. Sherrill asked if he could utilize Goga and Parker for team security, and McNamara gave his blessing. Both men came to like and admire Sherrill and his players.

"The whites and blacks got along very well," Parker said in 1998. "They could kid each other without anyone being offended. There was no racial discord. Jackie was able to relate very well to kids from all types of backgrounds."

"A lot of people are ashamed or embarrassed about their backgrounds, or the fact that they're from the ghetto," Sherrill once remarked. "One of the things I've tried to do with players is to make them feel comfortable or at peace with that part of their lives."

Parker came to recognize Sherrill's adherence to structure. "He [Jackie] was like a great golfer in that his routine and approach to things never wavered."

As part of the itinerary on the day of road games, Sherrill, Parker and Goga would play a hand or two of bridge before heading to the stadium. "Once, on the bus just as we were about to leave, Jackie said, 'Holy hell, Ray, we didn't play cards yet,'" said Goga.

The three men got off the bus, went inside the hotel lobby and played a hand of bridge. "Jackie wasn't very good at cards," said Goga.

Meanwhile, back in New Orleans after returning to the locker room with the Sugar Bowl victory in hand, Sherrill wanted to stage a brief ceremony to honor Chancellor Posvar and Cas Myslinski. Sherrill said: "So I turned to Parker and Goga, and I said, 'No one in but players, coaches, Cas and Posvar.' That's when Bozik started beating on the door and threatening Parker and Goga and saying, "You're fired" and all this stuff. They wouldn't let him [Bozik] in the locker room."

Alex Kramer stated: "Jackie told me not to let anybody in. He was very specific about Bozik; not letting Bozik in. I did not let him in. It was a raucous locker room. Happily raucous. I probably said something like, 'Coach doesn't want anybody in.' I'm sure if I hadn't said that, Bozik would have come in."

"He [Bozik] was very threatening and demanding in his desire to enter the locker room," Goga related many years later.

"I had Cas and Posvar get up on the table, and I told the players, 'Guys, this is why we have had a chance to be as good as we've been the last four years,'" said Sherrill. "Just giving them some recognition."

But still upset about the commotion at the locker room door, Sherrill requested a meeting with the chancellor. "Their attitude was like, 'Who in the hell do you think you are? I'll tell you when we'll have a meeting.'" So right then I thought, 'Screw it. You know, maybe it's getting to a point where a change has to be made.'"

"It made no sense whatever," Alex Kramer said when asked about the growing hostility between Sherrill and the administration. "There was a lot of jealousy and envy in regard to Jackie's success because Jackie did not bend his knee to those people [administrators]. He felt he didn't need their help unless he asked for it."

After returning to Pittsburgh, Sherrill was back on the road again, this time to California to coach in the East-West Shrine Game at Stanford Stadium on January 9, 1982. While there, he visited with his mentor and college coach, Paul "Bear" Bryant. The legendary Alabama coach confided to Sherrill that he was going to coach only one more season (1982) at Alabama and that Sherrill would be one of three men he was going to recommend as his successor. Steve Sloan and Ray Perkins were the other two. Perkins ultimately replaced Bryant, who died a short time later.

"If he [Bryant] had told me I was the one, I probably would have stayed at Pittsburgh [for the 1982 season]," Sherrill later admitted.

While in Palo Alto, Sherrill also caught up with Michigan coach Bo Schembechler and Dallas Cowboys' scouting director Gil Brandt. The three men discussed the possibility of Schembechler's opportunity to accept the coaching position at Texas A&M University. Schembechler was offered the job, but decided to remain in Ann Arbor.

The following week, back in Pittsburgh, Sherrill received a phone call from Gil Brandt. Would Sherrill be interested in the A&M job? He was.

Saturday, January 16 was a busy day on the Pitt sports front. The men's basketball team was in State College for a basketball game with Penn State. While in his room at the Nittany Lion Inn, Bob Smizik received a phone call from a sportswriter from Texas. Smizik said: "The guy called to tell me that there was talk that Jackie Sherrill was going to leave to go to Texas A&M. I told him that was utterly preposterous. He [Sherrill] has the Number One team in the country coming back, and there's no way he's leaving for Texas A&M." As a responsible reporter, Smizik went straight to the source. He placed a call to Sherrill's home in Oakland, only a few blocks from both Pitt Stadium and the Cathedral of Learning. Smizik recalled:

Jackie answered the phone. He denied the rumor. He was getting ready for a party that night, and I was told that some of the Texas A&M people were going to be there. I don't bear any grudge against Jackie. I understand there are certain times when people cannot tell you the truth, and that was one of them.

The recruiting party included coaches, Pitt players, recruits, and three gentlemen, dressed conservatively in business suits, whose identities were a mystery. The following morning, Sunday, January 17, Sherrill called Alex Kramer back to his home, where he invited his administrative aide to his study for a confidential meeting. Sherrill informed Kramer that the three strangers from the night before had been Dallas attorney William McKenzie, San Antonio oilman John Blocker, and James "Jimmy" Bond, general counsel for Texas A&M University. While Sherrill and his assistant coaches had been recruiting high school seniors, McKenzie, Blocker, and Bond had been there to recruit Sherrill to Texas A&M.

Sherrill explained to Kramer that he would be flying to College Station the next day, a Monday, to discuss the Texas A&M opportunity, and that he would keep Kramer informed of how the meetings went.

When he first came to Pittsburgh, Jackie Sherrill set a personal goal for himself; he wanted to be named Dapper Dan Man of the Year. It became a reality after the 1981 season, and Sherrill received that honor during the annual dinner ceremony at the Pittsburgh Hilton on Sunday night, January 17, 1982.

Outside the banquet room, WTAE TV's Stan Savran was preparing to conduct a live interview with Sherrill as part of the station's six o'clock news program; Savran said:

> As we were getting ready for Jackie to come over and do the interview, one of the producers back at Channel 4 told me the story had emanated out of Texas, maybe College Station, that Jackie Sherrill was under consideration to be the new A&M head coach. They told me that, literally, a minute or two before Jackie was going to do the interview. Naturally, I said, "Jackie, we're getting reports that you and Texas A&M might get together."

Sherrill was non-committal, trying to put Savran off as best he could, as Savran remembered:

He [Sherrill] said, "Well, I think we should enjoy this evening. It's a great honor. Pittsburgh's been great to me." It wasn't long before he accepted the [A&M] job. I don't know that I broke the story. I asked him the question, and of course by giving the answer that he did, that pretty much proved that he was going

Jackie Sherrill flew by private plane to College Station, Texas, on Monday, January 18, 1982 and accepted the dual positions of athletic director and head football coach. During the flight back to Pittsburgh, he called Jack Freeman, telling him of his decision, and recommended that Pitt hire Foge Fazio as his replacement.

Alex Kramer remembers the way Sherrill divulged the highly publicized deal in a phone call the same day. "Jackie told me, and I'll always remember this because he syllabified it, he said it was 'Un-be-lie-va-ble,'" said Kramer. "He broke it down into syllables."

Official word that Sherrill was leaving for Texas A&M had not been released, but Bob Smizik had an inkling. The morning after the Dapper Dan ceremony, he placed a call to Foge Fazio at Pitt's football offices. Bob Smizik said:

I called Foge under the ruse and congratulated him on becoming the new Pitt coach. He didn't quite know what to do, because it hadn't been announced, but being the genial guy that he was, he acknowledged that fact which gave us the scoop. We were an afternoon paper, so we were able to break the story.

Jackie Sherrill met with his players at Pitt Stadium at 4 p.m. on Tuesday afternoon to inform them that he was leaving, with J. C. Pelusi stating:

It was a little bit shocking. It did not surprise me that he left because you could see the tension in his last year, especially when we were at the Sugar Bowl. I was a little bit aware of it. I'm not sure others were. I could see the disconnect between Jackie and the athletic administration and maybe the administration overall.

"I was surprised that he left, but I was well aware that there was unhappiness on his [Sherrill's] part," said Smizik. "When the team was in New Orleans, it became clear that he was unhappy."

Pitt scheduled a joint press conference for Tuesday, January 19, during which Sherrill announced he had accepted the positions at Texas A&M,

followed by the introduction of Foge Fazio as Pitt's new head football coach. Sherrill, flanked at the podium by Dan Marino, wearing a T-shirt inscribed "No Where Else But Texas," was joined by teammates John Brown and J. C. Pelusi., Sherrill was somber as he talked about his decision to leave Pittsburgh: "If my decision had been made solely on emotion and sentiment, there's no question I'd be here. But you get to the point in your life where you start to think your family is important, and you start to think of your future financially."

Pitt officials made it clear that they were not going to engage in a bidding war for Sherrill's services. It would have been moot anyway. "They [Texas A&M] have more loyalty and allegiance to that school than anybody here can visualize," Sherrill explained. "A lot of football coaches would walk to Texas A&M to take that job."

"That's a very, very deep and rich school, financially," Dean Billick said of Texas A&M many years later. "They had great financial resources and they had much better facilities than what we had. Jackie had an opportunity that we could not match."

Sherrill expressed his gratefulness for the eight years he spent at Pitt, first as an assistant coach under John Majors, then as head coach from 1977 through 1981. "When I came here in 1973, I was a tough, abrasive football coach," he said. "Since I've been exposed to the city and people of Pittsburgh, it's put a lot of sandpaper on me."

Alex Kramer noted: "He [Sherrill] was devoted to winning. He did not interfere with his assistant coaches. He let them do what they were responsible for. He oversaw it all. I don't ever recall one instance where he intervened or interfered with one of the assistants during practice."

Coincidentally, around the same time that Sherrill was leaving Pitt, Joe Paterno had announced that he was relinquishing his duties as Penn State's athletic director. Sherrill was not impressed.

"Joe Paterno is still the athletic director at Penn State, regardless if he has the title or not," he said. "He'll still make the decisions. I don't see [Jim] Tarman telling Joe Paterno he can't do anything."

Sherrill's Pitt teams won fifty games, lost nine, and tied one. They won four of five bowl games, and finished four seasons ranked among the nation's Top Ten. He has the highest winning percentage of any football coach in Pitt history. Still, that abrasiveness rubbed many people the wrong way. He had his detractors.

Sam Sciullo, Sr., said: "I liked Jackie. There were people, Pitt people, who didn't like him, and the people who didn't like him vehemently didn't like him. All I know is that he was producing good football teams, and his players liked and respected him."

"He's always been loyal," Mark May said of Sherrill. "Jackie should be in the College Football Hall of Fame."

"Jackie knew the quality of an athlete," said Lloyd Weston. "He knew how to look at a kid and judge his talent, and he knew how to make him fit in."

Alex Kramer said: "There were no tears shed by the administration when Jackie left, but Jackie did a marvelous job, and he was not going to be beholden to anyone in getting the job done. That upset some people in the administration, but Jackie Sherrill made an inerasable impact on Pitt football."

Upon arriving in Texas, Jackie Sherrill hit Southwest Conference football like a storm, and the storm, primarily the media, hit back. Accustomed to coaches from the good ol' boy mode, Jackie Sherrill—sharply dressed, carrying himself in the manner of a CEO, provided a stark contrast to most of the coaching fraternity in that part of the country. Sherrill said:

> I never cultivated the media [in Texas]. Coach Bryant, back in his day, he thought if you gave 'em a steak and a bottle of whiskey, they were your friend. I was brash and different because I was not politically correct. I wasn't out drinking with them or playing cards with them. Barry [Switzer] cultivated a lot of them that way. I didn't do that. I'm not a guy who will go to a bar and just sit at a bar for hours. I don't do that. I never have.

At Pitt, Sherrill benefitted from the positive relationship he had working with Cas Myslinski, whose managerial skills drew varied assessments.

"Cas Myslinski let Jackie Sherrill do what Jackie Sherrill was paid to do, and that was win football games," said Alex Kramer.

"I thought Cas was smart enough to let his football coaches [Majors and Sherrill] run their programs, based on their backgrounds and previous experiences of where they'd been," said Dean Billick. "That was his method, and it worked."

Bill Hillgrove stated: "He [Myslinski] stayed out of the way. He let the coaches coach. His job was done once those people were in place. He was smart enough to let things happen. Any scrutiny of him, any criticism of him, is miniscule because you look at his results, he did a hell of a job."

Sam Sciullo, Sr., the longtime booster who did not have to worry about staying on the good side of Pitt administrators, offered a more balanced evaluation of Myslinski's background and business acumen:

> A lot of people thought Cas was a big galoot, but he wasn't. He was a West Point graduate. That had to mean something. You don't bluff your way through a place like that. Cas was no dummy, but he had no business sense. He'd come from the military, where he got three meals a day, his clothes and a nice paycheck. Everything was provided.

Cas Myslinski was all smiles when he stood at the podium to introduce forty-two-year-old Serafino Dante "Foge" Fazio as Pitt's new football coach. Fazio was confident the change at the top of the coaching structure was a mere formality.

"We're at the point where success breeds success," said Fazio of Pitt's program, which had won more games (sixty-two) than any other college program from 1976 through 1981. Still, he was humbled by the opportunity. Fazio continued:

> Being the head coach at the University of Pittsburgh is a great personal honor for me. It's an honor that doesn't come along too often. I'm really looking forward to the season. The magnitude of the responsibilities that goes along with the position are great, but the rewards are just as great.

Born in Diamond, West Virginia, Fazio was raised in Coraopolis, Pa., not far from Greater Pittsburgh Airport. He graduated from Pitt in 1960, where he had played linebacker and center. He had served stints as an assistant coach at Boston University, Harvard, and the University of Cincinnati. Pitt would be his first head coaching assignment.

Pitt's coaching staff remained largely intact for Fazio. Sherrill had asked Joe Daniels, Andy Urbanic, George Pugh, Bob Davie, and Alex Kramer to join him at Texas A&M, but only Pugh accepted the offer. Bob Matey and Bob Davie joined Sherrill in subsequent seasons.

Two new assistant coaches joined Fazio's staff at Pitt. Charlie Bailey had been assistant head coach and defensive coordinator at Kentucky in 1981. He would coordinate the defense as well as coach the linebackers at Pitt. Don Thompson came to Pitt from the University of Connecticut, where he had been coaching defensive ends and linebackers. Fazio appointed him to coach Pitt's defensive line. Fazio also promoted Joe Moore to the position of offensive coordinator: "I don't see any changes in our offensive or defensive philosophies. I don't consider this a changing of the guard, just a change within the program. We'll continue to be successful."

"Fazio has the nucleus of a team that many coaches spend nights dreaming about," was how Pitt's 1982 football media guide summarized the personnel on the roster. Indeed, eighteen starters were returning from an 11-1 team, including senior quarterback Dan Marino, who was the subject of a lavish feature article in *Sports Illustrated* in its college football preview issue. The only starters gone from the previous year were center Emil Boures and fullback Wayne DiBartola from the offense and linebacker Sal Sunseri and cornerback Pappy Thomas from the defense.

Pitt's 1982 freshman class included three local *Parade* All-Americans in quarterback Rich Bowen (Serra Catholic), defensive lineman Bob Schilken (Mt. Lebanon), and running back Matt Stennett (Shaler). Other prominent recruits were defensive lineman Bob Buczkowski (Gateway) and a versatile quarterback from Lauderdale Lakes, Fla. named John Congemi. Optimism was soaring throughout the summer of 1982. Pitt had a talented, experienced team returning, a new coach—and a new athletic director.

Cas Myslinski announced his retirement that summer, and Ed Bozik, who had worked with Chancellor Posvar at the Air Force Academy in Colorado, assumed his new duties at Pitt on September 1.

A native of Donora, Pa., Bozik graduated from California (Pa.) State in 1953, and served in the Air Force from 1953–1966. He earned a Ph.D. in political science from Georgetown University in 1968. In 1966, he joined the Air Force Academy as an instructor, and in 1971, he became chairman of the Department of Political Science. He was later head of faculty at the National War College in Washington, D.C.

Bozik was taking oversight of a football program ranked No. 1 in the nation in both wire service's preseason polls. But there were concerns, even then, about the direction and leadership within. One veteran observer recalled his initial impression of training camp at what is now Edinboro University, in August. Bill Hillgrove said:

> I remember his [Fazio's] first on field experience at training camp. Johnny Sauer was there with me. Johnny said to me, "Billy, he [Fazio] doesn't look comfortable. He's standing there whipping that whistle around his finger, and he just doesn't look comfortable as a head coach." And I don't think he was.

A member of the 1981 and 1982 teams, who asked not to be identified, was called to Bozik's office for a meeting before Fazio's first season. An anonymous Pitt football player said:

> He [Bozik] called me into his office, and we were talking about Foge, and he wanted to know my thoughts about Foge as a head coach. I said, "Foge is a great defensive coordinator. He's a great person, and he's probably too friendly with the players." You don't know if that equates into being a head coach as far as the discipline and some of the fear that you have to put into players, which Jackie had a good ability to do. You don't know if some coaches can go from being a great coordinator to being a head coach.

Alex Kramer witnessed an animated argument between two assistant coaches during training camp in which one had to be restrained from attacking the other. "That was a disruptive influence which I think carried over into the season," said Kramer. "I don't think that staff was fully committed at times."

The 1982 Panthers faced a rugged schedule to open the season. North Carolina, Florida State, Illinois, and West Virginia each appeared in the Top 10 on the day of the game. Pitt's first opponent was North Carolina, ranked No. 5 and featuring star running back Kelvin Bryant. As Jackie Sherrill had been, Foge Fazio was more than accommodating to the local media. He invited Bob Smizik to spend part of the day with the team at its Monroeville hotel as it prepared for that night's game.

"I thought they'd win 35-6," said Smizik. "I never thought 7-6. Talk about a harbinger!"

An enthusiastic crowd of 54,449 filled Three Rivers Stadium, but the game was a dud. Pitt trailed 3-0 at halftime. Its only score came in the third quarter when Marino tossed a 4-yard touchdown pass to Bryan Thomas. Marino also threw four interceptions in the game. Fortunately for Pitt, the defense was stout. Bill Maas was named Pitt's CBS Player of the Game.

"It wasn't very pretty," Foge Fazio noted afterward. "Offensively we were disappointing. We talked about stopping ourselves and making mistakes. I think the team was pressing."

"We tried to change up on Marino defensively because it's just impossible to totally shut him down," said North Carolina coach Dick Crum. "I thought he was impatient on those long balls for the interceptions."

The narrow victory dropped Pitt to No. 2 in the rankings as it prepared to visit Tallahassee and Florida State for a night game September 18. Years later, many Pitt fans would mistake this rain-soaked game with the disappointing 1980 loss to the Seminoles. The 1982 Panthers defeated Florida State, 37-17, after falling behind 10-0 early. Two touchdown runs by Marlon McIntyre aided the comeback as the first half ended 17-17. Then the torrential rains came, which seemed to help Pitt more than Florida State.

"We had to have an advantage, and we just didn't get it," FSU coach Bobby Bowden told the media. "When the rains came, it got cold. You ain't gonna believe it, but it was cold. They [Pitt] handled it better than we did."

"I told Coach Bowden after the game that it could have been a real high scoring game had the rain not come," said Foge Fazio.

Dan Marino threw touchdown passes to John Brown and Julius Dawkins in the fourth quarter. Art Lowery had to return a rain-induced punt only 5 yards for Pitt's other touchdown in the second half. The conditions limited Marino to 133 yards passing, while Bryan Thomas rushed for 95 yards.

The Panthers visited Illinois the following week and quickly fell behind 3-0. The Illini were driving for another score when Pitt's Dave Puzzuoli made the play of the game, intercepting a Tony Eason pass and rumbling 95 yards for a touchdown. "I was surprised," said Puzzuoli. "The ball was just in my chest. I didn't have to think. I must have had the wind at my back. I was just waiting for someone to catch me."

"They [Pitt] just knocked us upside down on offense," Illinois coach Mike White explained after the game. "We didn't allow for the fact that their defense was just going to shove us all over town."

Eason threw the ball fifty-eight times, but the Panthers recorded ten quarterback sacks. Marino passed for 215 yards, including a scoring strike to John Brown. The Panthers won, 20-3, but Marino was intercepted four times, giving him a total of nine through Pitt's first three games.

Both Pitt and West Virginia were undefeated when Don Nehlen brought the Mountaineers to Pitt Stadium on a glorious Saturday afternoon, October 2, 1982. Nehlen was in his third season in Morgantown, and Foge Fazio recognized the challenge his team faced during his weekly luncheon with the Pittsburgh media four days before the game. "That Don Nehlen, he's sitting down there in Morgantown, smiling away, keeping quiet when, in fact, he's got outstanding personnel this year," said Fazio. "It's his personnel that makes the big difference."

Headlining WVU's personnel was junior transfer quarterback Jeff Hostetler, who had left Penn State after the 1980 season in search of more playing time elsewhere. Hostetler and WVU had upset Oklahoma, 41-27, in Norman to open the season. Hostetler threw for 321 yards and four touchdowns in that game.

ABC TV was in Pittsburgh for a regional telecast of The Backyard Brawl. Again, Pitt's offense struggled early, and the Panthers trailed 3-0 at halftime. WVU led 6-0 entering the final quarter, and extended the lead to 13-0 when Darryl Talley blocked a punt for a touchdown early in the fourth quarter.

"They [Pitt players] got upset after that blocked punt," Foge Fazio remarked after the game. "I've never seen Bill Fralic so mad. Dan [Marino] bit his lip and gave me a look like he knew it was now or never."

The Panthers fought back, driving 83 yards on their ensuing possession, culminating in a 3-yard touchdown run by Bryan Thomas to close the deficit to 13-7. Pitt caught a break when West Virginia center Dave Johnson had to leave the game with an injury after Pitt kicked off. Hostetler could not handle the exchange from backup center Bill Legg, and the Panthers took over near midfield. Marino marched the Panthers downfield and hit Julius Dawkins for a touchdown from 6 yards out to put Pitt ahead 14-13. A Bill Maas sack of Hostetler in the end zone produced a safety and a 16-13 Pitt lead.

West Virginia had one last shot, a 52-yard field goal attempt by Paul Woodside in the closing seconds. The kick fell inches short, and Pitt had its seventh consecutive victory in the series with West Virginia. Foge Fazio noted: "Maybe I was taught that in the heat of the battle, you don't quit until the last whistle or like a boxer, hang in there until the fifteenth round or a last second knockout. I never doubted that we would come back."

Don Nehlen said: "It's a shame to lose a game like this, when your kids play so super. We went down, but we didn't go down without a fight. And if Marino's a Heisman Trophy candidate, so is Jeff Hostetler."

Hostetler, who was under relentless pressure from Pitt's defensive front the entire game, had to be helped to the team bus outside Gate 3 following the game.

Pitt suffered a key loss in the victory. Defensive end Michael Woods sustained a neck injury, ending his football career.

Meanwhile, approximately 1,300 miles from Pitt Stadium, at Kyle Field in College Station, Texas, Jackie Sherrill's Texas A&M Aggies had just lost to Texas Tech, 24-15. In the A&M locker room, a friend of Sherrill's from

Pittsburgh informed the coach that Pitt had rallied from a 13-0 deficit to defeat West Virginia. Sherrill raised his eyebrows in surprise. "They [Pitt] were able to come back like that because of their experience," he said.

Back in Pittsburgh, following a week off, the Panthers took a break from Top 20 opponents to welcome 3-3 Temple to Pitt Stadium for Homecoming. It was the final season for veteran coach Wayne Hardin, who had been a nemesis for Pitt, first at Navy, later at Temple. Scouts from the Sugar, Cotton, and Fiesta Bowls were there to watch Pitt.

The Panthers led 17-0 following an Eric Schubert field goal and a pair of touchdown passes from Marino to Dwight Collins. Temple quarterback Tim Riordan rallied the Owls with a pair of scoring passes, but Marino then hit Julius Dawkins for a touchdown followed by a scoring run by fullback Bill Beach. The Panthers won, 37-17. Marino threw for 344 yards, three touchdowns and three interceptions, and had begun to hear a smattering of boos from the hometown fans. Normally a willing subject in the locker room after games, the senior quarterback decided to do one interview only, with the assembled media, after the Temple game.

"It doesn't bother me," Marino answered in response to questions about the booing. "All I care about is my family, my close friends and the people in this locker room. I just go out to have fun and play football."

Smizik stated:

Marino was a fantastic player. Jackie Sherrill always used to say this about him: he was "raised right." He was. I agree with him. His parents were good people. He was cooperative with the media. He didn't really have a lot to say. I don't think he enjoyed the byplay with the media. A lot of guys on those teams, there were a lot of good talkers, but Dan wasn't one of them. That's why it surprised me a little that he went on to have the nice career in TV that he had.

A Carrier Dome crowd of 42,321 watched Pitt register its first shutout of the season, a 14-0 blanking of Syracuse on October 23, 1982. It was Pitt's tenth straight victory against Syracuse in the long rivalry.

Pitt's defense was the story in the win, limiting Syracuse to six first downs. The Orange never crossed Pitt's 20, and gained only 140 total yards. The Panthers scored touchdowns in the first and fourth quarters, a pass from Marino to Dawkins, and a short plunge by Joe McCall. Marino threw for 227 yards, a touchdown and three more interceptions. In his postgame remarks, Fazio accepted blame for some of the offense's inefficiency. "We started well, but the coach screwed up by not getting the plays into the game quickly enough," he said. "I take the blame for that. We lost our continuity because of that."

The offensive explosion everyone had been expecting from the 1982 Pitt offense finally came the following week when the Panthers scored nine touchdowns in a 63-14 defeat of Louisville at Pitt Stadium. Pitt led 49-7 at halftime, and amassed 522 yards in total offense in raising its record to 7-0. Bryan Thomas rushed for 119 yards on nine carries, while Dan Marino threw two touchdown passes. Tom Flynn returned a punt 63 yards for a touchdown and tight end Clint Wilson caught a pass for the first score of his career. Running back Mike Boyd ran 5 yards for his first career touchdown. Foge Fazio was asked if some of his offensive players had been short of confidence during the season. "We never lacked confidence," said Fazio. "If you know Dan Marino, Bryan Thomas, Bill Fralic and Jimbo Covert, you know that they don't lack confidence."

Pitt sustained a key injury, however, when cornerback Tim Lewis suffered a sprained ankle. "We needed a big game going into the Notre Dame game," said Thomas.

Back at No. 1 in the nation, the 7-0 Panthers prepared for 5-1-1 Notre Dame at Pitt Stadium on November 6. The Irish were coached by Gerry Faust, in his second season after making the jump from Cincinnati's Moeller High School to the college ranks.

A packed Pitt Stadium crowd of 60,162, reminiscent of the Penn State game the previous season, was there to watch Pitt and the Irish meet in Pittsburgh for the first time since 1977.

Before the game, Faust played the tradition card in the Irish locker room, reciting a list of past Notre Dame conquests of No. 1 teams on the road. It must have worked. Notre Dame stunned the Panthers, 31-16, dealing an almost certain fatal blow to the Panthers' hopes for a national championship. Statistically, the Pitt offense was impressive, outgaining Notre Dame 323 yards to 197, and collecting twenty-five first downs to only ten for the Irish. Dan Marino passed for 314 yards, but no touchdowns.

"We moved the ball well but we didn't get it into the end zone," said Foge Fazio. "Notre Dame played a great defensive game."

Pitt had to settle for a pair of Eric Schubert field goals in the first half, which ended with Notre Dame leading 10-6. Pitt went ahead 13-10 on a short run by Bryan Thomas late in the third quarter, but three Notre Dame touchdowns in the fourth quarter, one on a 54-yard flea flicker from Blair

Kiel to Joe Thomas gave the Irish the lead. Allen Pinkett added a pair of scoring runs to produce the final margin.

Pitt safety Tom Flynn had to leave the game with a sprained foot early in the first half, leaving the Panthers thin in the secondary.

"The kids are taking it pretty tough," Fazio told the media. "They felt they lost it, that they didn't get beat. But mistakes killed us."

"I can rank that one [Notre Dame] right up there as one of the low moments in my career," J. C. Pelusi said in 2019. "Tommy Flynn getting hurt cost us a lot in that game, but it's a team game."

The bitter defeat dropped Pitt to No. 7 (UPI) and No. 8 (AP). Adding insult to injury, Notre Dame proceeded to lose its next three games (Penn State, Air Force, and Southern California).

With no time to feel sorry for itself, Pitt traveled to cold, windy Michie Stadium at West Point the following week, and dispatched Army, 24-6. The Panthers scored all their points in the first half. Joe McCall ran for 129 yards on twenty-four carries. Dan Marino passed for only 71 yards, but three touchdowns, two to Dwight Collins and one to Julius Dawkins. He also threw three interceptions. The Panthers collected 366 total yards to only 90 for Army. Pitt's running game picked up 295 yards. With Cotton Bowl representatives watching, the Panthers raised their record to 8-1. Fazio was not too concerned about his team's scoreless second half. "I don't see why the bowl people would be disappointed with our performance," he said. "They saw the first half. They know what was going on."

A Pitt Stadium crowd braved a cold, rainy day to watch the Panthers defeat Rutgers, 52-6, in the final home appearance for Dan Marino and the rest of Pitt's seniors. Marino completed twenty-two of thirty passes for 262 yards and three touchdowns as the Panthers raised their record to 9-1. Julius Dawkins, Keith Williams, and Joe McCall caught touchdown passes from Marino, and Bryan Thomas ran for two scores in his final game at Pitt Stadium. The Panthers had 418 yards in total offense compared to 76 for Rutgers, which gained only 29 yards on the ground.

In the locker room after the game, Pitt officials accepted a bid to play SMU in the Cotton Bowl on New Year's Day 1983. "We want to express our appreciation to the Cotton Bowl people because they stuck with us and had confidence in us," said Foge Fazio. "It means a lot to us."

"I'm pleased about the Cotton Bowl bid, but we can't celebrate until we play the team coming up this week [Penn State]," added Dan Marino. "It was an emotional game, being the last home game for the seniors." Marino's jersey No. 13 was retired during a halftime ceremony.

For the fourth consecutive season, Pitt entered its season finale with Penn State with no more than one loss on its record. Both teams were 9-1, and the game had national title implications. Alabama had defeated Penn State, 42-21, earlier in the season, but Penn State was No. 2 and Pitt No. 5 as the teams prepared for their November 26 day after Thanksgiving showdown at Beaver Stadium.

The game was an NFL scout's dream, featuring nine players in the starting lineups who eventually were drafted in the first round. Dan Marino, Bill Fralic, Jimbo Covert, Chris Doleman, Bill Maas, and Tim Lewis were Pitt's future first round picks, while Todd Blackledge, Curt Warner, and Kenny Jackson were Penn State's top selections.

With virtually the same team from the year before, but a year older, the Panthers had a strong desire to erase the memory of the stinging 48-14 loss at Pitt Stadium in 1981. There would be no blowout this time. The first half was a defensive struggle. Penn State scored first on a 26-yard field goal by Nick Gancitano.

Late in the second quarter, with the Panthers driving, Marino sustained a shoulder injury, forcing him from the game. Danny Daniels replaced him, and Pitt took a 7-3 halftime lead when Bryan Thomas scored on a 4-yard run. It was Pitt's only touchdown in the game. Marino returned to the game after halftime, but facing a stiff wind, the Panthers were plagued by poor field position in the third quarter. They attempted only two passes, both incomplete.

Gancitano added three more field goals in the second half. Pitt's best chance came with seven minutes remaining. Trailing 16-7, the Panthers had the ball fourth and goal at the Penn State 1. Foge Fazio opted for an Eric Schubert field goal to make it 16-10, Fazio questioned himself after the game. "If I had to do it over, I probably would have gone for the touchdown," Fazio said. "I had a strong feeling we would come back and score. We had our opportunities."

The Nittany Lions then drove downfield and clinched the 19-10 victory on a 29-yard field goal by Gancitano. The loss spoiled a fine effort by Bryan Thomas, who carried the ball thirty-one times for 143 yards. Marino passed for 262 yards. Pitt outgained Penn State, 397 to 359, and had more first downs, twenty-two to the Lions' eighteen, but that was of little consolation. Pitt ended the regular season 9-2. Penn State, 10-1, went to the Sugar Bowl, where it defeated Georgia, 27-23, for the program's first national championship.

With the Cotton Bowl date with SMU looming, Pitt's troubles were only beginning.

Mark Hyman, a native Pennsylvanian then employed by *The Dallas Times-Herald*, was home for the holidays. Looking to gather some materials in advance of the Cotton Bowl, Hyman interviewed Pitt players Tim Lewis and Ron Sams in anticipation of the game in Dallas. Hyman could not have expected what the players told him. Both Lewis and Sams were quoted as being critical of wide receiver Julius Dawkins' effort that season, along with a general lack of discipline on the team. Hyman contacted Pitt beat writer Bob Smizik, informing him of what the players had told him. Hyman and Smizik went back and interviewed the players again to get corroboration. Their article appeared in both *The Dallas Times-Herald* and *The Pittsburgh Press* on Sunday, December 5, 1982.

Pitt responded quickly, scheduling a press conference for the following day, where Lewis and Sams did not say they had been misquoted, but that their comments had been taken out of context. Smizik, who was at the press conference, was not buying any of it. "It was exactly what was wrong with the Pitt team that year," Smizik said in 2019. "They [Pitt] were trying to diminish the story and diminish me."

"Bob's entitled to his opinion, and I'm entitled to mine," said Dean Billick, who arranged the news conference. "I thought it was appropriate to defend our coach [Fazio], our players and our university. I thought it was time to step up for our program, and I did."

After the press conference, a film crew from a Dallas TV station drove downtown to *The Pittsburgh Press* offices to interview Smizik. "They [TV people] were just aghast at how thin skinned Pitt was," said Smizik.

The day before the Pitt travel party was to leave for Fort Worth, where it would begin preparations for the Cotton Bowl, Alex Kramer received a visit from one of the players. It was Todd Becker, a sophomore linebacker from Fitchburg, Mass.

"Todd wanted to know if he could leave his car in 'The Hole' while we were in Texas," Kramer said in 2019. The Hole was a large dirt area inside Gate 3 of Pitt Stadium, leading down to the old basketball pavilion. Kramer continued:

Early the next morning [December 16, 1982], I received a call from Foge from UPMC Presby[terian Hospital]. He told me that Todd was there in very, very critical condition. I can't recall if Foge said he had already died. Foge decided that we were going to delay, for one day, going to the bowl game.

Becker, who had been suspended from the university dorms for squirting a fire extinguisher, was at a party at Brackenridge Hall on campus. An alarm had gone off, and the building had to be evacuated. Afraid of being recognized, Becker attempted to exit the building from a third-floor window, but landed head first on the concrete below. Rick Telander wrote a lengthy feature about the tragedy, and the state of Pitt football, for *Sports Illustrated* a year later.

Against a backdrop of controversy and tragedy, the Pitt football team flew to Texas for its second consecutive New Year's Day bowl game. It was not a particularly happy time.

"More often than not, the weather was not good, and I did not think the Cotton Bowl people did a very good job in entertaining the players," said Alex Kramer. "It was not as nice as the Sugar Bowl."

In SMU, Pitt was meeting a team that had gone 10-0-1 in the regular season, a tie with Arkansas being its only stain. The Mustangs also had a rookie head coach, Bobby Collins, and featured a dynamic pair of alternating tailbacks in Craig James and Eric Dickerson known as The Pony Express.

Five years later, SMU's football program would receive the NCAA's Death Penalty for a number of serious violations, and was forced to suspend its football operations for the 1987 and 1988 seasons.

New Year's Day 1983 arrived cold, wet, and raw in Dallas. The stadium lights were on before the game. The poor weather kept a significant portion of the crowd away, and 60,359 showed up to see the final collegiate games for stars Marino, Dickerson, and James. Included in the crowd was Jackie Sherrill.

The Panthers received the opening kickoff and drove downfield, but Joe McCall lost a fumble at the SMU one. Typical of the afternoon, the game's first six penalties all went against Pitt. Neither team was able to score in the first half.

Eric Schubert's 43-yard field goal with four minutes and thirty-four seconds remaining in the third quarter gave Pitt a 3-0 lead, but quarterback Lance McIlhenny's 9-yard run with thirteen minutes and forty-three seconds left put the Mustangs ahead, 7-3. Pitt's final drive was stopped when Marino was intercepted in the end zone. There was no more scoring. SMU pressured Marino more than any of Pitt's 1982 opponents. With Dan Marino on the field, Pitt's offense failed to score a touchdown in his last two collegiate games. It was Pitt's lowest-scoring output since the 17-0 shutout loss to Navy in 1975, and the first time Pitt lost consecutive games since the end of the 1978 season (Penn State and North Carolina State).

"The first half we had some excellent opportunities, we got the ball back in good field position, but we just couldn't get it in the end zone," said Foge Fazio in what had become a familiar refrain throughout the 1982 season. "We'll congratulate the seniors, and tell the younger players we have a lot of work to do."

J. C. Pelusi, Pitt's senior nose tackle in 1982, admitted many years later that he had never watched that Cotton Bowl game until finding it on a YouTube link in 2018. He did not like what he saw:

> That was a miserable day. I'm looking, and I just see the talent that we had on that offensive line, and Danny [Marino], and it's shocking that we had difficulty putting points on the board toward the end of the season. Sometimes you get a team with a lot of seniors on it, you can lose a team once in a while. I don't think that would have happened under Jackie, though. Jackie was a different type of coach.

Foge Fazio coached the Panthers for three more seasons. His second Pitt team (1983) went 8-3-1, including road wins at Tennessee and Notre Dame, a tie with Penn State, and a Fiesta Bowl loss to Ohio State. With much of the residual talent from Sherrill's teams gone, the floor collapsed in 1984. The Panthers lost their first four games, and stood 1-6 at one point. A 31-11 win at Penn State in the final game provided some degree of satisfaction, but 3-7-1 seasons were not what Pitt fans and administrators had come to expect from their football team. Fazio was dismissed following a 5-5-1 record in 1985.

In hindsight, almost forty years later, it is easy to say that the Bozik-Fazio combination could not measure up to what Myslinski-Majors-Sherrill had built. But, at the time, those associated with the program were not so sure. "There was a real strong feeling that Foge would be successful," said Dean Billick, "and I think the administration had the right to believe that."

Bill Hillgrove stated: "I thought we had it going, and that the 'Next Man Up' would work. I didn't know that Foge just wasn't ready for a head coaching position. He was a defensive coordinator, and there are people who fit that mold and, unfortunately, he was one of them." Hillgrove remembered what Johnny Sauer had said to him about Fazio's apparent discomfort during 1982 training camp:

How else can you explain the [1982 North] Carolina opening game? That was a tight Pitt football team. They were worried about the expectations, and the job of the head coach is to say, "Hey, let's just throw caution to the wind and go get it. Forget about all the outside stuff." I don't think Foge was able to do it.

The performance of the Pitt offense that year sticks in Hillgrove's memory. Dan Marino threw twenty-three interceptions that season, with a veteran offensive line and the same receivers from the year before when he passed for thirty-seven touchdowns. "Okay, but *were* they the same receivers?" Hillgrove asked. "What went wrong?"

Alex Kramer was optimistic that Pitt's football program remained in good hands following the departure of Jackie Sherrill. "I was confident because we had so many of our players coming back," he said. "Jackie did not leave the cupboard empty."

Billick stated: "He [Fazio] wasn't able to make the step from being an outstanding assistant coach to a head coach. It happens. There wasn't the need to go into a great search because he was the logical choice."

In 2020, Bob Smizik admitted he had written a glowing piece about Fazio being named to succeed Sherrill, but now believes he should have known better in 1982: "In retrospect, you do your due diligence, and Pitt was one of the best jobs in the country. You don't just turn it over to the most popular guy [Fazio]. But Pitt didn't do that, and that was a very important mark against Pitt."

Smizik, who attended virtually every practice session upon accepting the Pitt beat in 1978 through Fazio's early years, enjoyed the same journalistic freedom from Fazio that he did during Sherrill's term as coach, but that is where the similarity ended; Smizik said:

> You can't replace Jackie with Foge. I always said this about Jackie: respected, liked and feared. I believe all three of those were true with him. To me, that's the Bear Bryant in Jackie. With that being the situation in the players' eyes, Foge was not the person to replace him because he was too close to them, especially the defensive players.

As for the man who replaced Cas Myslinski as Pitt's athletic director in 1982, Bill Hillgrove recalls entering an establishment in Aspinwall, Pa., where he first heard the news from a former Pitt football great:

Who's the first person I see? Paul Martha. "Hey, Paul, how's it going?" He says, "Billy, you know you got a new athletic director?" I said, "Who?" He said, "Ed Bozik." I felt a sickening feeling in the pit of my stomach. I thought, "Okay, this is not going to be good. For anybody." You got an administrator meddling, dabbling, putting his nose in athletics. Never, never good. And it wasn't.

It is difficult for those who were associated with Pitt's football program during the 1970s and 1980s to discuss many of the key figures from that era, many of whom are deceased. Wesley Posvar (2001), Cas Myslinski (1993), Jack Freeman (2012), Ed Bozik (1994), and Foge Fazio (2009) are no longer here to give their versions of events.

"As we saw when Bozik took over, he was a very, very smart man," said Bob Smizik, "but he wasn't up for that particular job."

Dean Billick said:

Ed [Bozik] was very, very bright, one of the smartest individuals I've ever known. He wanted to leave the administration side of the university, and athletics was where he wanted to be. He once said to me, "I don't put up with fools easily." There was some clash between Pitt supporters and Doctor Ed during those years.

Foge Fazio was in his first year as Pitt's head coach and Dan Marino his last as a college player in 1982. The Panthers finished No. 10 in the nation. Through the 2019 season, that remains the last time a Pitt team finished that high in the final polls. Only once, when Dave Wannstedt's Panthers were 10-3 in 2009, has a Pitt team reached double figures in victories during that same time period. The Johnny Majors-Jackie Sherrill years at Pitt appear even more distant.

"College football today, it's such a production," said J. C. Pelusi, a senior on the 1982 team. "You have games on TV all day. Talk shows. At the time, you didn't realize how special a period that was for Pitt football."

Jackie Sherrill, who retired from coaching after thirteen seasons (1991–2003) at Mississippi State, was typically candid when asked about the role of a head football coach at any college or university:

We're hired to win games. We're not hired to graduate players. Everybody out there who says differently is crazy. The NCAA can say all it wants.

The college presidents can say it, too. But if that weren't the case, there'd be a lot of coaches out there who'd still be in their jobs, because they are good people. But they didn't win enough games.

Over the next few decades, Sherrill's theory, in Pitt's case, would prove to be correct.

7

CAN PITT BE GREAT AGAIN?

At Pitt, we don't just shoot ourselves in the foot. We take a cannon, and blow our whole goddamn leg off!

Sam Sciullo, Sr. (2009)

I think Pitt has done enough of the right things to show me that they're trying, they're at least trying, to have a solid, competitive football program.

Dean Billick (2020)

It had been a remarkable period in Pitt's long football history. From Tony Dorsett through Dan Marino (1973–1982), it brought ten consecutive winning seasons, a 7-2 record in bowl games, six Top Ten finishes, a national championship (1976), and a Heisman Trophy winner (Dorsett) that same season. In 1980 alone, Hugh Green won the Lombardi, Maxwell, and Walter Camp Awards, while Mark May earned the Outland Trophy. Pitt went 92-25-2, on the heels of nine straight non-winning seasons.

Fifteen players who entered Pitt during that time frame became All-Americans, plus four Academic All-Americans (Jeff Delaney, Rob Fada, J. C. Pelusi, and Greg Meisner). Eleven Panthers were selected in the first round of the NFL Draft. Five (Dorsett, Green, May, Marino, and Bill Fralic), along with coach John Majors, are now in the College Football Hall of Fame. Six (Dorsett, Marino, Chris Doleman, Jimbo Covert, Russ

Grimm, and Rickey Jackson) are now enshrined in the Pro Football Hall of Fame.

Pitt teams went 35-1 against Eastern rivals West Virginia (9-1) Syracuse (10-0), Boston College (7-0), and Temple (9-0). Only Penn State (3-7) held an edge against Pitt during that stretch. Pitt never lost more than two games in a row.

After leaving Pitt following the national championship season, John Majors spent sixteen seasons as head coach at Tennessee. He enjoyed eleven winning campaigns, and captured Southeastern Conference championships in 1985, 1989, and 1990. When Paul Hackett was fired as Pitt's coach after the 1992 season, Majors was brought back to Pittsburgh. He had been ousted at Tennessee in the wake of a messy conflict with interim coach Phillip Fulmer, when Majors was forced to take a break from coaching following heart surgery.

When Majors was hired at Pitt, times were different, and Majors was not the same coach. "Back to the Future" was how Pitt officials labeled his return. His first game, a 14-10 win at Southern Mississippi in the 1993 season opener, sparked hope that the veteran coach who had orchestrated Pitt's unprecedented turnaround during the 1970s might be able to do it again. But Southern Mississippi finished the season 2-8-1, and Pitt lost its next two games, both at Pitt Stadium, to Virginia Tech (63-21) and Ohio State (63-28).

Majors' final season (1996) was particularly difficult. The final record was 4-7, but some of the losses were disastrous. West Virginia beat Pitt, 34-0, in the opening game at Pitt Stadium in an ESPN telecast. Pitt also lost to Ohio State (72-0), Miami (45-0), Syracuse (55-7), and Notre Dame (60-6). Against the Irish in South Bend, the Panthers allowed three punt returns for touchdowns in the second quarter alone.

In the 1997, 1998, and 1999 NFL Drafts, not a single player from Pitt was selected. During Majors' second Pitt term, the only player who entered the program and was later drafted was defensive back Hank Poteat, selected by the Steelers in the third round in 2000. John Majors passed away June 3, 2020 at his home in Tennessee. He was aged eighty-five.

Jackie Sherrill, meanwhile, transformed Texas A&M from a perennial underachiever into a three time (1985-86-87) Southwest Conference champion before NCAA sanctions forced him to resign after the 1988 season. After spending two years away from football, involved in an automobile partnership in Baytown, Texas, Sherrill was hired by Mississippi State. He spent thirteen seasons with the Bulldogs, winning more games in Starkville than any previous coach. His 1998 team won the SEC's Western Division before losing to Tennessee, that year's national champion, in the conference title game. The NCAA followed Sherrill to Starkville, and the MSU program received NCAA probation late during his term. Sherrill does have a notable achievement on his coaching resume—seven consecutive wins against the University of Texas.

At Pitt, following Foge Fazio's dismissal as coach in 1985, by 2020 Pitt was on its eighth different head coach. Mike Gottfried (1986–1989), Paul Hackett (1989–1992), Majors (1993–1996), Walt Harris (1997–2004), Dave Wannstedt (2005–2010), Todd Graham (2011), Paul Chryst (2012–2014), and Pat Narduzzi have attempted to return Pitt's program to national stature. Gottfried, Harris, and Wannstedt each had winning records at Pitt, including wins against nationally ranked teams, but Pitt has not been able to regain a spot among college football's elite since Dan Marino was a senior in 1982. It begs the question, "Can Pitt be great again?"

Bill Hillgrove said:

That's a good question. I don't know. I know it's going to take a longer time because of the recruiting rules and regulations. John [Majors] was able to bring in that huge recruiting class the first year [1973], which ultimately became a great senior class. Plus, guys stuck around all four years, too. Back in those days there weren't as many restrictions.

Bob Smizik stated:

Not at Pitt. No way. College football has become the haves and have nots. It's almost getting like Major League baseball, where the Dodgers and Yankees have such an advantage. Maybe, some years, Pitt has a chance to win its division, and get to the title game, and if you don't have a juggernaut team like Clemson, maybe win the title game.

Pitt moved from the Big East to the Atlantic Coast Conference and began league play in 2013. While there has been a raging debate as to whether the move was good for the school's basketball program, much less has been said about the football aspect.

"I think Pitt is going to survive in the ACC," said longtime sportswriter Jerry DiPaola. "Whether they thrive there is going to depend. I think Pitt is in the right spot as far as conference affiliation."

"I don't subscribe to the 'never again' theory about how successful Pitt can be," said Alex Kramer. "I think Pitt can be a perennial contender for a championship. I don't think the conference affiliation is that significant in that regard."

"People are starting to understand that Pitt is as much a part of the ACC as North Carolina or Duke," said Jerry DiPaola. "I've made a lot of friends with people in the media around the ACC, and they have a lot of respect for Pittsburgh and Pitt."

"They're in the right league [ACC] where they can compete," said Dean Billick. "If they do a really good job, why can't they beat Clemson every now and then?"

Jerry DiPaola said:

Pitt can be nationally relevant again in football, but it's gonna take three or four or five really good recruiting classes. Pat Narduzzi's had five of them now, and they're still pretty mediocre, all things considered. But now he has to recruit against teams in Florida and against teams in the Carolinas. Maybe there are just fewer really good kids out there playing football these days.

Alex Kramer, who worked with each Pitt football coach from Jackie Sherrill through Paul Hackett, believes that two of Pitt coaches, if they had stayed or been given more time, could have elevated Pitt's program to national prominence:

I think Mike Gottfried had the program headed in the right direction. He recruited some outstanding players to Pitt. Had he continued to have successful seasons, he probably would have been lured away.

Walt Harris should not have been let go. When his agent made that remark [that the Pitt coaching job was not conducive to winning championships], he wasn't quoting Walt. He was speaking for himself. But I never, ever heard Walt reject that idea, or counter what his agent said. Had Walt stayed on, I think he would have done very well here.

Walt Harris was Pitt's coach in 1999 when the decision was made to demolish Pitt Stadium to make way for the Petersen Events Center, Pitt's arena for basketball and other university events. Pitt's Board of Trustees voted unanimously in favor of the move, and a public assembly was held on March 18, 1999 at the William Pitt (Student) Union on campus to make the announcement. "The University of Pittsburgh Board of Trustees today endorsed plans to move Pitt's home football games to the new stadium [Heinz Field] on Pittsburgh's North Shore, and to use the current ten-acre site of Pitt Stadium for its new convocation center," read the official press release from Pitt's Office of News and Information.

Steve Pederson, who replaced L. Oval Jaynes as director of athletics in 1996, and hired Walt Harris, was excited about the move.

"This is an opportunity that doesn't come along all that often," said Pederson. "For the first time, players and fans will be in a world class facility like other top ranked programs have."

"It was a mistake when they made that decision," said Dean Billick. "Pitt Stadium should have been renovated."

Pitt also moved its football offices and training facilities to the new UPMC Sports Performance Complex on the South Side, adjacent to those of the Pittsburgh Steelers, in 2000.

Pitt defeated Notre Dame, 37-27, in the final game at Pitt Stadium on November 13, 1999. Pitt played its home schedule at Three Rivers Stadium, in its final season, in 2000 before moving to Heinz Field in 2001.

"I think the effect by those who feel we have to have a campus stadium are really overemphasizing its importance," said Alex Kramer.

According to Billick, there was a proposal in place to put a dome over Pitt Stadium, and make a major reconstruction of the aging football facility, but the plan died. This was toward the end of Ed Bozik's term as director of athletics. Billick said:

> Pitt brought in the number one architect in the world relative to domed stadiums. He had done Olympic stadiums. Pitt spent $100,000 to have this man do a survey. Pitt wanted to know if Pitt Stadium's infrastructure was such that the stadium could be domed, and the answer was "yes." It would have been a double-decked facility seating 80,000 people. It could have been used for football and basketball.

Billick estimates the new stadium would have cost approximately $100 million. University officials approached an unnamed Pittsburgh businessman. "We asked him for thirty million dollars," said Billick. "We made a big pitch using a video presentation and things like that, but ultimately he turned us down." Shortly after Pitt's pitch was made, both Bozik and Pitt's chancellor, Wesley Posvar, retired.

"It [a renovated and domed Pitt Stadium] would have been beautiful," Billick said in 2020. "I don't know if a whole lot was known or written about it at the time, but it was a real idea, a real plan. But it's over and done with. There's no sense going on and on about it now."

The close proximity between Pitt and the Steelers goes back a long way in the city's sports history. During the 1930s, when Pitt football was riding high during the Jock Sutherland years, Steelers owner Art Rooney and the rest of the fledgling National Football League were trying to keep their collective heads above water. The Steelers, originally known as the Pirates, struggled to draw fans to wherever they could find a place to play, eventually settling at Forbes Field. In the 1950s, the Steelers approached Pitt about the idea of having the Steelers play their home games at Pitt Stadium.

Tom Hamilton, Pitt's director of athletics, viewing the Steelers and the NFL as a threat to Pitt's business, wanted no part of the arrangement. Rooney, however, had a key ally in longtime Pittsburgh mayor David L. Lawrence, along with many other important Pittsburgh political power brokers. The Steelers would get what they wanted, and the Pittsburgh sports pecking order was on its way to being changed forever. Art Rooney Jr. and author Roy McHugh, in *RUANAIDH, The Story of Art Rooney and His Clan*, summarized what happened next.

Art Rooney, Jr., and Roy McHugh wrote:

> Tom Hamilton was a visionary. Over the next twenty years, in all the cities where professional football had taken hold, the college teams lost their support base, the general public. Already, New York was more devoted to the Giants than to Army or Columbia; Philadelphia preferred the Eagles to Penn; Chicago belonged to the Bears, not to Northwestern.[1]

Penn State and West Virginia fans, in particular, enjoy pointing to Pitt's relatively unimpressive attendance figures as some type of indictment or attempt to delegitimize Pitt football. But current numbers support the claim made in the Rooney book. For example, in 2018, of the nation's top twenty college football single game attendance average leaders, nineteen of the schools were located in towns where there is no NFL team. The one exception was the University of Washington (Seattle), and it ranked nineteenth on the list.

The obvious, yet rarely mentioned reality, is that all college teams located in metropolitan locations struggle to increase their fan bases beyond students and *alumni*. The strength of the National Football League is that it appeals to all demographics, particularly blue collar, noncollege-educated people. Many of these people simply do not care about collegiate sports. The same can be said about the media in Pittsburgh, both sports and general. Many of them have their own collegiate preferences, and sports columnists, who have their choice of events to cover, have no problem staying away from college games for extended periods of times. They could not practice that brand of selectivity if they were working in a traditional college town. Think Penn State, Nebraska, Oklahoma, Alabama, North Carolina, Kentucky, or Kansas. Alex Kramer noted: "I don't think you can understate the impact and the hurt the Steelers, the Penguins and the Pirates have on Pitt football. When it comes to media attention, we're in fourth place. One way that can be corrected, of course, is by becoming big winners."

Expertly, by design, and to its credit, the National Football League has placed itself in the everyday news cycle twelve months a year with a number of events and activities, and its fans can't get enough. Talk about the Steelers and Penguins dominates the conversation on Pittsburgh's sports radio station 93.7 The Fan.

Jerry DiPaola, a graduate of Point Park College, began his career with *The Butler County News* before moving to the *Valley News-Dispatch* in 1979. He worked on the copy desk at *The Pittsburgh Press* until 1986. After *The Press* folded, he was picked up by the *Tribune-Review*. He has been covering Pitt football and basketball for a number of years, and has seen the balance of attention shift. DiPaola said:

> Pitt football would have to be behind the Steelers and Penguins for sure, and probably the Pirates. I'd have to say that they're in a three-way tie with Pitt basketball and high school football for attention in this city. Back in the day, in the 1980s, Pitt football would have been ahead of the Penguins, but not anymore.

DiPaola does not buy the claim, by some Pitt fans, that reporters and columnists in the local media are against Pitt, or hate Pitt: "I don't think that at all. The media people here who don't go to the games, don't cover the games, do so because they think Pitt is irrelevant in the grand scheme of things. I don't think anybody in the local media hates or dislikes Pitt."

With print newspapers fading from America, more people now get their information digitally, and there is no question what team attracts the most viewers in Pittsburgh. "Pitt doesn't get a whole lot of clicks from the people who read the stories online," said DiPaola, "All we have to do is put [former Steeler] Antonio Brown's name in a headline, and all of a sudden we get 10,000 clicks.

Dean Billick remembers his days as Pitt's sports information director when, routinely after work, he would drive downtown to the offices of *The Pittsburgh Press* and *Post-Gazette* and take sportswriters out to dinner. Bob Smizik, Roy McHugh, and Phil Musick were among his guests.

"I enjoyed doing that," he said. "I also felt that it was part of my job. I'm not so sure I'd want to do that now with some of the people who are covering Pitt."

During the 1970s, the beat writers who covered Pitt football had seats reserved for them on the team's charter flights to away games, and room reservations at the hotels where the Panthers were staying. Those days are gone.

Someone who has become exceedingly familiar with the digital age, and how it applies to Pitt athletics, is Chris Peak, publisher of the Panther-lair website. A 2001 Pitt graduate, Peak, who works from his home office, is on call twenty-four hours a day. "There's no closing whistle," he said. "I don't punch out and leave. If it's nine o'clock at night and a kid commits to Pitt, or someone gets arrested, I have to run downstairs, get on the computer and get to work."

Peak sees no point in pondering where Pitt ranks on the Pittsburgh sports totem pole, but he did not hesitate when asked his opinion. He answered the question with a question. "Fourth?" he replied. "It's not any higher than fourth, and it probably swaps between fourth and fifth. During those years Pitt basketball was doing well, it [football] might have been fifth. It's number four at best."

Given Pitt's standing in the public conscience, do the Panthers have to be that much better? Are they required to perform to a higher standard than a team in a conventional college town, or risk losing fan and media support? "They [Pitt] can't afford to be mediocre," said Jerry DiPaola. "They've been mediocre for a long time, and that's why you see a lot of yellow seats at Heinz Field."

Nothing excites college football fans throughout the year as much as recruiting news. Peak is at the center of it, calling coaches and recruits in search of information. He has an interesting take on how players in Pitt's hometown visualize the football program, stating:

When you look at juniors and seniors in high school [in 2020], you have to look at their formative years. What did they see from Pitt when they were in middle school? You take a high school junior or senior now, and go back when he was in middle school around 2014, when Pitt lost to Akron at home. Or go back a couple years, and a kid was in middle school when Pitt lost the season opener to Youngstown State at Heinz Field.

Cable television, the internet, and social media have made the country much smaller. High school players are now exposed to programs across the United States, and coaches have easy access to information about the recruits. "Recruiting has become so much more national now," said Peak. "You can find video online of any recruit in the country."

With Western Pennsylvania's population in decline, along with the number of boys playing high school football, the area is not the fertile recruiting ground it was during the Majors-Sherrill years. Chris Peak noted:

> People say, "Why can Pitt recruit Florida better than locally in Pennsylvania?" I say it's because kids here have become intimately aware of what's gone on here. It's not necessarily because of poor media perception. These kids have seen it for themselves. They've spent their formative years seeing this program flounder.

And there can be no denying that Pitt, at times during the 2000s, has been its own worst enemy. The firing of Dave Wannstedt; the hiring, then firing, of Mike Haywood a short time later because of a domestic violence charge; and Todd Graham bolting for Arizona State after one season at Pitt have all contributed to a sense of instability in Pitt's football program. "Those were the things that a lot of the top prospects in this area were witnessing at Pitt," said Peak. "Kids have had close proximity to everything that's happened here."

And while Pitt has shot itself in the foot a few times, certain national powers have dominated college football, not to mention the airwaves. Alabama, Clemson, Ohio State, Oregon, and Oklahoma can be seen every Saturday. DiPaola said:

> Seeing the national championship game, and all the glitter that goes with it, the confetti at the end of the game, kids want to go to a place where they can be a part of that, where they can win a national championship. A lot of them don't see that opportunity, or experience, right now [2020] at Pitt.

The pomp and ceremony attached to the national title game are enough to want to make a high school football player leave the Pittsburgh area for a more desirable football location. Perhaps provincial pride isn't what it once was. Or is it still a determining factor?

"Aaron Donald was one of the first guys I heard say that," said DiPaola. "'I want to play for my city. I want to win a championship for my city.' He didn't say 'for my university.'" DiPaola continued:

> I think that's important for some kids, but I don't think it's important to everybody. You can see all these other teams on TV now. Penn State and Ohio State were always successful in football, but they just seem to be more aggressive in recruiting in this area than maybe when Joe Paterno was, back in the day.

Dean Billick said: "Can they beat Penn State out for players? Sure they can. If you have the right coaching staff with enough resources to retain quality coaches who know the Xs and Os, and know how to recruit, and you have solid football facilities, they can be competitive."

"People ask, 'Is Pitt's Aliquippa High School pipeline broken?' said Chris Peak. "Who did (former Pitt and NFL star) Darrelle Revis talk to when he was in high school? He probably talked to Pitt and Penn State. Well, it's different now. Other schools can find these kids, and they can talk to them."

During the Majors-Sherrill years, Penn State successfully recruited a large number of good players from the Pittsburgh area, but the very few great ones—Dorsett, Gordon Jones, Covert, Marino, and Fralic—signed with Pitt. Probably the most hyped area prospect in this century, Jeannette High School's Terrelle Pryor, went to Ohio State.

Taking these factors into consideration, Can Pitt be great again? Dean Billick said:

> The answer to the question depends on what "great" means. Can Pitt put together a program in which they can be a perennial Top Twenty-Five contender? The answer is, if they have good leadership and they commit enough resources to it, the answer is "yes." As a Pitt fan, I would be disappointed if that isn't their goal.

Billick is a sentimentalist. He misses having a stadium on campus, but believes Pitt is doing what it can to accentuate what it has, rather than lament what no longer is. "These people who say it's a terrible situation, who want to make it a negative, I think most of them don't know what they're talking about," said Billick.

Billick spent several years in the athletic department at the University of Cincinnati, and got to know Pat Narduzzi when the Pitt head coach was there as the Bearcats' defensive coordinator. He believes Narduzzi has the right ideas at Pitt:

> I think they're trying to make the best of the situation. I don't think it's a terrible situation. What Pat Narduzzi is doing is a smart thing. He's using the pros [Steelers] as a positive, not a negative. He's telling recruits that they're gonna play where the Steelers are. They have scouts at every one of our home games. They train right next door to the Steelers. There are a lot of plusses in that.

Still, Billick can't help but think of the game day experience of a football Saturday on a college campus.

"You bring people back to your campus," he said. "You walk them across your campus every Saturday when you have a home game, and that's your ideal situation. But it's not what Pitt has now, and it's not what they have in their future."

Playing its home games at Heinz Field has produced some embarrassingly small crowds for home games. Pitt officials have done their best to promote the overall experience of attending a college football game as a prime selling point, but how effective that effort has been is debatable. The reality remains; college sports are a more difficult sell in a town dominated by professional teams. Some have suggested that certain sections of Heinz Field should be blocked off for Pitt games.

"This idea of tarping [the upper decks] of the stadium, I think is nonsense," said Dean Billick. "They just need to win more football games, and the size of the stadium won't be a problem."

Unlike the 1970s, when Pitt enjoyed great success in football without huge financial advantages, the university has made a solid commitment as the 2020s begin. "It's clear to me that the administration, and I'm starting at the top with the chancellor and the Board of Trustees, has made a commitment to attempt to be competitive in a Power Five conference," said Dean Billick:

> The football facilities over on the South Side are pretty good. They're not Clemson good. They're not Florida State good, but they're pretty good.

But if they have the right leadership and continue to do a good job on an annual basis to put a million, a million and a half dollars into facility upgrades, which is what they've been doing, they can be a Top Twenty, Top Twenty-Five, and every now and then a Top Ten program.

Chris Peak said:

You have to look at support at the top. I think this chancellor [Patrick Gallagher] is committed to athletics, and wants to improve athletics. I think he has a director of athletics [Heather Lyke] who is pretty driven herself, and she has the support of the chancellor, as does the football program. The resources are there. I think that's encouraging about the long term future of the program.

Some Personal Observations

August 30, 2014 was a difficult day for me. The occasion, the opening game of Pitt's football season, has always been something I have looked forward to, but this one came with a touch of sadness. It was the first Pitt football season I would be following without my father, who died on December 21, 2013.

From the time I was old enough to remember anything, Pitt football had always been a big part of my life, and I was able to share so much of it with my dad, who became involved as a Pitt booster when Dave Hart became head coach in 1966. He was recruited by another Pitt loyalist, Bob Miller, who had already been very active in the program. My dad and Bob Miller were two of the original members and founders of the Golden Panthers booster club in the early 1970s. Before that, however, during the Hart and early years of Carl DePasqua's term as coach, there was a loosely configured booster organization called the Pitt Prowling Panthers. In fact, they had gold tie clips made for the members, and my dad wore his for many years, well beyond Pitt's 1976 national championship season.

Because of my father's involvement, it would be fair to say I was both spoiled and privileged when it came to Pitt football. I started going to games in 1965, a few weeks after my sixth birthday. When I arrived at Pitt as a freshman in 1977, I had already been going to Pitt games, and close to the program, for twelve years. My dad and I saw the worst (three straight 1-9 seasons) and the best (the 1976 season) during that time period.

Pitt had little trouble with Delaware in that 2014 opener, winning easily 62-0. I have my choice of sitting in the stands or the press box at Pitt games. I always buy season tickets, and I decided to sit in my seat in Section 231 for this particular game. When the band played "Hail To Pitt" during its pregame performance, it was very emotional for me. So many memories of Pitt football that I shared with my dad returned, and it was a difficult experience.

For anyone to appreciate what he has, it is important to know and understand where he's been. Living through the Dave Hart-Carl DePasqua seasons at Pitt were all I knew as I was growing up. My dad and I went to all the home games, and some road trips, during those years.

A workaholic attorney, my dad and I had a routine for Saturday afternoon games at Pitt Stadium. Before heading to Oakland from our residence in Castle Shannon, we would head to his office at the Law & Finance Building downtown. He would work several hours, then we would leave for the games, which always started at 1:30 p.m. We might stop at Isaly's near campus for lunch, or go straight to the stadium. My father always had a parking pass through the athletic department.

I became immune to the losses during those seasons. I came to expect them. The experience of being there with my father was more than enough to create a pleasurable experience for a kid then in grade school.

My father became involved with recruiting football players during those years. In Carl DePasqua's first season (1969), recruits would come to the Student Union on campus for a brunch before heading to the game. My job was to stand at a table and pass out game programs to the recruits and anyone else who happened to be with them. My dad and I would sit with the recruits in the stands. At the Navy game in 1969, he and I had to make numerous trips up and down the stadium steps to purchase about forty Cokes for everyone!

It was also during this time when we began to host recruiting parties and dinners at our house. My dear mother, Ryta Sciullo, who passed away in January 2020, would prepare all the food. Catering was never considered when my parents entertained guests. Several times following basketball games on Saturday nights, my dad would call my mom from a pay phone inside the Pitt Field House after a game and tell her that he was bringing maybe ten or twelve people to the house. Regardless of the hour, my mom would spruce herself up and head to the kitchen, where she would prepare plenty of food for everyone. And this was well into the evening!

Around that time, Pitt booster Chris Passodelis brought Tony Dorsett to our home during the recruiting season. After they left, my mom, taking note of Dorsett's slight build, remarked, "That kid's a football player?"

One particularly memory from the DePasqua years stands out. An assistant coach, who shall go nameless, became extremely inebriated at one of our parties, so my dad and fellow booster Moe Lebow had to take him to another room, far from the festivities, to sober him with cups of coffee!

Glenn Hyde, a big defensive tackle from the Boston area, was a regular dinner guest at our home. After one meal, he leaned back in the wooden dining room chair—and broke it!

Gary Burley, the jovial defensive lineman who was a major cog in The Major Change, brought his wife to our house for dinner one night. He and I played one-on-one basketball on the back patio court afterward. It was impossible to get around him. I was a freshman in high school.

When Pitt made the decision to look for a new head football coach during the 1972 season, my father and Bob Miller, who were at the center of the search for Carl DePasqua's replacement, would speak on the phone regularly. He allowed me to listen in on another line in our house. I was thirteen at the time. When it came to Pitt football, my dad told me everything. Cas Myslinski called our house from Memphis, Tennessee, on the night of December 16, 1972 to tell my dad that John Majors had agreed to become Pitt's head coach.

I met Majors for the first time on December 31, 1972 on an escalator at Three Rivers Stadium. My father and I were attending the Steelers-Miami Dolphins AFC title game. That night, Majors and a few other couples came to our house for dinner.

Who hasn't seen the movie *The Wizard of Oz?* In one of the most dramatic scenes, a dreaming Dorothy is lying in bed while her house, lifted off the ground by a tornado, spins and spins before crashing to the ground. Until then, the movie was shot in black and white. When Dorothy awakens and goes outside, she is transformed to a land of brilliant colors, as is the viewing audience. The same can be said for the transformation when Pitt hired John Majors as football coach. Pitt's program went from the dark ages into modern living color.

There was not anything mythical or magical about the job Majors, his staff and players accomplished in taking Pitt from 1-10 to 12-0 in four years. Pitt had not been taking shortcuts. It was simply a product of hard work, enthusiasm, stellar recruiting, and a committed administration.

Along the way, Pitt gained a reputation for recruiting "bad kids" to its football program in those years. Speaking from personal observation, I can state with the utmost certainty that there were roughly the same number of off the field incidents involving Pitt football players during the Dave Hart-Carl DePasqua years as there were after John Majors arrived. I can recall two incidents in particular when my dad took phone calls at our house well past midnight, and had to leave to go get a player out of jail. One of the incidents occurred before Majors arrived in Pittsburgh, while the other happened when Jackie Sherrill was head coach. My father received occasional hate mail and prank phone calls during the course of his representation of a few Pitt football players in criminal cases. And he was not being paid for any of the work or attendant aggravation. All the legal work he did for Pitt was *pro bono*.

Jackie Sherrill is not easy to get to know. He is reserved. Unlike John Majors, he is not a gregarious storyteller. Majors was masterful in his ability to work a room or any type of crowd. He knew the right thing to say to flatter someone. He took a politician's approach to public relations where Sherrill did not. The media loved Majors because he gave "good quotes."

Jackie Sherrill is not remembered as reverently as Majors. He did not seduce the media, and he came painfully short of winning another national championship for Pitt in both 1980 and 1981. Perhaps if Pitt had been No. 1 in either, or both, of those years, a more hallowed spot would be reserved for Jackie Sherrill in Pitt history, but in today's "championship or nothing" sports culture, he who does not have the coveted "ring" cannot be included among his sport's elite, or so the thinking goes.

When Jackie Sherrill left Pitt for Texas A&M in early 1982, I had the good fortune to follow him. I worked in the sports media relations office there from 1982 until 1987. I came to know Sherrill much better than I had during his years in Pittsburgh. I later took numerous trips to Starkville to visit with him when he was coaching Mississippi State, and traveled to quite a few Mississippi State games across the South.

When Sherrill left Pitt, he made a remark to the effect that, "my heart remains in Pittsburgh." At least one Pittsburgh writer agreed, adding, "but his bank account is moving to College Station."

Several times during my time in Aggieland, while I would be standing along the sideline at Kyle Field watching practice, Sherrill would notice, and motion for me to join him on the field. While continuing to monitor the field, not looking at me, invariably he would ask the same question: "What do you hear out of Pittsburgh?"

While he was at Mississippi State, Sherrill would have returned to Pitt as head coach after the 1992 and 1996 seasons if Pitt had wanted him, but school officials, leery of his problems with the NCAA, begged off.

In retrospect, and having watched Pitt football during the almost forty years since Sherrill left, I have come to appreciate what he and John Majors meant to Pitt's program. They were special. Each possessed levels of shrewdness and savvy that, frankly, I have not seen in any Pitt coach since 1982. They saw and understood the big picture. They did not merely see themselves as football coaches, but as stewards of a growing, competitive business.

Can Pitt be great again? Absolutely, but it will not be easy. In some ways, Pitt has to be better. Being a college program in a pro town has that effect. While it does not affect Pitt's ability to field a better product, it definitely makes it harder for Pitt to expand its fan base and attract increased media coverage.

Unlike traditional college towns, where the entire community has grown up with the local college team and is familiar with its history, that is not the case in Pittsburgh. Pitt's basketball program is a perfect example of that model.

Pitt basketball's fan base has experienced two significant migrations in two different decades. When Pitt joined the Big East Conference in 1982, it was a perfect marriage. ESPN was establishing itself by televising large numbers of college basketball games. Pitt basketball became visible around the country, and the program began attracting players from outside the Pittsburgh area, players it had never been able to recruit in the past. Pitt basketball became a hot ticket, the thing to do, the place to be. Interest, along with season ticket sales, soared.

Pitt attracted a new wave of fans, folks in their twenties and thirties who had not grown up following it. Even local college graduates who had not gone to Pitt jumped on the bandwagon. In effect, Pitt basketball had become the city's *de facto* NBA team. Casual sports fans without college degrees joined the club, and the Panthers were riding high. Unfortunately, when the program began to decline in the mid-1990s, many of those fans, people who had no loyalty or natural allegiance to Pitt to begin with, abandoned ship.

A parallel migration happened when coaches Ben Howland, then Jamie Dixon, established Pitt as a national power after construction of the Petersen Events Center. "The Pete" became a magnet for local celebrities to sit at courtside and cheer the Panthers to victory. But when recruiting began to slip toward the end of Dixon's term, and the program bottomed out during Kevin Stallings' two seasons as head coach, attendance at Pitt basketball games plummeted.

At blue blood schools, where there is an ingrained loyalty to the program, where the college teams are the primary sports entertainment in town, those schools can afford a bad season or two without fan interest and support taking a hit. Pitt is not that fortunate.

There is no doubt in my mind that the presence and popularity of the professional sports teams affects Pitt's ability to attract more fans and receive greater coverage in the media throughout the year. I do not buy the line that "people only have so many entertainment dollars to spend." Generally speaking, people do want they want to do, whether they can afford it or not. They do that which they cannot resist. This is not an excuse, but a reason for some of Pitt's attendance problems. Pitt certainly has to do its part to field a more attractive product.

Sam Sciullo Jr.
February 24, 2020

ENDNOTES

Chapter 1

1 Smith, *Area Coaches Likely To Help Hart Hunt Stars, The Pittsburgh Press* (Dec. 8, 1965), p. 86.
2 Franke, *Pitt's Hour of Decision Nears, The Pittsburgh Press* (Dec. 5, 1965), sec. 4, p. 1.
3 McHugh, *Hart Wants To Take On The World, The Pittsburgh Press* (Dec. 7, 1965), p. 57.
4 Franke, *New Pitt Coach Enthusiastic, The Pittsburgh Press* (Dec. 7, 1965), p. 57
5 Franke, *Hart Bubbles With Enthusiasm, The Pittsburgh Press* (Dec. 7, 1965), p. 57.
6 Franke, *Lions Have Sympathy For Panthers, The Pittsburgh Press* (Nov. 24, 1968), sec. 4, p. 6.
7 Livingston, *Drumming Out Carl, The Pittsburgh Press* (Nov. 28, 1972), p. 37.

Chapter 2

1 Heufelder, *Rainy Day Arrives for Golden Panthers, The Pittsburgh Press* (Nov. 29, 1972), p. 75.
2 Franke, *New-Look Pitt Ties Georgia, 7-7, The Pittsburgh Press* (Sept. 16, 1973), sec. D, p. 1.
3 Heufelder, *Kush Not Interested In Panthers' Job, The Pittsburgh Press* (Nov. 28, 1972), p. 37.
4 Heufelder, *Winning Life or Death Matter, The Pittsburgh Press* (Dec. 20, 1972), p. 61.
5 Heufelder, *Winning Life or Death Matter, The Pittsburgh Press* (Dec. 20, 1972), p. 61
6 Smizik, *Pitt's Dorsett Stages Record-Topping Show, The Pittsburgh Press* (Nov. 11, 1973), sec. D, p. 2.
7 Sciullo, *Tales from the Pitt Panthers* (2004), p. 26.

Chapter 3

1 Livingston, *A Skilled Pick, The Pittsburgh Press* (Sept. 9, 1976), p. 31.
2 Franke, *Dorsett Sets Record, Pitt Romps, The Pittsburgh Press* (Oct. 24, 1976), sec. D, p. 1.
3 Franke, *Big 3 Makes Pitt Middle Solid, The Pittsburgh Press* (Sept. 5, 1976), sec. D, p. 7.
4 Livingston, *Dorsett: HE-IS-my-MAN, The Pittsburgh Press* (Nov. 26, 1976), p. 41.
5 Axelrod, *Majors-Players: Tearless Farewell, The Pittsburgh Post-Gazette* (Dec. 4, 1976), p. 6.
6 Axelrod, *Majors-Players: Tearless Farewell, The Pittsburgh Post-Gazette* (Dec. 4, 1976), p. 6.
7 Franke, *Pitt: How Sweet It Is!, The Pittsburgh Press* (Jan. 2, 1977), sec. D, p. 1.

Chapter 4

1 Livingston, *Panthers On a Hunch, The Pittsburgh Press* (Sept. 8, 1977), sec. D, p. 1.
2 Livingston, *Limited Offense, The Pittsburgh Press* (Sept. 13, 1977), sec. C, p. 1.
3 Franke, *Pitt's Basket Shortage Tough To Explain, The Pittsburgh Press* (Sept. 12, 1977), sec. C, p. 1.
4 Underwood, *Maybe It's The Luck Of The Irish, Sports Illustrated* (Sept. 19, 1977), p. 21.
5 Franke, *Cavanaugh Dazzles Record Crowd, The Pittsburgh Press* (Dec. 31, 1977), sec. A, p. 6.

Chapter 5

1 Burdick, *Awesome Panthers Rip Syracuse, Syracuse Herald-American* (Nov. 2, 1980), sec. D, p. 1.
2 Ibid.
3 Smizik, *Panthers' Big Plays Win Big One From Lions, The Pittsburgh Press* (Nov. 29, 1980), sec. A, p. 6.
4 Musick, *Tale of Two Plays: A Year of Anguish, The Pittsburgh Post-Gazette* (Nov. 29, 1980), p. 9.
5 Lyon, *Short yardage failures foil Lions, The Philadelphia Inquirer* (Nov. 29, 1980), sec. C, p. 1.
6 Looney, *When it comes to grit, Pitt is it*, Sports Illustrated (Dec. 8,
7 1980), p. 60.

Chapter 6

1 Smizik, *Pitt, Marino Regain Form, The Pittsburgh Press* (Oct. 17, 1982), sec. D, p. 1.

Chapter 7

1 *Rooney and McHugh, RUANAIDH, The Story of Art Rooney And His Clan* (2008), p. 172.

BIBLIOGRAPHY

Georgia Football 2019 Media Guide (University of Georgia, 2019)

The Owl (University of Pittsburgh, 1967-1972)

Panaccio, T., *Beast of the East: Penn State vs Pitt, a game-by-game history of America's greatest football rivalry* (Leisure Press, 1982)

Penn State Football 2019 Media Guide (Penn State University, 2019)

Pitt Football Media Guides (University of Pittsburgh, 1966-1983)

Rooney, A. J. Jr., and McHugh, R., *RUANAIDH, The Story of Art Rooney And His Clan* (2008)

Sciullo, S., *Tales from the Pitt Panthers* (Sports Publishing L.L.C., 2004)

Tennessee 1977 Football Media Guide (University of Tennessee, 1977)

INDEX